DEMOCRATISATION

Spectrum Law Series
Nigerian Law of Torts — *Kodilinye*
Nigerian Legal System — *Obilade*
An Introduction to Equity in Nigeria — *Kodilinye*
Nigerian Business Law — *Ezejiofor, Okonkwo and Ilegbune*
Nigerian Law of Contract — *Sagay*
Criminal Law in Nigeria — *Okonkwo and Naish*
The Law of Evidence — *Aguda*
Nigerian Tax Law — *Ayua*
Introduction to International Law — *Umozurike*
History and Sources of Nigerian Criminal Law — *Karibi-Whyte*
Sharia Law Reports of Nigeria Vol. 1 — *Yahaya Mahmood*
Law of Judicial Immunities in Nigeria — *Olowofoyeku*
Military Rule and Constitutionalism — *Nwabueze*
Military Rule and Social Justice — *Nwabueze*

DEMOCRATISATION

B. O. Nwabueze
LL.M LL.D (Lond.) Hon. LL.D (UNN) S.A.N. N.N.M.A.

Spectrum Law Publishing
Ibadan • Owerri • Kaduna • Lagos

Published by
Spectrum Law Publishing
a division of:

Spectrum Books Limited
Sunshine House
1, Emmanuel Alayande Street
Oluyole Industrial Estate
P.M.B. 5612
Ibadan, Nigeria

in association with
Safari Books (Export) Limited
Bel Royal House
Hilgrove Street
St. Helier, Jersey
Channel Islands, UK

ISBN: 978 246 172 5

Printed by Polygraphics Venture Limited Ibadan.

DEDICATION

To Chinazom, Adaeze and Uzoamaka with Love

Contents

Contents

Preface

This book has been inspired by the democracy movement now sweeping across the world, from the countries in the former Soviet Union and Eastern Europe to Africa and Asia. Democratisation is not only a concept, nor is it synonymous with multi-partyism; it is also concerned with certain conditions of things, conditions such as a virile civil society, a democratic society, a free society, a just society, equal treatment of all citizens by the state, an ordered, stable society, a society infused with the spirit of liberty, democracy, justice and equality. It is the thesis of the book therefore that, aside from multi-partyism, democratisation, in the fullest sense of the term, requires that the society, the economy, politics, the constitution of the state, the electoral system and the practice of government be democratised. Not only does the society need to be democratised, it must also be a society founded upon freedom, justice and the equal treatment of all citizens by the state; it must be an ordered, stable society, one infused with the spirit of democracy, liberty, justice, equality and order. These conditions are fully analysed in the book.

Of all these, it seems to me that the condition most crucial to democratisation in the emergent countries of the world, particularly in Africa, is the infusing of the spirit of liberty, democracy, justice, equality and order among the people. The chief problem of democratisation in these countries has to do, not with the inappropriateness of the underlying values and principles of liberty, democracy and social justice as with the inability of the people, the rulers and the ruled alike, to imbibe their spirit.

Democratisation involves also a process of experimentation over time. The listing above of the things required by democratisation does not, and is not intended to, carry the implication of preconditions or prerequisites without which democratisation cannot, and must not, be embarked upon. It is wrong to take the view that the experiment should not begin unless and until all the factors necessary for its success are present. These factors can be created or developed in the process of the experimentation. While it certainly functions better under conditions of modernity and development, constitutional democracy is not a form of government for civilised or developed societies only. In a society of men, whatever their state of development, and whatever their national character may be, whether self-restrained and public-spirited or not (savages or barbarians excepted), there is no other viable alternative form of government. This is the lesson of the collapse of socialism/communism in the former Soviet Union and Eastern Europe, and of the failure of one-party and military rule in Africa.

I am grateful to my Secretary, Mr Damian Obiefule, for his usual assiduity in typing the manuscript.

Ben Nwabueze
Lagos,
May, 1993.

Chapter 1

What Democratisation Involves

> We have no theories which could help us bring about, or even understand, the transition from socialism to the open society... The issue is how to establish the constitution of liberty and anchor it firmly. The heart of the problem lies in the incongruent time scales of the political, the economic and the social reforms needed to this end.
>
> Sir Ralf Dahrendorf

Dimensions of Democratisation

So much has been written and said in glorification of the events of 1989-90 ushering in the change from one-party, military or communist rule to multi-partyism in Eastern Europe, the former Soviet Union and Africa as if that is all that is entailed in democratisation — as if multi-partyism is synonymous with democracy. No doubt, the change from the political monopoly of one party decreed by law to a free political competition between rival parties is a momentous event, one which is made equally fantastic by the bewildering plethora of parties that in Africa has sprung up in its wake — 250 in Zaire, 100 in Congo, 68 in Cameroun, 30 in Senegal, 25 in Burkina Fasso, 17 in Benin and 16 in Guinea.

Yet it is important to enquire what the change has really meant in these countries. What actually has changed from what used to be? Would transition from one-party, military or communist rule to multi-partyism have changed much else where the same person(s) as before remains still in control? Have the new multi-party regimes shed the authoritarianism and autocracy of the one-party, military and communist regimes they supplanted? What changes besides that from one-party, military or communist rule to multi-partyism are required for full democratisation?

Democratisation, in the fullest sense of the term, has a much

1

wider meaning and compass than multi-partyism. It must seek, in addition, to democratise the society, the economy, politics, the constitution of the state, the electoral system and process, and the practice of government. Not only does the society need to be democratised, it must also be a society founded upon freedom, justice and the equal treatment of all citizens by the state; it must be an ordered, stable society, one infused with the spirit of liberty, justice, equality, the Rule of Law and order. In answer to the question of what democratisation means for the ordinary people, Claude Ake has said that "the democracy movement has gathered momentum as commodities disappeared from grocery stores in Lusaka and Dar es Salam, as unemployment and inflation got out of control in Kinshasa and Lagos, as a bankrupt government failed to pay wages in Cotonou, as the vanishing legitimacy of incompetent and corrupt managers of state power drove them to political repression in Nairobi, as poverty intensified everywhere defeating all possibilities of self-realization, threatening even mere physical existence. So, the democracy movement in Africa is, among other things, an expression of the will to survive. The survival strategies which the ordinary people spontaneously devised to cope with economic austerity and to reduce their vulnerability to a predatory state engendered popular empowerment, energised civil society and strengthened the will to struggle for democracy."[1]

In more specific terms, democratisation must involve the following twelve things:-

(i)   multi-partyism under a democratic constitution having the force of a supreme, overriding law;

(ii)   a complete change of guards and the exclusion of certain other categories of persons from participation in democratic politics and government;

(iii) a genuine and meaningful popular participation in politics and government;

---

1.   Claude Ake, "The Feasibility of Democracy in Africa," Keynote Address at the symposium on Democratic Transition in Africa organised by the Centre for Research, Documentation and University Exchange, University of Ibadan, 16-19 June, 1992.

(iv)   a virile civil society;
(v)   a democratic society;
(vi)   a free society;
(vii) a just society;
(viii) equal treatment of all citizens by the state;
(ix)   the Rule of Law;
(x)   an ordered, stable society;
(xi)   a society infused with the spirit of liberty, democracy and justice; and
(xii) an independent, self-reliant, prosperous market economy.

All these and their relevance to democratisation will be examined in the various chapters of this book.

We need to emphasise that, of all these things listed above, perhaps the one most crucial to democratisation in the emergent countries of the world, particularly in Africa, is the infusing of the spirit of liberty, democracy, justice, the Rule of Law and order among the people. The chief problem of democratisation in these countries has to do not with the inappropriateness of the underlying values and principles of liberty, democracy and social justice as with an inability to imbibe their spirit. These principles and concepts — elections, universal suffrage, political competition, representative government, separation of powers, limitations upon government for the protection of liberty, bill of rights, the Rule of Law, the welfare state, social equality, etc. have a universal appropriateness and validity; it is only some of the institutional forms, trappings and practices — ballot boxes, ballot papers, secret ballot, winner-take-all, etc. — that may be inappropriate in the conditions of mass illiteracy and poverty prevalent in the emergent countries, and which may therefore need to be done away with. Liberty, democracy and social justice are not faring well in these countries simply because of the inability of the people — rulers and the governed alike — to imbibe their spirit, not because of the inappropriateness of their underlying values and principles. Democratisation must therefore involve concerted effort to instil the spirit of liberty, democracy and social justice in the people.

Democratisation Involves a Process of Experimentation Over Time

The listing above of the things involved in democratisation does not, and is not intended to, carry the implication of pre-conditions or pre-requisites without which democratisation cannot, and must not, be embarked upon. Constitutional democracy, like other forms of government, is an art which has to be learnt and developed, and the learning involves a process of experimentation over time, of trial and error. It is wrong therefore to think that the experiment should not begin unless and until all the factors necessary for its success are present. These factors can be created or developed in the course of the experimentation. While certainly it functions better under conditions of modernity and development, constitutional democracy is not a form of government for civilised or developed societies only. In a society of men, whatever their state of development, and whatever their national character may be, whether self-restrained and public-spirited or not, there is no other viable alternative form of government. We are not of course talking of a nation of savages or barbarians.

John Stuart Mill (1859) thinks, however, that liberty is not meant for backward societies, or for a people of violent disposition, or a people lacking in public spiritedness, or in a sense of civic responsibility. "Despotism," he asserts, "is a legitimate mode of government in dealing with barbarians, provided the end be their improvement, and the means justified by actually effecting that end. Liberty, as a principle, has no application to any state of things anterior to the time when mankind have become capable of being improved by free and equal discussion. Until then, there is nothing for them but implicit obedience to an Akbar or a Charlemagne, if they are so fortunate to find one."[2] He concedes, happily, that "all nations with whom we need here concern ourselves" have "long since

---

2.   J.S. Mill, *On Liberty* (1859); reprinted in *Unitarianism, Liberty and Representative Government* (1910) Everyman's Library, pp. 78-79 and pp. 191-192.

reached" the state of maturity to embark on the experimentation with liberty and democracy, and can over time, learn their ways and habits.

But Lord Bryce, writing in 1920, was uncompromising. He strenuously maintained that democracy and free government were not suitable nor meant for, and should not be embarked upon by, "backward peoples" among whom he classified the rest of mankind apart from Britain, Europe, North America, Australia, New Zealand and Japan;[3] despotism, he said, is what is good for them, and the democratic "experiments that are now being tried might have been better left untried."[4] And if at all "the work of fitting" such peoples for self-government is to be attempted, it should be done by "slow degrees."[5] It did not occur to him that a world, half free and half unfree, is hardly realistic nor even possible in our present conditions of mass education, of enormous intellectual development and of fast communications which have brought it closer and closer together in feelings, aspirations and outlook; and that the capacity of self-government, which took the advanced countries centuries to acquire, may today, given the free flow of ideas and under the stimulus of influences from the advanced peoples, be acquired in a comparatively shorter time.

What we say is that liberty and democracy, if they are to take firm root and thrive (not if they are to be embarked upon at all) must have a foundation in certain shared sentiments that bind a society to respect human rights and to behave democratically, common sentiments expressed in habits, traditions, attitudes, a moral sense and a transcendental spirit. "The ultimate foundation of a free society," Justice Frankfurter has remarked, "is the binding tie of cohesive sentiment."[6]

---

3. James Bryce, *Modern Democracies* Vol. 2 (1920), chap. LXXI, titled "Democracy and the Backward Races," pp. 545-568.
4. *ibid*, p. 549.
5. *ibid*, p. 566.
6. *Minersville School District v. Gobitis*, 310 U.S. 596 (1940).

Chapter 2

The Current Transition From One-Party, Military or Communist Rule to Multi-Partyism

> The unrestrained liberty of association for political purposes is the last degree of liberty which a people is fit for
>
> Alexis de Tocqueville

Political and Institutional Mechanisms for Transition

Transition to multi-partyism has taken three forms or patterns, which are here considered in turns, namely

    (i)   transition voluntarily embarked upon by the incumbent regime;

    (ii)   transition by constitutional but forced process; and

    (iii) transition by revolution.

(The pattern of transition in Bulgaria is altogether unique, and will be considered in chapter 3).

(i) Transition Embarked upon Voluntarily by the Incumbent Regime

This is the form of transition adopted by the military regimes in Ghana and Nigeria. Ghana has had two previous democratic transitions in October 1969 and September 1979, and Nigeria one in 1976-79. Both are presently embarked on another one. The processes were essentially the same in the two countries, and terminated in the hand-over of government by the military, under a new constitution, to a civilian government chosen by means of multi-party democratic elections conducted by an Electoral Commission which was independent of the contestants. However, the democratic character of the elections in the on-going transition in Nigeria has been seriously attenuated by the fact that they were conducted on the basis of two parties established *by name* by Decree, with constitutions and manifestoes drawn up for them by the Electoral Commission; in the result, what the parties stand for in terms of policies, objectives and ideology is hardly understood by the members, let alone the wider public. The elections were thus fought, not on the basis of issues, but of mere trivialities — mud-slinging between the parties and denigration of each other's emblems or symbols, the National Republican Convention's (NRC's) eagle and the Social Democratic Party's (SDP's) horse. The one was depicted as a "vicious predator" and the other as treacherous, with a propensity for looting and falsehood.[1] The campaigns have aptly been described as "phoney," "a veritable war of the symbols."[2] As one commentator has remarked: "We expected to hear of the long and short-term plans to improve the standard of living for the masses. But they are busy reducing the argument to what a terrible animal the horse or the bird is."[3]

A significant difference between the first and the on-going transitions in Nigeria is that, whereas in 1976-79 the coming into force of the new Constitution and the handing-over of government to democratically elected rulers were brought about in a single act, the commencement of the 1989 Constitution and the hand-over of power are being effected in phases, spaced, that is, over appropriate intervals of time, starting with the installation of elected local governments, followed by the election and swearing-in of the state governments, and ending with the election and swearing-in of the federal government. Only the provisions of the Constitution relevant to each phase are brought into force with it, so that the entire Constitution only comes into force with the installation of an elected federal government scheduled for 27 August 1993. In the meantime and until then, the powers of the Federal Military Government

---

1.   Olatunji Dare, "As the transition unfolds," *The Guardian,* Tuesday, December 17, 1991, p. 15.
2.   Mary Kanu, "A phoney election," *The Guardian,* Tuesday, December, 17, 1991, p. 15.
3.   Mary Kanu, loc. cit.

(FMG) remain as absolute, unlimited and as supreme as ever, the democratically elected local and state governments being entirely subordinate to, and dependent upon, it just as when the states were ruled by military governors appointed by it.

There is a lot to be said for a stage by stage transition. It would enable the military government to monitor the conduct of government by elected civilian functionaries at the two lower tiers of government to ensure that they conform with the standards of the new political culture required of them. The transition is thus to be a period of learning the art of good leadership and followership under the surveillance of the military government. The continued presence of the military government, armed with the power of correction or removal, would, it is hoped, instil sufficient sense of disciplined behaviour among the civilian political operators at each of the lower stages of democratic transition. The arrangement would also enable the military government to adjust any structural defects or contradictions observed during the transition period.

But the true nature of this arrangement needs to be emphasised. It implies no diarchy at all, as is commonly but erroneously thought. A diarchy is a power-sharing arrangement instituted by a supreme constitution and which, accordingly, is not amenable to unilateral alteration by either party to it. A supreme constitution cannot exist alongside an absolute military government. So long as the FMG remains in existence, the 1989 Constitution (or rather so much of it as is brought into operation), being its creation, can have no greater force than any other enactment of the FMG, and is liable to modification or abrogation by a subsequent Decree. In other words, the absolutism and supremacy of the FMG remain the *grundnorm* of the Nigerian legal order until its (i.e. the FMG's) regime is brought to an end on 27 August, 1993. The true position, then, is that, until the FMG terminates its own life in August, 1993, the government of the country remains a military government, not a diarchy. The elected state and local governments are simply agents or instruments of the FMG to exercise powers delegated to them under a Decree of the FMG.

However, whilst the FMG remains supreme over the 1989 Constitution, the installation of constitutional democracy at the state and local government levels calls for much greater self-restraint on the part of the FMG in the exercise of its absolute power. In its relations with elected state and local governments, particularly as regards the division of powers, the allocation of revenue and the tenure of office of elected functionaries, both executive and legislative, it should as much as possible let the Constitution govern and abide by its provisions, resorting to its autocratic power only in a situation imperatively calling for corrective action of a revolutionary nature. But this is no more than a moral exhortation with no legal force whatever. As a matter of law, the absolute power of the FMG continues to extend to the whole field of government until it is finally relinquished.

(ii) Transition by Forced Constitutional Process

The characteristic features of this form of transition are, first, that it is not voluntary but rather forced upon a reluctant regime by popular agitation in the form of demonstrations and rallies organised by opposition groups operating either separately or under an umbrella organisation, the now famous *Forums*, like the Civil Forum in Czechoslovakia, the New Forum in East Germany, Democractic Forum in Hungary and the Forum for the Restoration of Democracy (FORD) in Kenya. (In Poland the opposition umbrella organisation was called Solidarity and in Zambia, the Movement for Multi-party Democracy). These opposition umbrella organisations have been described as a bridge from authoritarianism, absolutism or totalitarianism to democracy. Sometimes the agitations are accompanied by a general strike of workers, uprisings or revolts, culminating in the regime being forced to talks with the pro-democracy groups at a Round Table — the form of the table became a symbolic characteristic feature in the countries of Eastern Europe.

The second characteristic feature of this form of transition is the fact that it is effected under, and in conformity with, the existing constitution, either a new constitution or the old constitution which, using the prescribed procedure for constitutional change, is first amended to drop the word People from the name of the state and to remove the monopoly of the single party and allow for freedom of political association and the rule of law. This is followed thereafter by multi-party general elections for the election of a new government.

This form of transition was originated by the countries in Eastern Europe including, it should be noted, East Germany (but not Romania). As Timothy Garton Ash observed, "in East Germany, as in Poland, Hungary and Czechoslovakia, the Round Table briefly became the highest instance in the land. Here, too, they at once set a date for free elections, and the pseudo-parliament voted to remove from the constitution all reference to the leading role of the Party. Here, too, the membership and power of that Party evaporated at quite breath-taking speed, taking with it the most formidable security apparatus in Europe."[4] (The multi-party elections took place on 18 March, 1990 one week before Hungary held its own). What was different in the case of East Germany is its post-transition re-unification with West Germany on October 3, 1990.

From Eastern Europe, it was adopted in some of the Soviet Republics and in the former Soviet Union itself where, following pressures from reformist elements within the Communist Party and massive popular demonstrations in Moscow and other cities demanding an end to Communist monopoly of power and a full multi- party system, President Gorbachev announced, after a meeting of the Central Committee in February 1990, the Party's decision to renounce its guaranteed monopoly of power and to accommodate the democratic process. In March 1990, the Congress of the People's Deputies (the enlarged Soviet parliament) voted to repeal the article of the Constitution (art. 6) which guaranteed the Communist Party's leading role. A law on establishing new political parties was announced to be in the process of being drafted.

The pattern has also been followed in a number of African countries — Cote d'Ivoire, Zambia, Burkina Fasso, Gabon, Zaire, Sao Tome and Principe, and Kenya and is also being followed in Tanzania — all one-party states. There are other African one-party regimes, for example, Angola and Mozambique, where, although the one-party system has been publicly renounced and the decision announced to replace it with a multi-party system under a new constitution to be

4.   Timothy G. Ash, *We the People* (1990) pp. 74-75.

adopted through a referendum, the transition process is either yet to begin or is yet to be completed. The announcement by President Joaquim Chissano of Mozambique in August 1990 acknowledged that events in Eastern Europe and their fall-out effects in other African countries as well as agitations within the country itself were the major factors that led his Government to re-think its position on the issue of democracy. He should have mentioned as one of the factors, the new policy of the advanced Western democracies to tie military and economic aid to democratisation.

Needless to say, there are variations in the countries in which the pattern has been adopted, especially as regards the space of time within which the change was effected, the absence of round-table talks and the creation of transitional coalition governments pending multi-party general elections. The round-table talks between the incumbent regime and the pro-democracy groups were not a feature of the process in the former Soviet Union and in the African countries as they were in those of Eastern Europe. And in Czechoslovakia, because of the great rapidity of the transition (24 days as against 10 months in Hungary, 10 weeks in East Germany and 10 years in Poland), a transitional all-parties but Forum-dominated government was put in place pending new parliamentary elections scheduled to take place in six months' time; in the meantime too, the Forum leader was elected President of the Republic by the existing communist parliament. On the other hand, Hungary proceeded straight with a free multi-party parliamentary elections in March 1990 to replace the old parliament of the communist regime. A referendum had earlier been held on the opposition's demand that the President of the Republic should be elected, not by the old parliament, but by the new one to be constituted after the free, multi-party parliamentary elections; the proposal was approved by an overwhelming majority at the referendum.

In the multi-party general elections for the president and members of parliament in Zambia in November 1991, incumbent President Kenneth Kaunda and his United National Independence Party (UNIP) were heavily defeated by the Movement for Multi- party Democracy (MMD), thus bringing to an end Kaunda's rule and UNIP's monopoly of power which had lasted for 27 and 18 years respectively. In Cote d'Ivoire, on the other hand, incumbent President Felix Houphouet-Boigny, who has been in office since November 1960, emerged victorious against the pro-democracy party candidate. Also in Burkina Fasso, incumbent President Blaise Compaore won as a sole candidate, the pro-democracy parties having boycotted the election in protest against Compaore's candidature, which has thus cast the gloom of a crisis on the transition process.

Multi-party elections are yet to take place in Tanzania after the constitutional amendment. Also, except in Lithuania, no multi-party election and no non-communist coalition government have been held or formed in the former Soviet Union before the dissolution of the Communist Party and the subsequent disintegration of the Union itself.

Timothy Garton Ash has raised the question "whether what happened in Poland, Hungary, Bulgaria or even Czechoslovakia and East Germany, actually qualified for anything but a very loose usage of the term 'revolution'. "Should popular movements", he asked, "which, however spontaneous, massive and effective, were almost entirely non-violent, really be described by a word so closely associated with violence?"[5] Although he thinks that the events are perhaps best described as "revolution", he seems nevertheless to regard them as amounting to a revolution because, he says, "the change of government, no, the change of life, in all these other countries was scarcely less profound than in Romania. By a mixture of popular protest and elite negotiation, prisoners became prime ministers and prime ministers became prisoners."[6]

From the juristic point of view, a revolution is determined, not by the profundity of a change or its consequences or the means employed, violent or non-violent, but rather by whether it is effected in an unconstitutional manner. "A revolution", writes the German legal philosopher, Hans Kelsen, "occurs whenever the legal order of a community is nullified and replaced by a new order in an illegitimate way, that is, in a way not prescribed by the first order itself... From the juristic point

5.   op. cit. p. 20.
6.   loc. cit.

of view, the decisive criterion of a revolution is that the order in force is overthrown and replaced by a new order in a way which the former had not itself anticipated."[7] Kelsen's definition has been affirmed by the courts in decided cases in at least four countries.[8] As the Pakistani Supreme Court puts it, "a revolution is generally associated with public tumult, mutiny, violence and bloodshed but from a juristic point of view, the method by which, and the persons by whom, a revolution is brought about is wholly immaterial. The change may be attended by violence or it may be perfectly peaceful... For the purposes of the doctrine here explained a change is, in law, a revolution if it annuls the constitution and the annulment is effective."[9]

Insofar, therefore, as the transitions under this pattern took place in conformity with the existing constitutions of the countries concerned, they are not a revolution in the strict juristic sense of the term. They certainly do not have the same juristic character as the French Revolution of 1789. In their profundity and abruptness, however, the changes of 1989-90 in some countries of Eastern Europe, Africa and the former Soviet Union are unquestionably of revolutionary proportions.

(iii) Transition by Revolution

The transition to multi-partyism in Romania is indisputably a revolution, because it was brought about by the violent overthrow of the incumbent communist regime without first amending the existing Constitution accordingly. (The Communist Party was made illegal soon after the revolution). Power was thus assumed by the new multi-party regime, not by the authority of the pre-existing Constitution, but by virtue of the successful seizure of the state by one of the pro-democracy groups which, by seizing the radio and television stations and

---

7.   *General Theory of Law and State* (1945), pp. 111-118.
8.   *The State v. Dosso*, P.L.D. 1958, S.C. 533 (Pakistan); *Madzimbamuto v. Lardner-Burke* (1969) 1 A.C. 645 (Privy Council on an appeal from Rhodesia); *Uganda v. Commissioner of Prisons, Ex parte Matovu* (1966) E.A. 514; *Lakanmi v. The Att Gen (West)*, S.C. 58/69 decided on April 24, 1970 (Nigeria).
9.   *The State v. Dosso* ibid pp. 538-9.

obtaining the backing of the military commanders, was able to get itself installed as the new revolutionary government.[10]

The revolutionary course was dictated by the fact that the ousted regime, instead of engaging the pro-democracy agitators in negotiations at a round table, as in the other East European countries, resorted to armed force to subdue the agitation, which resulted in the massacre of peaceful demonstrators. What began as a peaceful popular agitation then turned into a violent revolt in the course of which the army withdrew its support and stopped firing; angry crowds in the streets then ran amok setting government buildings aflame, stormed the presidential palace, and the hated dictator was seized, put up against a wall and shot. Following upon this, multi-party general elections for both the president and members of parliament were held in May 1990 (the overthrow occurred in December, 1989), from which the pro-democracy party in control of the revolutionary government emerged the winner with overwhelming majority against three other pro-democracy parties.[11]

Among African countries, the Republic of Benin was the pace-setter in democratisation by revolution, although in this case the revolution was not a people's revolution as in Romania but one by way of "national conference", which is really in the nature of a *coup d'etat*; besides, it involved no violence as in Romania. In response to popular agitation featuring mass demonstrations supported by an umbrella organisation called the Assembly of Democratic Forces comprising four different movements, the one-party regime of President Mathew Kerekou in January 1990 officially renounced Marxism-Leninism, and appointed a National Conference on democratic reforms, with members drawn from the government, the ruling party, the National Assembly, the military, trade unions, opposition parties, the University and Beninoise in exile.[12]

The Conference, at its meeting on February 21, 1990, declared itself, without due authorisation, as having power to

---

10.   Gwyn Prins ed., *Spring in Winter: The 1989 Revolutions* (1990), p. 157.
11.   Misha Glenny, *The Rebirth of History* (1990) pp. 98-99.
12.   Ralph Uweche ed., *Africa Today*, 2nd ed. (1991), pp. 543-545.

draft a new constitution, to give binding effect to its decisions and to implement them accordingly; in other words, constituting itself a revolutionary authority for the government of the country. Against protestations by President Kerekou that the Conference had not been set up as a constituent assembly and could not turn itself into one, or otherwise arrogate to itself authority for the government of the country, the Conference proceeded, in line with its earlier declaration, to take decisions on multi- party presidential elections to be held on January 27, 1991, a reduction in the powers of Kerekou as a transitional President pending the elections, and on the appointment of a prime minister, which took effect on March 12, 1990 with the appointment of Nicophore Soglo as Prime Minister to head a new cabinet of predominantly pro-democracy members.

More significantly, it created what was called as *Haut Conseil pour la Republique* or a High Council of the Republic (HCR) to oversee the executive, supervise the elections, approve the draft constitution, choose one of its members to act as President or Prime Minister in the event of a vacancy, and generally to oversee the transition to a new constitution. Included in the Council were four former Presidents of the Republic and the Conference Chairman (a bishop). At the same time, the country was re-named the "Republic of Benin", thus dropping the word "People's".[13]

On April 12, 1990 the draft constitution for a multi-party democracy under a presidential system, which had been drafted by a commission set up by the Conference, was submitted to the HCR and approved at a referendum on December 2, 1990 by 95.8 per cent of the votes cast. Parliamentary elections, contested by 17 political parties, were held in February 1991, and presidential elections in March at which, after two round of voting, Soglo emerged the winner, defeating Kerekou.

The transition process in Benin was certainly, "one of the most remarkable changes among the many moves by African states towards democracy in 1990."[14] It was both remarkable

---

13. Ralph Uwechue, loc cit.
14. Ralph Uwechue, op. cit. p. 544.

and novel. It blazed a trail, a revolutionary trail, which a number of other African countries have followed — Togo, Niger, Ethiopia, Congo and Mali (all five, as well as Benin, were one-party regimes). Yet, it is a trail that seems almost guaranteed to lead to conflict and crisis for those who follow it. For, not every President would be as acquiescent as Kerekou was, and take lying down, such palpable usurpation of power by a body which, unlike in Romania, is not the product of a popular revolution. Not surprisingly, therefore, both Togo and Congo are now in the grips of crises resulting from a conflict between the incumbent Presidents and the interim governments appointed by the National Conference and headed by the leaders of the pro-democracy parties.

In Togo, President Eyadema, stripped of most of his powers and reduced virtually to a ceremonial President by the National Conference, has resorted to the army which, in loyalty to him, laid a siege on the interim government and surrounded the Prime Minister's residence, thereby putting the government out of action, unless and until certain of its policies were reversed, especially the ban on Eyadema's party and its exclusion from the interim government. After days of the siege during which some 43 people were reported killed, the Prime Minister, under duress, accepted the lifting of the ban on Eyadema's party and its inclusion in the interim government, just so as to avoid further bloodshed. Two weeks later, the army struck again, this time demanding an end to the interim government, particularly its legislative arm, the High Council of the Republic (HCR). Happily, a reconciliation was effected in January 1992 with the formation of a new interim cabinet in which Eyadema's party is included. A new constitution, drafted since December 1991 by a constitutional commission appointed by the Eyadema regime, was adopted by a national referendum on February 16, 1992, but general elections under the new constitution are yet to be held.

Surely, the ban on a whole political party and the denial of its members' democratic right to associate together for political purposes seem rather a negation of the very idea of multi-partyism. It is a totally different thing from the ban on an individual(s) to which different considerations apply.

In Congo too, the interim government appointed by the

National Conference was sacked in January, 1992 by the army apparently at the behest of President Nguesso to whom it still remains loyal. It seems, however, that the army's action was not a take-over, in view of the re-affirmation of their commitment to the democratisation process and the call on the High Council of the Republic (HCR) of the National Conference to appoint a new interim government in place of the ousted one, which is of course not accepting its ouster.

Although a National Conference was set up in Zaire, it is not of the revolutionary type as in the other countries. It was not meant as a mechanism for democratic transition nor has it functioned as such, transition having already been effected by a law of December, 1990 which permitted parties to be formed without any limit as to number, unlike an earlier law of July 1990 protested by the pro-democracy parties because it restricted the number to three. (By December 1991, some 250 parties were said to have sprouted up, although only 19 were registered by the government to contest the parliamentary elections fixed for 1992).

In setting up the National Conference alongside a transitional government of "public salvation" made up predominantly of ministers from the pro-democracy parties with a pro-democracy Prime Minister, President Mobutu was merely looking for a way to salvage his decadent and tottering regime from imminent collapse. But, finding himself at loggerheads with the transitional government right from the beginning, he promptly sacked it, and appointed another in its place. In a situation where the sacked transitional government is not accepting its sack, the country has been plunged into an explosive crisis, with marauding troops frequently on the streets, looting, killing defenceless people and generally endangering the security of lives and property to the extent that foreigners have had to be evacuated out of the country. Subsequently on January 19, 1992, he (President Mobutu) suspended the National Conference on the ground that several of its resolutions were unconstitutional and inconsistent with the terms of reference given to it by the government. An attempt to overthrow the regime by a military coup on January 23, 1992 failed, although the international airport was reported to be occupied by some troops the following day. To complicate matters further for the

President, the U.S. had earlier in November 1990 cut off all military aid to the country (amounting to $4 million per annum), and stipulated progress towards democratisation as a condition for further economic aid. But embattled President Mobutu is still hanging on precariously to power.

In Ethiopia too, the National Conference was of an altogether different character. It was not in the nature of a *coup d'etat* or a usurpation of the powers of an existing government, the one-party Marxist-socialist cum military government of Col. Mengistu Haile Mariam, described as the most repressive, terroristic and murderous regime of tyranny in Ethiopia's 3000 years of recorded history, having been driven out on 28 May, 1991 by a civilian armed resistance force, the Ethiopian Peoples Revolutionary Democratic Front (EPRDF), which overran Addis Ababa and took control of the country.[15] Following agreement among the warring nationalities and political groups at the Peace Talks held in London, a National Conference was convened and held in Addis Ababa from 1-3 July, 1991. The Conference was able to agree on the structure of a provisional government under a Provisional Charter which was to serve as the supreme law of the land for a two-year transitional period during which a new Constitution would be adopted and a new government elected to take over from the provisional one. The provisional government, which is still in control, is thus expected to hand over to a democratically elected government in July 1993.

The procedure of a national conference is certainly an ill wind. It is important that the foundation of the emerging democratic regimes in Africa should be laid in legality and legitimacy. Apart from Benin, only in Mali and Niger does the procedure of a national conference appear to have worked without too much friction. In Mali, a new multi-party constitution drafted under the auspices of an interim government appointed by the National Conference was approved at a referendum in January 1992, and election for

---

15. Samuel M. Woldu, "Democratic Transition in Africa: A Case Study of Ethiopia," in B. Caron, *et al, Democratic Transition in Africa* (1992), pp. 69-80.

local government councils contested by 20 parties have also been held. In Niger, as in the other countries, a national conference, inaugurated on 29 July, 1991 with 1200 delegates representing trade unions, students' unions, 30 political parties, the chamber of commerce, voluntary associations and the civil service, had constituted itself by sheer arrogation, the supreme authority for the government of the country, reducing Ali Saibou to a mere ceremonial Head of State. And when it wound up in November 1991, it had an interim government installed to rule the country for 15 months when general elections would then be held. (Even here, in Niger, the army was split between those supporting and those opposed to the national conference, resulting in an uprising in which the former took over the radio station, arrested some members of Saibou's regime and forced the dissolution of his council of ministers.)

It must not be thought that the procedure of a national conference is without merit altogether. In Niger, for example, it is said to have fostered the passion for liberty throughout the country, and to have generated very wide public interest in politics which expressed itself through popular participation in political discussion in the newspapers, three of which had sprung up during the period, and through numerous petitions for investigations into corrupt practices and other abuses.[16] It "reversed the marginality of the population and the will and determination for popular participation in politics became the order of the day."[17]

Constitutional Mechanism for Transition

It needs hardly be stated that the radical constitutional transformation demanded by the events of 1989-90 cannot be brought about merely by removing through constitutional amendment, the provisions in the existing constitution establishing a socialist socio-economic order and a socialist

---

16.   Jibrin Ibrahim, "From Political Exclusion to Popular Participation: Democratic Transition in Niger Republic," in B. Caron et al. *Democratic Transition in Africa* (1992), p. 65.

17.   Jibrin Ibrahim, loc. cit.

political system, and by replacing the guaranteed political monopoly of the communist or single party with multi-partyism. A new constitution is needed, and must possess two attributes if transition from one-party, military or communist rule to multi-partyism is to contribute meaningfully towards the achievement of the objective of democratisation. First, it must be a democratic constitution, that is to say, a constitution adopted by the people at a referendum or through a constituent assembly specially elected and mandated for the purpose by the people. Second, the constitution must have the force of a supreme, overriding law.

(i) A New Democratic Constitution

With the exception of the Bulgarian Constitution which was adopted by a national referendum on 16 May, 1971, none of the constitutions in force in the communist countries of Eastern Europe and the Soviet Union at the time of the revolutions of 1989-90 was a democratic constitution. They were all enacted by the several parliaments. This is perhaps in consonance with the socialist ideology which recognised sovereignty as belonging only to the working people, not the entire people. In communist ideology too, parliament represents and embodies the sovereignty of the working people. It should be stated in parenthesis that, with the transition of society to the full-scale construction of communism in the Soviet Union, the concept of sovereignty as belonging to the working people only was considered in 1961 to have served its function, and was, accordingly, abandoned in favour of a new conception of the state as a state of the whole people − a socialist all-people state. This new concept was explicitly affirmed in the 1977 Constitution. Yet, notwithstanding the recognition in the Constitution of a referendum of all the people as a method of deciding certain questions of national importance, the making of a constitution or its amendment was still reserved exclusively to the Supreme Soviet of the USSR (parliament). Apparently, the societies of the countries of Eastern Europe had not progressed to the full-scale construction of communism, since the constitutions of most of them still speak of the sovereignty of the working people.

As at February 1992, two of the countries of Eastern Europe, Bulgaria and Romania, have, since the revolutions there, adopted new constitutions; in both cases the method used was democratic, the constitutions having been adopted by a constituent assembly in the case of Bulgaria (Grand National Assembly as it is styled) or, in the case of Romania, by a referendum after approval by a constituent assembly. (A new constitution for Poland, which was expected in 1991, had still not been finalised by February 1991).

In Africa, most of the countries affected have since also adopted new democratic constitutions by a referendum or through a constituent assembly. The processes and the requirements for a transition to a democratic constitution are perhaps best discussed by reference to the Nigerian experience. The first transition there (1976-79) involved, among other things, four processes, viz the setting up of a Constitution Drafting Committee of experts, 49 in all, appointed by the Federal Military Government (FMG) from various fields of specialisation; public discussion of the constitutional proposals; convening of a Constituent Assembly, and, finally, promulgation of a new Constitution by the FMG.

The Constituent Assembly was established by a Decree of 1977, with 230 members, twenty of whom were appointed by the federal military government while seven were the chairman of the Constitution Drafting Committee and the chairmen of its six sub-committees. (There were a chairman and a deputy chairman of the Assembly appointed by the government but without a vote either original or casting). The remaining 203 members were elected, not directly by the people but by the local councils acting as electoral colleges. Clearly, a constituent assembly elected in this way could not claim to have the people's mandate to adopt a constitution on their behalf. The local government councils had no such mandate themselves and could not confer it on the Constituent Assembly which, being at one remove from the people, is indeed, as regards reflecting the popular will, in a position inferior to that of a national assembly which constitutes itself into a constituent assembly without a prior popular mandate. Besides, the composition of the local government councils had not been fully democratic. Election in many cases was by indirect method or by selection by village or family heads, while in some places traditional members were brought in by nomination.

There is next the question of the role of the Constituent Assembly in the adoption of the Constitution. Its constituent statute defined its role as being to "deliberate upon the draft Constitution of the Federal Republic of Nigeria drawn up by the Constitution Drafting Committee appointed by the Federal Military Government."[18] There would seem to be implied in this provision a suggestion that the Assembly had no power to decide the substantive content of the Constitution, or, if it had, that its decisions would only be by way of recommendation, which might be accepted or rejected by the FMG. This is not of course to say that the Assembly was a mere deliberative body, with no power to take decision on the form and content of the Constitution. The draft Constitution was presented to it in the form of a bill, and its proceedings on it were, by the terms of the governing statute, to be conducted in accordance with prescribed regulations which clearly required that it should take decisions on the form and content of the Constitution following a procedure of first and second readings and detailed consideration in a committee of the whole Assembly.[19] And the procedure left the Assembly pretty ample scope for meaningful choice. The proposals contained in the draft constitution bill presented to it, being those of a committee of forty-nine independent people chosen for their specialist knowledge or background, did not carry the somewhat inhibiting force of government proposals. More important, the procedure did not preclude departure from these proposals. An amendment seeking to replace the presidential system proposed in the draft bill with a parliamentary system of cabinet government was in fact vigorously urged upon the assembly in two different forms and lost.[20]

But the really critical point, which nearly created a stalemate between the Assembly and the FMG, was whether the decisions

---

18.   Constituent Assembly Decree 1977 S.1.
19.   s. 4 ibid.
20.   Proceedings of the Constituent Assembly, Official Report, vol. 11, cols. 1943-55; cols. 1981-8.

of the Assembly were to have finality or be open to change by the Supreme Military Council. The threatened stalemate was averted by a verbal assurance by the FMG of non-interference with the decisions of the Assembly. This assurance was however not kept, as the government, in enacting the decisions of the Assembly into law, made a considerable number of amendments to them. The mere fact of a substantive amendment, as distinct from a purely formal one, seems, irrespective of its nature or importance, to have further eroded the basis of the Constitution as an original act of the people. And, while the form and structures of the government have remained as they were approved by the Constituent Assembly, the changes resulting from the amendments are in many cases of far-reaching significance. Such are the amendments radically limiting the guarantee of property rights; abolishing the quota system in the composition of the officer corps of the armed forces; attenuating the procedure for the removal of judges; removing the disqualification imposed on candidates for the first election who had been found guilty of corruption, unjust enrichment or abuse of office by a tribunal of enquiry since October 1960; incorporating into the Constitution the provisions of the Decrees of the FMG on Land Use, Public Complaints, National Security Organisation, and the National Youth Service Corps; prohibiting designated public officers from having foreign accounts, and so on.

The merely deliberative role of the Assembly and the fact that its decisions were in the nature of recommendations which the Supreme Military Council (SMC) might approve, reject or modify are put beyond question by the Constitution of the Federal Republic of Nigeria (Enactment) Decree 1978, which declares as follows in a preamble:-

"Whereas the Constituent Assembly established by the Constituent Assembly Decree 1977 and as empowered by the Decree has *deliberated* upon the draft Constitution drawn up by the Constitution Drafting Committee and presented the result of its deliberations to the Supreme Military Council and the Supreme Military Council has *approved* the same subject to such changes as it has deemed necessary in the public interest and for purposes of fostering the promotion of the welfare of the people of Nigeria." (my italic)

Thus it was the Supreme Military Council, not the Constituent Assembly, that adopted the Constitution. The Assembly merely acted in an advisory role to the SMC.

For these reasons, the 1979 Constitution can hardly be regarded as an emanation of the popular will and choice. The FMG was not, at the time of the adoption of the Constitution, relinquishing constituent power to the people through the Constituent Assembly. There was as yet no restoration of constituent power to the people. But this conclusion does not flow from the mere fact that the Constitution was promulgated into law by the FMG.[21] If the substantive content of a constitution is agreed by the people either in a referendum or through a constituent assembly specially elected for that specific purpose, then it is their act, although promulgation may, in the interest of formalism and regularity, have been done by an existing state authority. Promulgation in the context is a purely formal act, which should not detract from the popular will.

The second (on-going) democratic transition is programmed over a eight-year period, 1986-93 and also, as in 1976-79, features, among other things, the setting up of a 17-member Political Bureau, a Constitution Review Committee, a Constituent Assembly and promulgation of a new Constitution by the FMG.

Inaugurated on January 13, 1986, the Bureau was charged, among other things, to "gather, collate and evaluate the contributions of Nigerians to the search for a viable political future." (The debate kicked off formally on February 3, 1986). People were mobilised at the grassroots and as members of various professional, academic, economic and social groups and organisations to participate in the debate through memoranda and newspaper articles, radio and television discussions, seminars, conferences, and symposia on specific issues identified by the Bureau.[22] To assist in further

---

21. See Constitution of the Federal Republic of Nigeria (Enactment) Decree 1978.
22. Report of the Political Bureau, Fed. Govt Printer Lagos, March 1987; and Govt White Paper on the Report, Fed Govt Printer, Lagos, March 1987.

mobilising the people for full participation, publicity and enlightenment committees were established in all the states and local government areas to publicise the debate and enlighten people on the specific issues to be focused on. The Bureau also toured all 301 local government areas in the country and conducted public hearings in all the state capitals. Participation in the debate was thus said "to cut across all social, economic and professional groups — urban elites, including businessmen, medical doctors, university teachers and administrators, lawyers and journalists, traditional rulers, market men and women, farmers, youths, students and workers."[23] The Bureau expressed itself satisfied with the general response of the Nigerian people to the debate, and emphatically denied the view expressed in some quarters that it was "an elitist affair."

Its recommendation in favour of the presidential system and federalism was based, it said, on the mass of public support for them, but there is nothing in the report to indicate that many of its other recommendations have also a basis in mass public support. They seem clearly to have been based on the Bureau's evaluation of their intrinsic merit.

On the basis of the Bureau's recommendations, and before a Constituent Assembly was set up to consider them, the FMG took decisions approving certain vital institutions and aspects of a new constitution for the country, and declared them to be "no-go areas" — the presidential system, two terms of four years each for the president and state governors, federalism, a bicameral legislature at the federal level and a two-party system. It also rejected constitutional rotation of the presidency and special representation for women and for organised labour.

For the rest, the process followed in the making of the Constitution was the same as in 1976-78, viz, the preparation of a draft Constitution by the Constitution Review Committee appointed by the FMG, public discussion of the constitutional proposals, formalised discussion and adoption by a Constituent Assembly established by Decree and consisting of a Chairman

23. Report, op. cit. para. 0.011.

and a Deputy Chairman appointed by the FMG, 450 members elected by existing local government councils functioning as electoral colleges and 111 other members nominated by the FMG, and the promulgation of the approved proposals, with modifications, into law by the FMG — the Constitution of the Federal Republic of Nigeria (Promulgation) Decree 1989. The Constituent Assembly functioned in much the same way and with the same procedure as in 1977.

(ii) A Constitution Having the Force of a Supreme, Overriding Law

Since an authoritarian or autocratic regime is, by definition, a government inadequately limited by, or which, in the case of an autocracy, is not subject at all to, a constitution having the force of a supreme, overriding law, such a constitution is, accordingly, a necessary condition in any scheme of transition from authoritarianism or autocracy to constitutional democracy. There is a mutual antagonism between the communist/totalitarian conception of government and the notion of a constitution as a supreme law which limits the powers of government and renders void all inconsistent governmental acts, legislative and executive. In communist theory and practice, a constitution is conceived rather as essentially a political, economic and social charter consisting largely of declarations of objectives and directive principles of government as well as a description of the organs of government in terms that import no enforceable legal restraints. A communist constitution has essentially a political existence, its provisions are political, serving mainly to exhort, to direct and to inspire governmental action, and to bestow upon it the stamp of legitimacy. Its contents are rooted in ideology, society, politics and economics. Thus, the earlier 1936 Constitution of the former Soviet Union and the earlier constitutions of the other communist states modelled upon it read more like manifestoes of social, political, economic and ideological goals to be pursued by the state together with a description of the institutions and procedures for realising them. No doubt, the later generations of communist constitutions, e.g. the 1977 constitution of the former Soviet Union, has tended to assume a somewhat more normative character;[24] even so, they are only normative, not coercive; they command no coercive legal force or sanction, such as to render void any inconsistent governmental action.

Constitutionality is judged in terms of the performance of government in "the realisation of socialist democratism,"[25] of its ability to realise in practical terms the political, economic and social goals of the socialist order, and to this end everything else, including human rights, is subordinated. The paramount duty of all state institutions as indeed all social organisations is to "promote, with special diligence, the realisation of the aims set precisely in the constitution."[26] And all powers necessary for the accomplishment of the socio-economic objectives and goals of the socialist order are deemed to be granted by the constitution, and are therefore legitimate. A communist constitution is considered to be faithfully implemented when the material conditions of socialism are fully realised. This is really what "socialist legality" is about. As was said by the President of the Soviet Supreme Court, "communism means not the victory of socialist law, but the victory of socialism over any law."[27]

The constitution purports to guarantee individual rights, but the so-called guarantee has no more effect than a declaration of objectives. In the 1936 Constitution of the Soviet Union and in those of the other communist countries modelled on it, certain rights were declared as either "an indefeasible law", e.g. equality of rights of citizens,[28] or "as guaranteed or protected by law," e.g. freedom of speech, press and assembly,[29] the inviolability of the homes of citizens and privacy of correspondence.[30] What law is referred to here, the law of the constitution or some other law? A proper interpretation would seem to suggest that the Constitution itself (1936) created no

---

24. See Williams Simons, ed. *The Constitutions of the Communist World* (1980), Introduction, p. xi.
25. G. Antaliffy, "The Amendment of the Constitution of Hungary," *Hungarian Law*, 1-2 (1984), p. 13.
26. G. Antaliffy, op. cit.
27. Quoted in Hayek, *The Constitution of Liberty* (1960), p. 240.
28. Art. 123.
29. Art. 125.
30. Art. 128.

legal guarantee of rights which the individual may assert against the state. Furthermore, the stipulation that the freedom of speech, press and assembly was guaranteed "in conformity with the interests of the working people, and in order to strengthen the socialist system"[31] made the guarantee subject to what the communist rulers considered was required by the interests of the working people or by the socialist system.[32]

The provisions relating to individual rights and duties contained in the later generation of constitutions of the countries of Eastern Europe and the 1977 Constitution of the Soviet Union which, interestingly, was greatly influenced by the former, are framed like a Bill of Rights properly so-called, although in all of them social, economic and cultural rights were given more prominence than civil and political rights.[33] As they were however embodied in a constitution that did not have the force of a supreme, overriding law, they could not have imposed a legal restraint enforceable against the state (especially the legislative organ) at the instance of the individual. In any case, we do know as a fact that they did not prevent "the *nomenklatura* in all communist countries from arbitrarily arresting and torturing people, from censoring all publications, from stopping people travelling and choosing their employment, or from curtailing other elementary liberties."[34]

Democratisation in the countries of Eastern Europe and the former Soviet Union needs therefore to be accompanied by a radical change in the way a constitution and constitutionality are conceived, framed and applied. Happily, the Constitutions adopted in 1991 by Bulgaria and Romania conform to the notion of a constitution as a supreme, overriding law, as does also Czechoslovakia's Charter of Fundamental Rights and Freedoms (1991) enacted by Constitutional Law Act No. 23/91.

---

31. Art. 125.
32. See Williams G. Andrews, ed., *Constitutions and Constitutionalism*, 2nd ed. (1963), p. 152.
33. Chap. 3, arts 34- 65, Bulgaria; chap. 2, arts 19-38, Czechoslovakia; Part II, chap. 1, arts 19-40, German Democratic Republic (GDR); chap 2 arts 54-70, Hungary; chap 8, arts 67-93, Poland; chap. 2, arts 17-41, Romania; chap. 7, arts 39-69, USSR; chap. 2, arts 280-281, Yulgoslavia.
34. Ralf Dahrendorf, *Reflections on the Revolution in Europe* (1990), p. 80.

The Constitution of Bulgaria (1991), in explicit terms, proclaims itself the supreme law, which must not be contravened by any other law; it also proclaims the rule of law as a fundamental principle of the state.[35] The pattern thus established by these three former communist countries may probably be followed by the others when they come to adopt new constitutions.

The constitutions of the one-party regimes in the ex-French African countries have the character of a supreme law, in both the normative and coercive senses, although in those of them which are based on the French conception of a constitution their coercive force is limited to the executive, and does not avail against the legislature whose acts can only be pronounced void for unconstitutionality by a special body, the Constitutional Council. The Council is a special device because it does not form part of the ordinary court system, is composed of non-permanent members appointed or elected in prescribed proportions by the executive and legislature for a specific, non-renewable term of years — nine years. (All past Presidents of the Republic are life members).

A body outside the ordinary court system, with a non-permanent membership, is no doubt intended as part of the answer to the objections against the review of statutes by an oligarchy of permanent, virtually irremovable judges. But for France it seems to be a design not to give the constitution a coercive force against acts of the legislature, rather in the manner of the British system. The Constitutional Council is neither a court nor are its functions judicial; this is because its ruling on the question of constitutionality can be rendered only before a legislative measure, whether a regulation, statute or organic law, is actually promulgated into law or before it is put into effect, and then only on a reference to the Council by the President of the Republic, the premier, the president of the Assembly, president of the senate, sixty deputies or sixty senators, but not by a private person.[36] A law declared unconstitutional may not be promulgated or put into effect.[37]

---

35.   Arts 4 and 5.
36.   Art. 61; arts. 56-63.
37.   Art. 62.

Whilst it has value in enabling unconstitutional or illegal acts to be nipped in the bud, a ruling given even by an ordinary court on a legislative measure before its promulgation into law or before it comes into operation and before a dispute has arisen on its application or threatened application to identifiable persons is not a judicial decision[38] because the issue on which it is given is not a justiciable one;[39] it is only an advisory opinion.[40] It is true that, unlike an advisory opinion strictly so-called, the French Constitutional Council's rulings are expressly made "binding upon the governing authorities and all administrative and judicial authorities" and are not "subject to review,[41] yet this fact has the effect of removing from the ordinary courts, power to review statutes for constitutionality, at any rate in cases where a matter has been ruled upon by the Council. It is a total rejection of the judicial review of statutes by the ordinary courts and of the coercive force of the constitution against the acts of the legislature.

Commenting on the Constitution of the Third French Republic, Dicey was thus prompted to say that "the restrictions (it) placed on the action of the legislature are not in reality laws, since they are not rules which in the last resort will be enforced by the courts. Their true character is that of maxims of political morality, which derive whatever strength they possess from being formally inscribed in the Constitution, and from the resulting support of public opinion."[42] For the African one-party states whose constitutions are based on this French system, democratisation should, ideally, involve a change to the notion of the constitution as a supreme law in the strict, orthodox sense of overriding all inconsistent acts of government, executive as well as legislative. The constitutions of the one-party states in Commonwealth Africa all conform to this notion.

---

38. *Hayburn's Case* 2 Dall 409 (1792); *United States v. Ferreira* 13 How 40 (1851); *United States v. Evans* 213 U.S. 297, pp. 300-1 (1909).
39. *Att- Gen for Ontario v. Att-Gen for the Dominion* (1896) A.C. 348 (P.C.).
40. On the difference between judicial decision and an advisory opinion, see Nwabueze, *Judicialism in Commonwealth Africa* (1977), pp. 84-97.
41. Art. 62.
42. A.V. Dicey, *The Law of the Constitution,* 3rd ed. p. 157.

Whether Freedom of Political Association Should be Entirely Unrestrained

Indisputably, democracy requires freedom to organise in opposition to the government in office. Next to the right of acting for himself, the most natural right of the individual is that of combining with others in a common effort and action. Freedom of political association, as an aspect of the general right of association, is important to participatory democracy because, while free discussion assures to the community information on, and a say in, public affairs, freedom to form a political party enables those who are politically inclined and share common ideas about government to associate and organise together in order to make their advocacy of their ideas more effective, and to seek, eventually, an opportunity to implement them by persuading people to vote them into power on the basis of those ideas. Political parties are the traditional platforms for organising and carrying on political activity.[43] Politics in our modern complex society would be virtually impossible to conduct effectively, nor would elections be possible to organise properly, without political parties. And democracy itself has little meaning without a free competition for power between associations of persons with opposing ideas about government. A political association unites into one the opinions of different people, and bestows upon the united opinion an authority which, because of the numbers it represents, necessarily commands greater attention and respect than the opinion of one individual. Political parties are therefore "a necessary evil in free government."[44]

Without an organised party in opposition, government may tend to take the people for granted, and may become unresponsive to their feelings. The political responsibility of the government to the governed can only be realised in the context of an organised opposition party alert to expose to the public the weaknesses and failure of the government, and capable of

---

43. See *Sweezy v. New Hampshire*, 334 U.S. 254 (1957).
44. Alexis de Tocqueville, *Democracy in America* (1835) edited Richard Heffner (1956), p. 88.

accepting the mantle of office should the people be inclined to bestow that upon it. In such role, therefore, the liberty of association is "a necessary guarantee against the tyranny of the majority."[45] "All change," said the U.S. Supreme Court, "is, to a certain extent, achieved by the opposition of the new to the old, and in so far as it is within the law, such peaceful opposition ... is recognised as a symbol of independent thought containing the promise of progress."[46]

The great advantage of political parties lies thus in ensuring that government and politics are conducted upon the basis of principles of government of fundamental moral significance to society, and not merely for motives of selfish gain or the aggrandisement of private interests. The issues of principle may concern, for example, the structure of society, the limits of state power over the individual, equality, social justice and such like. Where the existence and operations of political parties do not rest on, or are not informed by, any differences of opinion on fundamental issues of principle, then, their value is greatly reduced.

Where political parties are not formed along the lines of fundamental differences on issues of principle, politics may become dominated by minor controversies about details of administration. Moreover, there may then be an inclination to resort more to violence rather than try to win the support of the majority through persuasion by relying on the merit of each party's principle about how society should be better managed.

Granted the indispensability of competition among opposing political parties to democracy, the question is whether freedom to form political associations should be entirely unrestrained. In itself, a combination of persons is, like thought and conscience, perfectly innocuous, as it can impinge on no one's rights, neither those of other individuals nor of society at large. It is the *purpose* for which an association is formed, not the mere fact of people combining together, that has a potentiality for evil. The purpose of an association is invariably in the nature of an activity, and like other human activities, it should

45.   de Tocqueville, op. cit. p. 97.
46.   *Stromberg v. California,* 238 U.S. 359 (1931).

be subject to control. Political activity is no doubt of greater importance to the life of a community than economic or social activities, deserving therefore to be accorded more respect and protection, but it has also a greater potentiality to impinge on society's interest in order and security as to justify even greater control by the state. It is an evil, albeit an eminently necessary one.

Alexis de Tocqueville strenuously maintains that "the *unlimited* liberty of political association cannot be entirely assimilated to the liberty of the press. The one is at the same time less necessary, and more dangerous, than the other. A nation may confine it within certain limits without forfeiting any part of its self-directing power; and it may sometimes be obliged to do so, in order to maintain its own authority,"[47] adding that "the unrestrained liberty of association for political purposes is the last degree of liberty which a people is fit for."[48] He thinks it unwise therefore for a nation to "invest its citizens with an absolute right of association for political purposes" or to "set no limits" to it, since "if it does not throw them into anarchy, it perpetually brings them, as it were, to the verge of it."[49]

The limits which it may be necessary to set to freedom of political association must take into account a country's history and culture, the character of its people, its social structure and other relevant factors, in particular the extent to which people have accepted the object of politics as being to persuade and convince rather than to fight. Such a culture is difficult to get established and accepted where political parties are founded upon racial or ethnic group interests and where, consequently, minority parties have no hope of ever winning over the majority to vote them into power and are reduced to fighting as the only way to justify their continued existence. A country is thus entitled to set reasonable restrictions on the freedom of political association in order to curb this danger.

But perhaps the greatest danger of an unrestricted freedom

---

47. *Democracy in America* (1835), ed. Heffner (1956), p. 97.
48. ibid p. 209.
49. at p. 209.

of political association is that it may throw up an undesirably large and unmanageable number of political parties. This was the experience of Nigeria in 1978. Within days of the lifting of the ban on politics by the military government in preparation for the return to democractic rule scheduled for 1979, 53 political parties had sprouted up. The number of parties was 250 in Zaire, 100 in Congo, 68 in Cameroun, 30 in Senegal, 25 in Burkina Fasso, 17 in Benin and 16 in Guinea. It is difficult to see how a large number of parties can ever be in the interest of a country. Whilst meaningful elections presuppose a choice between alternative programmes presented by the contestants for political office, it is doubtful whether a society's problems admit of more than a limited number of credible and relevant programmes at any one time; moreover, a large proliferation of programmes may only confuse the electorate. Given a large number of political parties, their purpose in politics can hardly be to persuade the majority to support their programmes but rather to fight, so that violence becomes inevitable in that kind of situation.

Where the society is a plural one consisting of multifarious ethnic or racial groups marked apart by wide and deep differences in culture, outlook, education, language and economics, there is the even graver danger that the parties would be formed around the nucleus of the major groups. The major racial or ethnic groups provide the base for party formation, serving as a focus of appeal for support.

In such a situation, the parties not only represent the various ethnic or racial groups around which they are formed, they also institutionalise the divergent interests of the groups. Their activities are informed primarily and predominantly by ethnic or racial, rather than by national, interests. And because the interests of the groups are opposed to each other, relations among the parties are transformed from normal political competition into a feud, elections become a life and death struggle featuring thuggery, violence and all kinds of electoral malpractices, and government is turned into an instrument for the aggrandisement of the victorious group to the exclusion of the others. The groups so excluded become resentful and alienated, smacking under a fear of permanent domination by the victorious group. The affairs of the nation, indeed its entire life, are thoroughly overshadowed by the struggle for the control of the state and its resources. Politics looms larger than the nation itself, submerging everything else; it comes to matter too much, to dominate the thoughts and actions of people. Instability in society and in government reigns. Nationalistic feeling and pride are killed, and progress and development are held up. Such a situation of tribalised politics has been aptly described by the Donoughmore Commission on a Constitution for Ceylon (1928) as "a canker in the body politic, eating deeper and deeper into the vital energies of the people, breeding self-interest, suspicion and animosity, poisoning the new growth of political consciousness and effectively preventing the development of a national or corporate spirit."

It is probably inescapable that the struggle for the control of the state would, in the context of a multi-ethnic or multi-racial society, produce ethnic or racial parties, whether the system is unitary or federal. However, federalism provides an institutional base for the propagation of ethnicism or racism in politics. It enables the parties in control of the regional governments to use the institutionalised power to champion, at both the regional and federal levels, the interests of the tribes or races they represent. The effect of this at the federal level is to cause the federal government to be regarded as but a huge cake, already baked, and which it is the duty of each ethnic or racial party to secure for its ethnic or racial group as large a share as possible. This was the kind of perverted attitude that characterised the relations of the parties and their members at the federal level in Nigeria before the military take-over in January 1966. Every question, whether it be the award of scholarships or contracts, appointments in the federal public service, economic development or the siting of industrial projects, was viewed from the viewpoint of ethnic advantage, and support for, or opposition to, it depended upon whether or not it advanced the interest of one's tribe.

The experience of Nigeria is of course by no means peculiar to it. The danger has also been experienced to a greater or less extent in other African countries, and has been a major factor in the imposition of one-party system in many of them.

A country faced with this kind of danger is entitled to set restrictions on the freedom of political association without forfeiting its claim to be a democracy. All the Bills of Rights in the Commonwealth recognise the legitimacy of reasonable restrictions for this purpose, but the problem is to determine what restrictions may be considered as reasonably compatible with democracy. Is it a reasonable restriction to prescribe minimum conditions of eligibility to sponsor candidates for elections or minimum conditions for registration as a political party or to set a limit to the number of parties permitted to exist, and if so, what number? What can be asserted right away is that limiting the number to only one is not a permissible restriction conformable with the standard of democracy.

Political opinions divide broadly into seven — the far left, the left, the inside left, the centre, the inside right, the right and the far right — although these may be subsumed into three broader divisions, right, left and centre. This suggests that the largest number of political parties to be allowed to sponsor candidates for elections in a country should not be more than seven at most. Beyond this, political parties can no longer be said to be based on principle, but on personal or sectional interests. It follows therefore that the number of political parties to be recognised to sponsor candidates for elections should be limited in the Constitution to seven, and at the same time conditions of eligibility should be stipulated in the Constitution such that in practice no more than two or three would be able to meet them to qualify for recognition for purposes of sponsoring candidates for elections. It is hoped that in this way a two-party or a three-party system will eventually evolve on its own.

The conditions of eligibility should include the following:-

(i)   Membership must be open to all citizens irrespective of place of origin, sex, religion or ethnic identity.

(ii) The principal officers and members of the national executive committee or other governing body must be drawn from two-thirds of the local government areas in the country and the constitution of the party must provide for their election on a democratic basis for periods not exceeding five years.

(iii) It must be well-established in the capital and in the headquarters of two-thirds of the local government areas, judged by the number of registered members and administrative organisation at each of these places. Parliament is to prescribe by law the size of membership and the kind of administrative organisation required for this purpose.

(iv) The name, emblem or motto of the party must not contain any ethnic or religious connotation or give the appearance that its activities are confined only to a part of the geographical area of the country.

(v) The party's manifesto must show how it intends to tackle the various socio-economic and political problems facing the country, as, for example, problems of economic and social development, including rural development, corruption and indiscipline in society, national unity, stability and ethnic harmony, local government, the bureaucracy and social security.

(vi) Its aims and objects must conform with the fundamental objectives of the nation as may be laid down by law.

The responsibility for deciding whether a political party has met with the stipulated conditions of eligibility and for according its recognition accordingly shall vest in the electoral body so constituted however as to be representative of all political parties. A recognised political party shall be required to register the following particulars with the electoral body:-

(i) Its constitution which must be in such form as may be prescribed by Parliament; any alteration in the registered constitution must also be registered with the electoral body;

(ii) The names and addresses of its national officers and members of its national executive committee or other governing body;

(iii) Its emblem or motto, and

(iv) Any other information relating to the political party as may be required by the electoral body.

What is here suggested involves a distinction between *registered* political parties and those of them that are *recognised* as having met the prescribed conditions of eligibility to sponsor candidates for elections. There should be no substantive restrictions on the registration of political parties and any number may be registered in accordance with the law governing such registration. A registered political party may, on application, be accorded recognition by the electoral body as having met the stipulated conditions of eligibility to sponsor candidates for elections. This distinction is a necessary one because, in the nature of things, a political party, after its formation and registration, needs to have been in existence for a period of time to be able to meet the prescribed conditions for recognition. They are certainly not conditions that can be met at the time of registration as a political party.

Chapter 3

Exclusions From Participation in Democratic Politics and Government During and After the Current Transition

> I am in agreement with the majority of deputies, political parties and a large part of our public that this law — extraordinary and exceptional, as it may be — is necessary because many people linked with the totalitarian regime, who had for years taken an active part in crushing human rights in the land have not ... spontaneously renounced their leading functions in the State and public life ... and are halting or hindering the formation of a true democratic order.
>
> — President Vaclav Havel

One particular problem of the current transition from one-party, military or communist rule to multi-party democracy that has generated so much controversy and acrimony and which has a special relevance to the meaningfulness of democratisation is the question of the exclusion of certain categories of persons from participation in democratic politics and government on the grounds of their political antecedents or past involvement in corruption, human rights violation, abuse of office or mismanagement or for other reasons. The issue has assumed more serious proportions in Eastern Europe than in Africa because of the nature and methods of communist rule and the larger number of persons affected by the exclusions.

Necessity for Complete Change of Guards on Transition from One-Party, Military or Communist Rule to Multi-Party Democracy

The events of 1989 in Eastern Europe are generally regarded as a revolution. What makes it meaningful so to regard them is because they resulted in the removal of the former communist rulers and the delegitimation of a whole ruling class. Had the former rulers been permitted to contest the multi-party elections and had won, there would have been no real revolution, but only a change from the communist party's monopoly of power to multi-partyism which by itself alone would hardly qualify the events as revolutionary. The events are of a revolutionary character principally because they resulted in the ouster, the sweeping away, of the former communist dictators. We could not meaningfully talk of a revolution if, after the change to multi-partyism, Nicolai Ceausescu had continued in power in Romania, Jamos Kadar in Hungary, Honecker in East Germany, Todor Zhivkov in Bulgaria, Gustav Husak in Czechoslovakia or General Jaruzelski in Poland. The abolition of the communist party's monopoly of power is no doubt an important part of those events but it is the removal of the former rulers from power more than the abolition of the communist party's monopoly of power that gave them their revolutionary character. They derive their revolutionary character more from the fact that, in the words of Timothy Garton Ash in his book, *We the People* (1990), "prisoners became prime ministers and prime ministers became prisoners."

It is therefore appropriate to, indeed it is required by, the character of those events that the former rulers, even if they had not been put in jail, should be barred from putting themselves for re-election after the transition to multi-partyism. In Africa, incumbent Presidents Eyadema of Togo and Nguesso of Congo have been barred from contesting the multi-party presidential elections. It is right that they should have been barred because they represent, or at least symbolise, a rejected system of rule. To allow them to continue under the new system would involve a palpable contradiction.

The change to multi-partyism in Cape Verde Island, Zambia and Benin has meaning because Aristides Pereira, Kenneth Kaunda and Mathew Kerekou, Presidents under the one-party system, lost the multi-party presidential elections to the leaders of the democratisation movement. In Cote d'Ivoire, Burkina Fasso, and Kenya, where the multi-party presidential elections were won by Felix Houphouet-Boigny, Blaise Compaore and Arap Moi, Presidents under the former one-party system (the multi-party election in Ghana was won by Jerry Rawlings, the former military ruler), the change to multi-partyism lost much of its meaning. They should not have contested at all, but should have stepped down on their own if they had any sense of propriety or self-respect. In the advanced parliamentary democracies, established convention requires the government to quit when it is defeated on an important issue of policy. Surely, when a system, not just a policy with which a President has been identified for years and which he has come to represent and symbolise, is unequivocally rejected by the people, he should have the good sense and the self-respect to quit. In Burkina Fasso, the parties in the democratisation movement had boycotted the multi-party presidential elections in protest against incumbent President Blaise Compaore's candidature, but he stood all the same, and got himself declared winner as sole candidate. The country is now in the grips of a crisis as a result of this.

The question that arises from such a shameless act of hanging on to power is this: having stood and "won", can such leaders be expected to shed the authoritarian style of rule to which they have been used over the years? Experience shows that where — as in Togo in January 1972, Benin in February 1980 and Liberia in January 1986 — a military ruler succeeded himself upon the change from military to civilian rule, it is as if nothing had changed. The habits of authoritarian or autocratic rule, indulged in, or even cultivated, over many years, cannot be shed overnight just because of a formal change in the structures of power. Samuel Doe as civilian president from January 6, 1986 until his murder on September 10, 1990 remained largely as repressive and authoritarian as he was as a military ruler for six years (April 12, 1980 to January 6, 1986). So were Mathew Kerekou of Benin (October 26, 1972 to February 6, 1980 as military ruler, and February 6, 1980 to March 1990 as civilian ruler under a one- party system) and Eyadema of Togo (January 13, 1967 to January 9, 1972 as military ruler, and January 9, 1972 to 1991 as civilian ruler in a one-party regime).

As it is with military rulers, so also it is with civilian ones. Since his re-election at the multi-party presidential elections on October 28, 1990, Felix Houphouet-Boigny's authoritarian style of rule has not changed from what it was during his 30 years' rule under the one-party system from the time of independence on November 27, 1960. It is too much to expect him to shed a style of rule which, after 30 years in office as President in a one-party regime, has become rooted in him as part of his personality.

The lesson of all this is that these rulers should not have permitted themselves or been permitted to continue, even though they have not been found guilty of corruption, abuse of office or mismanagement. They should be barred. The ban should cover not the top man alone but all those who have held political offices in the government at any time, ministers and others as well as the leading members of the ruling party. It is a contradiction, and an affront to our intelligence, that anyone who, as minister or secretary to the government, had been actively involved in the formulation, articulation and implementation of the policies of a one-party or military regime, should turn round, in a campaign for election as president in the on-going transition, to denounce those same policies and to assure the people that he would reverse them if elected. No country ought to accept that from anyone. The problem today in some of the countries of Eastern Europe, notably Romania and Bulgaria, is that, while the communist party's monopoly of power has been abolished, some leading members of the party have managed to gain control of the government under the newly established multi-party system.

What happened in Bulgaria in 1989 was only a palace revolution, not a people's revolution as in the other East European countries. It arose from a division within the Bulgarian Communist Party (BCP) between a reformist group led by Mladenov, Foreign Minister for the previous 18 years, and a conservative group supporting Zhivkov who had ruled the country for more than 35 years. The reformists' opposition to Zhivkov was not just on the issue of reform; they also resented his personalised style of rule, particularly the decision, taken without consultation with the Politburo, to assimilate forcibly the Turkish minority in the country. Zhivkov's repressive handling of the Turkish minority question, the mass exodus of some 350,000 ethnic Turks, his generally appalling human rights record and the economic mismanagement with its resultant acute shortages of essential items, the endless queues at the shops and general deterioration in living standards had created widespread anger and hatred against the regime. There had been demonstrations on October 26 and again on November 3, 1989. The stage was then set for the reformist group within the BCP to act. At a meeting of the Party's Central Committee on November 10, 1989, they, with the support of Moscow, got Zhivkov removed, and replaced him with Mladenov. Zhivkov was immediately put under house arrest.[1]

Thus, the revolution in Bulgaria was largely an internal affair of BCP in which the pro-democracy groups played but minimal role. Nor were they really in a position to have played a significant role. Indeed the oldest of them, the Independent Society for Human Rights, only came into existence in 1988; however, by July 1989, three others had sprung up, viz the Independent Discussion Club for the Support of Perestroika and Glasnost, Ecoglasnost (an environmental group) and the Citizens Initiative. But, apart from being new and inexperienced, they were not well organised, and had no clear programme of action. Their coming together under one umbrella organisation by the name of Union of Democratic Forces (UDF) only came about in December 1989, some one month after the palace revolution. Other opposition groups, such as the Social Democratic Party (SDP), the Agrarian Party, the Greens and the Movement for Rights and Freedom (MRF) had also sprung up.

The revolution in Bulgaria resulted therefore only in the ouster of Zhivkov and the renunciation by the BCP of its guaranteed monopoly of power in favour of multi-partyism, but it did not bring about the overthrow of the Party's control of the government. The man who replaced the ousted Zhivkov had, as earlier noted, been Foreign Minister for the preceding 18 years and the rest of the Party's leadership remained, except for Zhivkov's closest associates. What is more, at the multi-party elections held on 10 and 17 June, 1990, the BCP, now renamed the Bulgarian Socialist Party (BSP), emerged

---

1.   *Tearing Down The Curtain,* The Observer Publication (1990) pp. 83-99; Misha Glenny, *The Rebirth of History* (1990) pp. 164-182.

victorious, with 211 seats in a 400-member Parliament, which proceeded to re-elect Mladenov as President (The BSP secured 47 per cent of the popular votes). In our view, it is immaterial that, as Misha Glenny tells us, "the Communist Party, at the time of the Bulgarian elections, was already a very different organisation, in ideological terms, from the enormous instrument of personal power that Bulgaria's dictator, Todor Zhivkov, had wielded for over thirty-five years until his fall in November 1989".[2] As Misha Glenny himself states the BCP remained an "instrument of political repression."[3]

The situation that emerged in Bulgaria thus prompts the question whether there had been any real revolution. It seems so far to contradict the revolution as to rob it of much of its meaning. Spurred on by a large body of students, UDF had therefore mounted a campaign for the revival of the revolution, and is demanding an end to BSP's continued monopoly on power. This led to the formation of what is known as "City of Truth" in the capital, Sofia, and other cities. The "Cities", it has been said, represented "an important extension of the revolution";[4] they had "a cathartic effect and eventually pushed the BSP towards more concessions, helping moderates in the party to weaken the hard-liners".[5] They (the Cities) even succeeded in forcing the resignation of Mladenov as President because of a statement he made in Parliament to the effect that the best thing to do, in handling opposition demonstrations, was "to let the tanks come", which was interpreted as showing that he had not cast off communist authoritarianism, and that he lacked a commitment to democracy. The BSP-dominated Parliament then elected the UDF leader, Zhelev, as President to replace Mladenov. But an invitation by BSP to UDF to join it in a coalition government was rightly rejected by UDF for fear that such a collaboration with the former Communist Party might destroy its credibility and public image as a pro-democracy movement.

---

2.   op. cit. p. 164.
3.   ibid p. 165.
4.   Misha Glenny op. cit. p. 178.
5.   Misha Glenny op. cit. p. 179.

The BSP had also been obliged to capitulate "on a series of other opposition demands as well, including greatly improved access to television... This had gone a long way in diffusing the political tension in the country, which at one point almost threatened to explode into an orgy of violence that would have pitted town against country".[6] In August 1990, for instance, demonstrators had ransacked and set fire on BSP's headquarters, giving rise to heightened tension and violent clashes. But the fact that these concessions were not voluntary but were forced out of the BSP showed how incompatible the continued control of the government by former communists was with the transition to democracy. Truly, therefore, has it been said that Bulgaria has "bucked the trend", the new democratisation trend in Eastern Europe. The revolution in Bulgaria is, happily, continuing; and it will not be complete until the BSP is liquidated as a political party — not of course by the totalitarian method of a formal ban, but rather through the electoral process as was the case in Hungary, Poland and East Germany.

The Romanian revolution which overthrew the hated dictator, Ceausescu, and the Romanian Communist Party (RCP) — outlawed soon after the revolution — saw the communists still in control of the government under a new name, the National Salvation Front (NSF), even winning the multi-party presidential and parliamentary elections held on May 20, 1990 with an overwhelming majority — about 82 per cent of the votes. The NSF had been described as "a phoenix that had risen effortlessly from the ashes of Ceausescu's RCP",[7] and as "assimilating the entire power structure" of that Party as well as its traditions, including its strong-arm tactic and frequent resort to armed force represented by the secret police, many of whose old members had been fully rehabilitated. The orientations and sentiments of the NSF were unmistakably anti-democratic. Its leader, Iliescu, is said to be an unrepentant, unconverted socialist politician of the old order. The Party "did not hide the fact that it was, in fact, the

---

6. Misha Glenny loc. cit.
7. Misha Glenny, op. cit. p. 98.

Communist Party with a reformist face."[8]

The Party was able to win the May elections by pandering to the public during its immediate post-revolution rule by means of equitable distribution of food, promise of social security for all, cutting working hours and increasing wages. This had the desired effect that "for the great majority of Romanians, the Front, and above all its president, Ian Iliescu, was synonymous with the overthrow of Ceausescu and the restoration of economic justice."[9]

The performance of the NSF Government since the May 1990 elections has been marked by intolerance, human rights violations and the persecution and repression of the opposition through the use of fascist-type violence, as in June 1990 when some 20,000 miners, at the instigation of the government, descended upon members of the opposition and beat them up senseless regardless of gender, age or nationality. Misha Glenny has expressed the view that "Romania bucked the trend in a much more fundamental way than did Bulgaria."[10]

The evidence thus shows that in Bulgaria, Romania, Cote d'Ivoire and Burkina Fasso the transition from communist or one-party rule to multi-party democracy has not brought an end to authoritarianism and repression, and that this will not come about unless and until the ruling party and its leaders under the former regime have been driven out of power. The transition to democracy in those countries remains therefore incomplete.

Exclusion by Means of Disqualification or Removal for Corruption, Abuse of Power or Mismanagement

The controversy and acrimony generated by the issue of exclusion is particularly acute where the exclusion is by means of disqualification from participation or removal from an office already held. It becomes necessary, then, to enquire into the

---

8.   ibid p. 115.
9.   ibid p. 98.
10.   ibid p. 164.

nature of disqualification or removal as a penalty for involvement in corruption, abuse of power or mismanagement. What are their consequences and incidents?

Nature of Removal and Disqualification as a Penalty

Disqualification from holding a public office has quite serious consequences. It entails a disability, a denial of a right, privilege or capacity possessed and enjoyed by the generality of the citizenry. In short, it is a denial of a person's status as a *full* member of his community. Admittedly, no one has a right to a public office. Whilst our humanity gives us a right to work, it does not entitle us to be employed by another, whether the state, a corporate person or an individual. But a citizen does have the privilege to contest or compete for a public office on equal terms with other citizens; to disqualify him from doing so on the ground of corruption, corrupt practices, abuse of power or mismanagement is indisputably a disability. On the face of it, removal from office in pursuance of a law is not quite the same thing as disqualification, since it does not wear the appearance of a formal disability, but it is as much a disability in its practical effect as a disqualification.

The consequences of disqualification are even more serious when it bars a person from participating in politics, as by membership of a political party, the expression of political opinion, campaigning or canvassing for partisan political support, donation to the funds of a political party, etc. It is then not merely the withholding of a privilege conferred by membership of society, but rather the deprivation of a fundamental right inherent in every individual by virtue of his humanity. The right to hold political opinions, to express or advocate them and to act in furtherance thereof is inherent in every person. Next to the right of acting for himself, the most natural right of the individual is that of combining with others in common advocacy and action. Disqualifying a person from participating in politics is thus a more serious matter than merely denying him the privilege of competing for an appointive public office or contesting for an elective one.

Yet, serious as are the consequences of disqualification or removal imposed by law for corruption, corrupt practices, abuse of power or mismanagement, it is only a disciplinary penalty for the purification of public life, and not a punishment for a criminal offence. Furthermore, whilst it implies guilt for some wrong-doing, it is not a conviction for a criminal offence. Thus, where a statute enacted by the Ceylonese legislature in 1965 vacated the parliamentary seats of certain named persons who had been found guilty of bribery by a commission of inquiry, the Judicial Committee of the Privy Council, on appeal from Ceylon, held the removal of the culprits from their parliamentary seats not to be punishment for a criminal offence, as to render the statute unconstitutional and void.[11] It was intended, said the Privy Council, not really to punish, but to discipline and to "keep public life clean for the public good."[12] Emphasising the difference between a disciplinary penalty of this kind and a punishment for a criminal offence, it said, quoting the words of Justice Frankfurter of the U.S. Supreme Court:[13] "The fact that harm is inflicted by governmental authority does not make it punishment. Figuratively speaking all discomforting action may be deemed punishment because it deprives of what otherwise would be enjoyed. But there may be reasons other than punitive for such deprivation."

The difference between the guilt implied by disqualification or removal and conviction for a criminal offence is of the utmost significance. Criminal conviction is an expression of society's condemnation of a person as unworthy of its membership, and is usually accompanied by punishment in the form of such unwelcome incarceration, like imprisonment. There is yet another significant difference. Disqualification as a disciplinary penalty is usually temporary in duration, whereas the taint of a conviction and some of its other incidents (it is also usually a bar to employment) are permanent. Disqualification as a permanent bar to employment is perhaps more in the nature of a punishment than a disciplinary penalty, and ought to be subjected to similar safeguards.

---

11. *Kariapper v. Wijesinha*, [1967] 3 All E.R. 485.
12. ibid at p. 491.
13. *United States v. Lovett*, 328 U.S. 303 (1945).

To condemn a person as unworthy of the membership of society and to punish him accordingly, imperatively requires that the process used must be such as guarantees the independence and impartiality of the tribunal and the other democratic safeguards of a fair trial, such as the presumption of innocence, the requirement of proof beyond reasonable doubt, the rules of admissibility or inadmissibility of evidence, etc. It also requires the safeguard of non-retroactivity in penal legislation. This is necessary in order to guard against, as much as possible, the possibility of an innocent person being convicted and punished. The injustice of a false conviction and punishment is the worst injustice imaginable. Nothing outrages human feelings and depresses the spirit more than a false conviction for a criminal offence and the infliction of punishment on an innocent person for it. These safeguards and considerations are inapplicable where all that is involved is, not conviction and punishment for a criminal offence, but only civil culpability or guilt as a basis for the imposition of a temporary disciplinary penalty for the purification of public life.

But since disqualification or removal implies culpability or guilt, the question still remains as to how the culpability or guilt is to be established as a basis for the imposition of the penalty, whether it has to be proved before an impartial, though not necessarily independent, tribunal, such as a judicial tribunal of inquiry, whether proof by means of an administrative enquiry suffices or whether it can be presumed from circumstances.

A finding of guilt for corruption, corrupt practices, abuse of power or mismanagement by a judicial commission of enquiry seems to provide a justifiable basis for disqualification. For, the procedure by which a commission of inquiry is conducted is sufficiently akin to that of a court to make its finding acceptable for this purpose. Unless otherwise directed, a commission of inquiry is by law required to conduct a public hearing at which evidence and arguments are presented just as in a court hearing. Also like a court, it has power to compel the attendance of witnesses and the production of documents or other things as evidence, to procure any other evidence, written or oral, as it may consider necessary or desirable, and to listen to arguments by counsel, representation by counsel being specifically authorised by law. Its members, like those of a court, are under oath to discharge their function faithfully and impartially. A commission of inquiry is not of course bound by any strict rules of evidence and procedure, such as govern court proceedings, but this ought not to affect the acceptability of its finding. On the contrary, its being exonerated from strict rules of evidence and procedure, and the absence of the intimidating atmosphere of a court place it in a better position than a court to obtain information and to expose the truth.

Although an administrative inquiry functions entirely informally and may not be characterised by impartiality to the same degree as a judicial commission of inquiry, its finding is also acceptable for this purpose, provided the person accused of corruption, abuse of office or mismanagement is given adequate opportunity to be heard in his own defence.

It is therefore right and proper for the Nigerian legislation on the matter, the Participation in Politics and Elections (Prohibition) Decree 1987, to disqualify public office-holders found guilty or who may be found guilty by any tribunal (civil or military), assets or special investigation panel, judicial commission of enquiry or administrative enquiry for involvement in corruption, corrupt practices, other official misconduct or any offence or misdeed whatever committed during a tenure of office between October 1, 1960 and the end of the transition period (August 27, 1993) as well as

(a)   persons in both the public and private sectors (including military and police personnel) who have been or will be dismissed from any office or any employment during the same period;

(b)   all military and police personnel who held office during the same period who were removed from office otherwise than by dismissal; and

(c)   persons not in the public service found guilty by any tribunal, assets or special investigation panel, judicial commission of enquiry or administrative enquiry for corrupting public office-holders during the same period. The inclusion in the disqualification of persons removed from office for corruption, abuse of office or other misconduct is also right and proper, provided that, as in the case of persons found guilty of such misdeeds after due enquiry, they were given an opportunity to be heard in their own defence.

All those covered in these various categories are for ever barred from contesting any elective office and from holding any public or party political office. Disqualification for life, even for corruption, is, as earlier stated, more in the nature of punishment which ought not to be imposed except on the finding of an independent and impartial tribunal. Since the purpose of exclusion is the purification of public life, rehabilitation should be allowed on the assumption that the culprit may have reformed himself after being under the clouds of disability for a period of time.

Disqualification under the Decree is, however, not self-enforcing. A body, the National Electoral Commission (NEC), is interposed for the purpose, with power to declare any person appointed or elected to any public or political party office or nominated to contest such office to be a person affected by a disqualification, and thereupon his nomination, election or appointment shall stand nullified. A declaration by the Commission may be made either on its own motion or upon objection by anyone after an opportunity for a hearing is given to the affected person. The Commission may also, on the application of anyone, conduct an investigation to determine whether the applicant is a person affected or not.

The Nigerian Decree goes further than this, for it also makes a ground for disqualification, the holding or the fact of having held designated offices between October 1, 1960 and January 15, 1966 or between October 1, 1979 and December 30, 1983 in the case of civilians or between January 16, 1966 and the end of the transition period in the case of military and police personnel, although no offence or misdeed is proved against them personally. This raises the question, which is the real bone of contention in this whole matter, whether culpability or guilt for corruption, abuse of power or mismanagement may justifiably be presumed from circumstances without positive proof after due enquiry.

(i) Presumption of Culpability or Guilt for Purposes of Disqualification or Removal on the Ground of Corruption.

In considering this question, the enormity and the all-pervading incidence of corruption in developing countries must be borne in mind. We are talking, not merely of simple bribery by an individual public officer or even the ordinary 10 per cent rake-off on contracts, but about corruption of the more buccaneering type involving billions of public money embezzled in many cases direct from the public treasury by those entrusted with its control and management, about political corruption by the means of which immense suffering was inflicted on the people.

Political corruption, with the economic adversity which it inflicts upon the people, is an offence against the people directly, involving as it does a criminal betrayal of trust. It is not really an offence against the state in its corporate capacity as a government, since government cannot commit a crime against itself. It is treason, not against the state but against the people. Every citizen, both old and young, is entitled to feel personally cheated.

The question whether guilt for corruption may be presumed from circumstances must therefore be viewed against the background that political corruption is the greatest social malady afflicting developing countries. In dealing with it, therefore, some departure from normal democratic standards might well be necessary.

Its incidence is so all-pervading and notorious as not to require to be substantiated with concrete cases. It is a fact of life, firmly rooted in the society. Although concrete cases may be difficult to prove conclusively, the forms of corruption are well known: the percentage on contracts, the rake-off on land, business, supplies and so on purchased on behalf of government at grossly inflated prices, or on licences issued or on other patronages dispensed. However its commonest and meanest form is bribery — the taking of money or other valuable things as a condition or inducement for the performance of an official act in favour of a person or for forbearing action.

Its manifestations are also clearly visible: an expensive and extravagant life style, lavish and ostentatious display of wealth, bulging bank accounts, large personal donation at private functions, ownership of private jets or fleet of expensive cars and so forth. Its extent is apparent. It runs right through the entire body politic from top to bottom, from the head of a ministry or department down to the messenger. It has broken loose of all restraints, and become completely buccaneering. It is now a plunder brazenly perpetrated. Its magnitude in terms of the amount of money involved is simply colossal. It extends over the entire area of public expenditure. The amount of money involved runs therefore into billions, and represents a large proportion of revenue that would otherwise have been used for the benefit of the community.

Corruption is an abuse of office both because of the huge loss and waste it inflicts on the nation, and also because it has meant that official acts — whether it be the siting of projects, investment decisions, the choice of contractors, suppliers or agents, or the granting of licences — are motivated or influenced not solely by considerations of the public interest but also by those of private or political gain, which sometimes is the predominating factor. Corrupt motives have often led to inefficiency in the disbursement and management of public funds and of public affairs generally. It has sometimes meant that money that would have been used in development along lines beneficial to the public is wasted in unprofitable, politically motivated enterprises or diverted into private coffers for electioneering or propaganda purposes of the ruling parties or otherwise for the enrichment of their members. By far the most tragic consequence of corruption is its effects upon the attitudes and mentality of the people. It has created a widespread feeling of frustration, of disgust and cynicism, which has in its turn undermined enthusiasm for, and faith in, the state. It has also left in its trail the terrible spectacle of public buildings burnt down as a cover-up for the embezzlement of public money or other types of fraud.

In the light of its incidence, extent and the enormous amount of loss corruption inflicts on the nation, it seems quite justifiable that the Code of Conduct for Public Officers enshrined in the 1979 Constitution of Nigeria should provide that "any property or assets acquired by a public officer after any declaration (of assets) and which are not fairly attributable to income, gift, or loan approved by this Code shall be deemed to have been acquired in breach of this Code unless the contrary is proved." By this provision, the onus normally placed on one who asserts something to prove it, is inverted. In such a case, it is right and proper that the excess assets should raise a presumption of guilt for corruption, thus throwing on to the person accused, the onus of proving his innocence.

It seems also right and proper that a presumption of guilt should be made against all those connected or associated with government in such capacities as president, governor, minister, senate president, speaker, ruling party chairman, etc. To presume guilt by association against such office-holders is not really subversive of democracy in the case of corruption; to purify democracy by this means cannot be undemocratic. Nor is such a presumption irrational, for in most of the developing countries, hardly anyone who has held any of the offices concerned can, in good conscience, claim never to have indulged in corruption or corrupt practice at elections to a greater or less degree. None can swear publicly upon it. The fact that he has not been investigated and found guilty or has, after investigation, been found not guilty for lack of sufficient or credible evidence ought not to be conclusive of his innocence. The involvement of all such office-holders in corruption is a notorious fact of which we are entitled to take notice unless and until the contrary is proved. Moreover, all have, during their tenure in office, acquired assets far in excess of what could be attributed to their legitimate earnings. But even if any one of them could be said not to have enriched himself personally by corruption, still he must share in the blame for the corrupt motive that influenced many investments and other similar projects undertaken by the regime.

The 1987 Decree of the military government in Nigeria which disqualified certain categories of persons simply on the basis of having held designated offices in the past, irrespective of guilt or innocence for corruption, rationalised the exclusion on the same ground but in rather subtle language by saying that the purpose was to assure "a clean break with the past and to establish a strong and stable foundation for the future." The statement clearly imputes collective wrong-doing and discredit to the past and to all those who held the designated offices in it, or else a clean break with it and with them would not have been decreed. Surely, if the past was a glorious era of civic virtue devoid of corruption, corrupt practices, abuse of power and mismanagement, we should want to continue it and its legacy into the present and the future rather than having a clean break with it.

The Decree did not of course mean to suggest that a clean break with a past that was ridden with corruption necessarily guarantees a corruption-free future. Corruption is a deeply embedded legacy that permeates the entire culture of the developing countries, and it is in the context of a culture so permeated that a new political system and its operators are going to function. Yet, whilst a clean break with the past cannot by itself alone eradicate corruption, it certainly adds to the armoury of weapons for combating it. The fact that corruption has so far defied all the measures mounted against it is no reason for not adding more or for giving up the effort. The fight against corruption must remain a central concern of social policy in these countries.

The disqualification under the Nigerian Decree was repealed in December 1991 for those who have not been found guilty of any misdeed. It seems a mistake to have totally lifted the ban on this category of people. What had made the ban so blatantly objectionable was its extension, by an amending Decree of 1989, to bar not only the holding of office but also participation in politics. To ban a citizen from participating in politics is, as earlier stated, to deprive him of fundamental rights inherent in him, and is clearly undemocratic and without justification. And it makes no sense anyway. Is it really practicable to stop a person from holding or expressing political opinions or from manifesting support for a political party in other ways? The prohibition simply manifests a failure to differentiate between what is realistic and what is not. When the Transition to Civil Rule Tribunal began issuing bench warrant for the arrest of former State Governors arraigned before it for having sponsored political parties and candidates for election, or refused bail to a former minister charged with the same offence in order to enable him attend his daughter's wedding, it was obvious that things were being pushed to rather absurd limits, and that the absurdity might rebound. Besides, coming after local and state governments elections had been completed, leaving only presidential and national assembly elections, the timing of the lifting of the ban seems capable of injecting into the transition programme, a considerable amount of confusion which may be expected to arise from the acrimonious rivalry for presidential candidature and for the leadership of the two political parties between the oldbreed and the newbreed politicians. It may be wondered whether the lifting of the ban at such a time was really an "act of grace" or part of a "hidden agenda"!

(ii) Presumption of Culpability or Guilt for Purposes of Disqualification or Removal for Involvement in Human Rights Abuses

Abuse or misuse of power takes many forms of which corruption is one. Another form of abuse or misuse of power which is of far greater concern to mankind is violation of human rights and other civil rights. As with corruption, it is generally agreed that public life should be purged of persons who actively and knowingly took part in human rights abuses. Exclusion from participation in public life on this ground is legitimate and justified therefore where it is established that a former office-holder had, during the erstwhile regime, committed violations of human or civil rights. The question again is whether there are circumstances when guilt for such violation might justifiably be presumed without positive proof.

As in the case of corruption, we would again strongly maintain that where human rights violations were a notorious feature of a former regime, as it was under communist rule in the USSR and Eastern Europe, collective responsibility and culpability for them should justifiably be visited upon all those who belonged to the regime in the sense of being members of its directing organs whatever might be the capacity in which they functioned, whether as party leader, secretary-general, president, minister, politburo member, etc. Each and every office-holder who can rightly be categorised as being part of the directing authority of the regime must bear a share of the responsibility or blame for such violations, and it should not be permissible for any one of them to say that, as an individual, he did not support, or even that he opposed, the abuses. The fact of having remained in office without resigning as a mark of conscientious objection is enough to fix him with responsibility or blame, at least as an aider and abetter who, in law, is as blameworthy as the principal offender. In the emphatic words of the new Constitution of Romania (1991), "each member of the government is politically accountable, jointly with the other members, for the activity and acts of the government."[14]

Apart from membership of the directing organs of a repressive regime, there are also other capacities in which involvement in such a regime may support a presumption of guilt against an individual. It is well known that a terroristic secret police was the main instrument employed by the communist regimes in Eastern Europe and the former Soviet Union to commit human rights violations. It seems right and proper that members of the organisation, at least those in positions of authority, should be presumed to be implicated to a greater or less degree in the abuses. Their exclusion from holding offices that have a direct bearing on human rights protection or the security of the state in the new democratic dispensation seems therefore justified. The outlook nurtured in them by their work in the former regime and the methods to which they had become accustomed disqualify them from participation in similar assignments under the new democratic polity, if not indeed in all public assignments in which a democratic and liberal outlook is needed.

A Czechoslovak law, the Screening Act, enacted in 1991, in fact makes employment as a member of the Secret Police in the former communist regime a disqualification for holding office in the new democratic regime. (The Act is discussed in detail below.) Also in Germany, personnel in the public service are required to complete questionnaire on whether during their time in the former East Germany (GDR), they had, among other things, been reproached or suspected of having violated fundamental principles of humanity, and many have been dismissed on the basis of their answers to the questionnaire.

(iii) Presumption of Culpability or Guilt for Purposes of Disqualification or Removal for Involvement in General Wrong-doing by an Evil Regime

Disqualification or removal generates even more controversy

---

14. Art. 108 (1).

and acrimony when culpability or blame is to be presumed, not for specific misdeeds like corruption and human rights violations, but for involvement in general wrong-doing by an evil regime. Exclusion on such wide and non-specific grounds must necessarily involve a large number of persons, which therefore makes it more difficult to justify.

The first problem is to define what amounts to involvement for this purpose. To begin with, it must be conscious and active involvement. In the second place, it must involve the performance or discharge of a function or role relating to the control, direction or management of society or the administration of public affairs. Thus, mere membership of the ruling party is not enough to establish involvement. While the holding of a public office or a political party office is the usual criterion, it is not the exclusive requirement; active and conscious collaboration in some form or other by a person who does not hold any such office may suffice, as in the case of a secret agent. Thus, the Czechoslovak Screening Act 1991 (referred to earlier) covers within the categories of disqualified persons, any one who, during the period 25 February, 1948 to 17 November, 1989 was a member or secretary of the committees, bureaus or other organs of the communist party at district and central levels (but not an ordinary member of the party), member of staff of any of those organs, a member of the People's Militia, member of an Action Committee of the National Front, member of the Screening Committee, member of the National Security Corps detailed to any state security section and a student of the USSR ideological school; also covered are persons listed in the files of the State Security as a confidant, a secret collaborator of confidential contacts and knowledge provided that "they knew they were in contact with a member of the National Security Corps and were giving him information in the form of clandestine contacts or were implementing tasks set by him," or as agent, an informer or a holder of a conspiratorial apartment.

Persons falling within these categories are for a period of five years disqualified from holding or liable to removal from *all* offices in the public service (both appointive and elective offices), in state enterprises, state organisations, in the joint ventures in which the state is the majority share- holder and in international trade agencies. The number of people likely to be affected by the exclusions is put at over one million.

The Act places upon a person holding or seeking any of these offices, the primary responsibility to show that he is not affected by the exclusions by swearing to an affidavit to that effect, or by obtaining from the Ministry of the Interior a certificate to the same effect, or a statement issued by a Commission of 15 members established by the Act, according to which of these methods of proof is required in his case. An application for a certificate may also be made by the organ or institution to which the office relates. In the case of a person already holding an office affected, termination or dismissal (depending on which is specified in the Act for a particular case) is prescribed as a penalty for failure to obtain and submit the necessary proof within the time specified in the Act or where his collaboration or involvement is confirmed in the certificate.

The truth of the statement in the affidavit or certificate is to be verified by the Commission referred to above, on the application of the person claiming not to be affected or by any one asserting its falsity. A finding by the Commission that a person is not affected concludes the matter, but one to the opposite effect may be questioned by the person affected before the district court equally as where he alleges the invalidity of the termination of his appointment. The Act is silent on whether the decision of the district court is appealable to a higher court, but presumably it is.

The Act was passed to meet growing public demand for the purification of the public institutions to rid them of the agents of communist misrule and their active collaborators, persons who, as the President of the country, Vaclav Havel, puts it, having taken active part in crushing human rights under the former regime, have not spontaneously renounced their public functions, and are hindering, in many institutions, the creation of a true democratic order. Similar demands are being mounted in other parts of Eastern Europe and the former Soviet Union, e.g., Bulgaria, Latvia and Lithuania, where legislation along similar lines is said to be under way.

Objections have been taken to the Czechoslovak Act by the Trade Union Association of Bohemia, Moravia and Slovakia

(Os-CMS) and by the Czech and Slovak Confederation of Trade Unions (CS-KOS), both of which had lodged a complaint with the International Labour Organisation (ILO) alleging that the Act violated the Discrimination (Employment and Occupation) Convention 1958 (No. 111) under which a ratifying state undertakes, inter alia, not to permit within its territory, any discrimination in employment or occupation except such as is based on the inherent requirements of a particular job or as regards measures against a person justifiably suspected of, or found to have engaged in, activities prejudicial to the security of the State. Discrimination is defined in the Convention to include "any distinction, exclusion or preference made on the basis of race, colour, sex, religion, political opinion, national extraction or social origin, which has the effect of nullifying or impairing equality of opportunity or treatment in employment or occupation." Czechoslovakia had ratified the Convention which, by virtue of Constitutional Act No. 23/91, formed part of its law, overriding any inconsistent local legislation. Also Czechoslovakia's Charter of Fundamental Rights and Freedoms enacted by the same Act 23/91 guarantees to all citizens equality of rights without distinction on any grounds whatsoever, including the ground of political opinion. All laws and regulations are required to be brought into harmony with the Charter by 31 December, 1991 while all provisions contrary thereto cease to have effect as from that date.

The exclusions imposed by the Act were also attacked as having been based on an irrebuttable presumption of collective guilt and as disregarding the presumption of innocence and the inadmissibility of retroactivity in penal legislation. Even President Vaclav Havel thought the provisions of the Act as enacted (which by reason of amendments made to it in parliament, differed substantially from the version initiated by the government) to be contrary in their spirit to the established foundations of a democratic legal order and that they could give rise to new injustices and inequities which, at the dawn of the new democratic system, might create troublesome precedents, a view also concurred in by the President of the Federal Assembly, Professor Alexander Dubcek. President Havel accordingly called for its amendment by Parliament.

In response to the complaints lodged with it by the two Trade

Unions, the ILO had set up a Committee to examine the allegations. The Committee reported that the exclusions imposed by the Act appear to be "based essentially on political or ideological opinions or on action linked thereto," and therefore constitute discrimination within the meaning of the Discrimination (Employment and Occupation) Convention 1958, except to the extent that they or any of them fall within the two exceptions mentioned earlier, and it then went on to examine in some detail the extent to which they are covered by the exceptions. We are not here concerned with the latter question, but only with the general conclusion that the exclusions appear to be based essentially on political or ideological opinions.

There is no warrant for saying that the persons affected by the exclusions are being discriminated against on account of their past membership of the communist party or for expressions of opinion, either alone or collectively with others, in support of its doctrines and ideology, since ordinary members of the party were not affected. The exclusions are based essentially on their activities in *managing* the communist party, which was not just a political party but also the vanguard and the leading organ of both the state and society, both of which it integrated into itself (or so it professed to have done). It is not in dispute that the communist party, with its monopoly of power and its role as the leading organ of the socialist socio-economic order, misdirected and mismanaged the society, the economy and the state, inflicted untold economic misery and suffering on the people, and committed flagrant abuses of human rights. All the members of its directing organs — its various committees and bureaus at least at the levels of the district and the centre — must be held collectively responsible, and each must bear a share of that responsibility. In effect, therefore, the persons affected by the exclusions are being penalised, not for the propagation of socialist doctrines or the collective advocacy of socialist ideology within the organisational framework of the communist party, but for mismanaging the society, the economy and the state and thereby inflicting misery and suffering on the people. Surely, it is not for human rights violations alone that the managers and directors of the communist party should be accountable, for their evil-doings were not limited to that.

The fact that they did these things in furtherance of the doctrines or ideology of the communist party should make no difference. The Discrimination (Employment and Occupation) Convention 1958 speaks only of "political opinion", not political action. The distinction between propagation of political doctrines or ideology and actions done in furtherance thereof is one familiar to the law.[15] (Discussed in chapter 12). The courts' decisions even recognise that advocacy of a political opinion or doctrine might overstep the limits of expression and become incitement to violent action punishable as sedition or subversion. The ILO Committee of Experts also excepts the "advocacy of violent methods to bring about" changes in the institutions of the State propagated in the doctrines of a political organisation.[16] (The reference in article 4 of the Convention to *activities* prejudicial to the security of the State" has more relevance to the other grounds of discrimination specified in article 1, religion, national extraction, social origin, race or colour, than to political opinion). If a political doctrine propagates the extermination of a particular racial group, as did Nazism, and the extermination is actually carried out by some adherents of the doctrine, as did the Nazi leaders, surely the penalization of the latter for that act cannot be discrimination based on political opinion.

The exclusions imposed by the Czechoslovak Act can also be defended on the further ground that the past activities of the affected persons as managers and directors of the socialist socio-economic order are prejudicial to the interests and the security of the new democratic system. It cannot be too often emphasised that socialist/communist rule, with its totalitarian methods and its appalling record of human rights abuses, stands in irreconcilable antagonism to democracy. It would be a contradiction, and would tend to lower the status of the new democracy and to endanger the maintenance of the standards of behaviour it requires and even its very survival, to permit

---

15.   See *Denis v. United States*, 341 U.S. 494 (1951).
16.   General Survey on "Equality in Employment and Occupation" (1988), para. 57.

anyone to hold office under it who had knowingly and actively participated in the "construction" of socialism/communism and in the mismanagement of the society, the economy and the state under its rule.

But having said this, it must be admitted that the net of exclusions under the Act seems to have been too widely spread as regards both the persons and the offices affected. There appears to be an injustice in the exclusion of those compelled to collaborate with the State Security under threat of death or of grievous harm to their families or dear ones or who did so in aid of the pro-democracy movements. In the second place, it is hardly just that the persons affected should be excluded from *all* employment in the state and its agencies and enterprises. The exclusions should be restricted to employment in political positions or functions involved in the administration of the state or those of a sensitive or confidential nature and others relevant to the maintenance of democracy.

In view of the point made earlier, the argument about presumption of innocence and the inadmissibility of retroactivity of penal legislation is misplaced. The Act is not a penal legislation. The activities penalised by exclusions are not thereby made criminal offences, and the penalty of exclusion is not a punishment. The presumption of innocence and the inadmissibility of retroactivity have thus no application in this case.

Exclusion Otherwise than by Disqualification or Removal for Corruption, Abuse of Office or Mismanagement

Where exclusion is not by means of disqualification or removal, and does not therefore carry the disability attendant upon disqualification or removal, then, all the considerations discussed earlier about how guilt implied by disqualification is to be established, particularly the vexed question of presuming guilt from circumstances, do not apply.

In Nigeria, the National Electoral Commission has been given additional power by a Decree of 25 November, 1991 to bar a person from standing for any election, including party primaries, or from holding any elective office, if it considers him or her on any ground whatsoever, to be not a fit and proper person to stand for such election or to hold such office, and the ground on which the Commission may come to such an opinion may include the fact that —

(a)   the activities of such person are inimical or are not in consonance with public order, public morality, law and order;

(b)   he is a person who is likely to —

   (i)   disturb or disrupt the process of democracy and peaceful transition to civil rule, having regard to his said activities;

   (ii)   hinder or prevent the progress and process of the grassroot democracy as established by the transition to civil rule programme;

(c)   he is a person whose loyalty, patriotism and attitude towards a peaceful and orderly democratic election are questionable;

(d)   he is a person whose participation in the democratic process may seriously put in doubt and jeopardy the legitimacy or credibility of such an election.

This seems to give to the Commission an undesirably wide discretion, especially as it is not explicitly required to grant a hearing as a basis for its opinion as to the fitness or otherwise of a person to stand election or hold a public office.

Procedure for Review

Whilst, as earlier stated, the finding of a commission of enquiry, an administrative enquiry or, in appropriate cases, a presumption of guilt based on the circumstances provides an acceptable basis for the infliction of the disability attendant upon disqualification, it is desirable that such finding or presumption should be open to review by a court of law or other independent and impartial tribunal, so as to afford an opportunity for testing its correctness and for correcting errors. Without the opportunity for a review by such a tribunal, it is unjustifiable to inflict disqualification, removal or other forms of exclusion upon people who might be the unfortunate victims of errors of judgment or even of deliberate perversion. The disability attendant upon disqualification or removal is too severe a penalty to be inflicted upon citizens in a democracy without the opportunity of a review by an independent and impartial tribunal.

Under the Nigerian legislation referred to earlier, the decision of the National Electoral Commission (NEC) declaring or pronouncing a person as one affected by a disqualification is, at the instance of any one dissatisfied with it, reviewable, not by a court but a special tribunal established by statute, the Transition to Civil Rule Tribunal, with a membership consisting of a serving or retired judge as chairman and four other members of whom one shall be a serving member of the armed forces.[17] All the members are appointed by the President. Also, the decision of the Commission barring any person from contesting an election or from holding any office under the additional powers given to it by the Decree of 25 November, 1991 is reviewable by the Tribunal. The Tribunal's decision is final and binding, and no suit or legal proceedings in respect of any ban, disqualification or any other matter covered by, or arising from, the enabling Decree shall be instituted in, or be entertained by, any other tribunal or court.

A tribunal constituted in the manner of the Nigerian Tribunal certainly does not meet the democratic standards needed for a satisfactory review of a decision to disqualify or ban a citizen from contesting an election for an office or from holding an office or to remove him from one which he is already holding, on the ground of some wrong-doing or for some other reason. For, the Tribunal is clearly not an independent body both because all its members are appointed and removable by the chief executive of the government (the President) and because an executive personnel of the government (an officer of the armed forces) is a mandatory member. Furthermore, there is nothing to stop the President, in the exercise of his unfettered power from appointing the other three members of the Tribunal from the personnel of the civil service, the police or the armed forces. (In point of fact, the three other members are independent private people.) A Tribunal so constituted may well be impartial in practice, but it is more important that it should manifestly appear to be so in the eyes of the public, and

---

17. Transition to Civil Rule (Political Programme) Decree 1987, s. 9.

independence is necessary to make it appear so. The reviewing function should have been entrusted to an ordinary court or else the appointment of the members of the special tribunal should be vested in the Chief Justice, with a specific direction to appoint only independent persons.

The procedure for review under the Nigerian legislation thus contrasts unfavourably with that under the Czechoslovak Act which makes a finding that a person is affected by the exclusions reviewable by the district court with a possible right of further appeal to higher courts. But the Czechoslovak procedure has been criticised by the Committee set up by the ILO on the ground that the Commission empowered to make the finding does not meet the requisite standard of objectivity and independence in that, of its 15 members, six are government officials appointed and removable by the heads of the responsible government departments, and that, while the other nine members are independent private citizens appointed and removable by the Presidiums of the legislative assemblies, the quorum for meetings (nine) means that the Commission can validly function with government officials forming the majority of the members present at a meeting; furthermore, by the terms of the Act, the Commission is established under the auspices of the Federal Ministry of the Interior which is also responsible for its functioning.

These criticisms seem misconceived. The Commission is not a reviewing or appellate body; its function is merely to conduct original or first instance investigation as to the truth or otherwise of the statement contained in an affidavit sworn to by a person claiming not to be affected by the exclusions or in a certificate issued by the Federal Ministry of the Interior. Its function thus combines those of both a commission of inquiry or an administrative enquiry and the National Electoral Commission (NEC) under the Nigerian legislation. It has been shown that, since conviction and punishment for a criminal offence are not involved, independence in the investigating body is not a necessity at the stage of first instance investigation, provided that the procedure affords adequate opportunity for the person affected by the exclusion to be heard in his own defence and that the finding of the investigating body is open to review by a court or other independent and impartial tribunal to enable the correctness of the finding to be tested and errors to be corrected.

Chapter 4

A Genuine and Meaningful Popular Participation in Politics and Government

> By a democracy I do not mean something as vague as 'the rule of the people' or 'the rule of the majority', but a set of institutions (among them especially general elections, i.e., the right of the people to dismiss their government) which permit public control of rulers and their dismissal by the ruled, and which make it possible for the ruled to obtain reforms without using violence, even against the will of the rulers.
>
> — Sir Karl Popper

The Reality and Meaningfulness of the Process of Elections and Referenda as Means of Popular Participation

The transition from one-party or communist rule to multi-partyism is intended to make more meaningful and real, popular participation in politics and government by means of referenda for the purpose of deciding specific questions including the approval of specific legislative proposals, and elections for choosing those to govern. Given a free competition between political parties, democratisation is not so much concerned with the nature and normal operations of these two means of popular participation, as formal institutions of democracy; it is concerned with them only insofar as the institution of popular elections for the choice of rulers suffers from certain short-comings, which makes the use of referenda necessary to supplement it. Nor is democratisation so much concerned with the meaning of democracy, however it may be defined.

Because it takes place at intervals of four or five years and never calls for judgment on specific questions, voting at elections does not give sufficient reality to the people's

68

participation in government. It needs to be supplemented by further *direct* contacts between the people and the government during the interval between one election and another by means of a referendum to decide specific questions including the approval of specific legislative proposals. Voting at a referenda thus carries participation a step further; it is a return to the form in which democracy originally began in the ancient Greek city states.

From its origins in the United States and Switzerland, the referendum, i.e., the submission for popular decision, of questions or legislative measures proposed by government, is today a common feature of modern democracy widely used throughout the world. Indeed, in some Swiss cantons, all legislative proposals originated by government, in particular constitutional amendments, are required to be submitted for popular approval or adoption whilst in other cantons as in the Confederation itself and also in the American States submission is optional at the instance of the government or a prescribed number of citizens. Apart from the submission, whether compulsory or optional, of legislative proposals originated by government, there is also the method, known as the initiative, whereby a prescribed number of citizens can themselves originate legislative proposals and have them submitted to the people for enactment into law, although the procedure is still restricted in its application to only a few countries, notably the Swiss Confederation as respects constitutional amendments as also many of the cantons and many American States as respects both constitutional amendments and ordinary law-making.[1] The initiative is an example *par excellence* of a means whereby the people could obtain needed reforms in a constitutional manner, even against the will of the rulers.

Both the referendum and the initiative are meant to supplement representative government, and to correct some of its shortcomings, including inadequacies on the part of representatives themselves. Representative government is afterall only resorted to as a substitute for direct democracy

---

1.   James Bryce, *Modern Democracies* Vol. 2 (1920), p. 460.

because of the impossibility, the inconvenience and expense in a large country of having every question touching upon its government decided by the people at large. But a substitute, a simulation, is scarcely ever quite the same as the real thing. When the people vote directly on specific questions or legislative proposals whose significance cuts across all sectional boundaries, the influence of class, party and other group interests and sentiments is considerably reduced. On the other hand, elections (even voting in the chambers of legislative assemblies) are dominated by party interests and spirit, so that the real mind of the people does not receive as full an expression as might be desired. Voting at referenda is largely free of the dominating influence of partisan interests and spirit, depending of course on the question submitted.

The referendum and the initiative have the further advantage that they increase the opportunities for the people's political education, and they do so in a way unequalled by elections, because they oblige those who take part in them to try to understand the question submitted, and to reach a conclusion on it. The public discussion of the question in the media and at public meetings that precede the voting is a source of education for all, even for those who abstain from voting. And they permit a closer scrutiny of the merits and demerits of the questions or proposals submitted than would otherwise be possible.

Yet they have a limited use. The limits of their application are implied, firstly, in the reasons creating the necessity for representative government — the great inconvenience, expense and time involved in a frequent resort to the people in a large modern state; secondly, the fact that their ability to produce dispassionate decisions presupposes that only questions of great importance cutting across sectional interests should be submitted; thirdly, low turn-out due to apathy or the absence of adequate publicity by means of organised campaigns unless when the political parties are sufficiently interested to call out their supporters; and fourthly, the fact that the questions submitted may be beyond the knowledge and competence of the mass of the people to understand and judge properly, and the danger that a desirable measure may be rejected out of ignorance on the part of the people. On the whole, however, referenda seem to have produced satisfactory results; witness, for example, the referendum in South Africa in March 1992 when the white electorate voted overwhelmingly in support of negotiations to end apartheid.

The real issue raised by democratisation is that participation by means of referenda and elections would not have been really and meaningfully democratised unless referenda and election are free and fair so as to enable the people to effectively exercise their political rights, the right to decide questions that may be referred to them, to choose the rulers, to control their actions and, above all, to dismiss a government of which they disapprove. This is what democratisation is or should be concerned with, not just transition to multi-partyism, universal suffrage, or majority rule important as these are as formal institutions of democracy.

Electoral Malpractices and the Reality of Popular Participation

The conditions for a free and fair election or referendum are, then, a matter of crucial importance to democratisation. Free and fair election or referendum requires that —

(a) every adult of sound mind shall be free to contest an election and to campaign for votes, to register as a voter, to choose the candidate for whom to cast his vote and vote accordingly, uninhibited and unimpeded by official interference, discrimination on the ground of sex, race, colour, wealth and so on, by physical restraint, intimidation, bribery, treating, undue influence or other such factors that endanger his personal security or otherwise obstruct his freedom of action;

(b) there is equality between the voters, none being allowed to cast more than one vote or to have greater weight attached to his vote;

(c) political parties are free to sponsor candidates and canvass for votes in a truly competitive sense;

(d) the territorial units of representation are demarcated as to be nearly equal in population as possible and so as not to favour some people against the others;

(e) those entrusted with the conduct of an election are not agents of, or are not subject to direction by, any of the contestants;

(f)   the contest is conducted according to laid down rules accepted by all as binding;

(g)   the contest is in fact conducted impartially, giving no advantage to one candidate against another;

(h)   the results are based on, and truly reflect the votes lawfully cast at the election by voters and are free from falsification, inflation or other fraudulent manipulation of figures;

(i)   the winner is determined by a majority or the highest number of such lawful votes.

While the constitution and the electoral laws can guarantee the conditions in (a) - (e) above, they cannot guarantee that individuals will not in fact pervert the established electoral process and rig an election. It is thus largely a matter of indifference for present purposes what type of electoral system is in use — winner-take-all or proportional representation; secret or open balloting, etc. They are all amenable, to a greater or less degree, to malpractices if people are minded and determined to do so. Yet to secure these conditions must be the concern of democratisation. For there is no democracy unless and until they are secured. Securing them is more a matter of inculcating the democratic spirit among the people, rulers and the ruled alike.

Among the greatest challenges of democracy in Africa and some other developing countries of the world today is wholesale electoral malpractices, in particular, rigging, by which governments in these countries keep themselves in power against the wishes of a majority of the people as expressed in their votes. The challenge is indeed a grave one because of the forms electoral malpractices take, their extent and ever recurrent incidence, of which Nigeria provides perhaps the most blatant manifestation.

Wholesale rigging of elections in Nigeria began with the federal elections of 1964, the first in the country since the departure of the British. By the time of the election, the coalition between the Northern Peoples Party (NPC) and the National Council of Nigerian Citizens (NCNC), which had ruled the country since 1959, had fallen apart, and each party had chosen a new bed-fellow for the purpose of the election and was determined to exert itself to the utmost to win it. The new alliances were the Nigerian National Alliance (NNA) between the NPC and Chief Akintola's Nigerian National Democratic Party (NNDP), and the United Progressive Grand Alliance (UPGA) between the NCNC and the Action Group (AG). Each party professed its desire to make the contest free and fair. At a conference of all the parties convened by the prime minister, agreements were reached on measures to be taken to ensure that the election would be conducted in a peaceful atmosphere; bans on processions and public meetings were to be lifted; discrimination in the grant of permits for election meetings was to be removed, while each party undertook to restrain its thugs. None of these agreements was ever observed. The UPGA complained that it had been unable to campaign in the North owing to the refusal of the Native Authorities to grant permits for campaign meetings, and to the mass arrest of their campaigners and agents for allegedly holding meetings without permit and for other trumped-up charges. A new element had also been introduced into the election. The technique was to get as many government party candidates as possible returned unopposed by preventing the opposition parties from filing nomination papers within the prescribed time. This result was achieved by abducting opposition candidates and their nominators and putting them away until the nomination time expired. In this way the NPC was able to get sixty of its candidates returned unopposed. In a documented memorandum submitted to the president of the republic, supported by sworn affidavits from the victims, the UPGA listed specific cases of intimidation, lynching, arbitrary arrest and imprisonment, abduction and other acts of persecution committed against its members by the NPC and its agents, and demanded the postponement of the election. When it failed to get the elections postponed, the UPGA decided to boycott them, but in spite of the boycott the elections went on in the Northern and Western Regions where the NNA government were in control, and also in the federal territory of Lagos. The boycott was thus effective only in the East and Mid-West, the areas controlled by the NCNC. In the West the boycott enabled the NNDP to win the election as it were by default, with votes so low in many places as to make a mockery of the whole exercise. In the North too the NPC swept through virtually all the constituencies.

The techniques used in the Western Regional election of 1965 were more brazen than those of 1964. The returning officers provided the main tool. Many deserted their posts after accepting nomination papers from government party candidates, thereby making it impossible for opposition candidates to file their own. Or, if a returning officer remained at his post he might refuse to accept an opposition candidate's nomination paper on some alleged technical fault. A returning officer refusing to desert his post might be abducted after having received the government candidate's nomination. And lastly, returning officers who had accepted nomination papers from opposition candidates and even issued certificates of validity had their appointments revoked, and their successors refused to recognise the validity of such certificates or to accept new nomination papers. By these means, the ruling party, the NNDP, was able at the close of the nomination to get as many as sixteen candidates declared unopposed. Then there was the illegal trafficking in ballot papers by the government party agents. Large bundles of ballot papers deposited with the police for safe-keeping found their way into the boxes of government candidates. Wads of ballot papers were also found in the possession of unauthorised persons. When all these failed and an opposition candidate was elected, the result might be reversed in favour of the defeated government candidate who would then be promptly announced on the government radio as the winner. "The most notorious example of this travesty was the case of a man who won the election in one of the Owo constituencies. His opponent was declared the victor. He thereupon announced that he had decided to join the NNDP. A few days after this announcement, the Electoral Commission declared him the successful candidate and quietly dropped his opponent."[2] Before the election, the regional premier, Chief Akintola, had boasted that "whether the people voted for them or not, the NNDP would be returned to power." And so it was, though the party had thereby overreached itself. For rather than swallow such an injury to their right to choose who should govern them, the people of Western Nigeria took the law

---

2.   Arikpo, *The Development of Modern Nigeria* (1967), p. 141.

into their own hands and launched a regime of violence and arson that held the region in its bloody grip until the military take-over of January 1966 intervened to flush out the politicians.

Thus, by the closing year of the Nigerian First Republic the institution of free elections, that cornerstone of democracy, had ceased to have any meaning in Nigeria, so blatantly had it been perverted. As long as an election posed any possibility of defeat for the government, the same perverse techniques, perfected at every turn, would again be called into use to avert the imminence of defeat.

In the 1983 federal and state elections, while some of the other rigging techniques of 1964 and 1965 were again employed, dumping of ballot papers and falsification of results provided the main methods used. In one case a team of party thugs was said to have invaded forty polling stations, drove away the agents of other parties, overpowered the police and forced the few presiding officers who were unable to escape to produce all available ballot papers, which they then thumb-marked and dumped into the ballot boxes.[3] In a few cases the police actually caught some persons in illegal possession of ballot boxes and papers or in the act of thumb-marking ballot papers in private houses with a view to dumping them into ballot boxes later.[4]

The key agents in the dumping of ballot papers were the presiding officers and poll clerks at the polling stations. Their active co-operation was needed before thumb-marked ballot papers could be dumped into the ballot box in use at the polling station or before a ballot box stuffed with thumb-marked ballot papers could be brought to the polling station and exchanged for the one in use there. And the ballot papers to be used for the purpose would have to come from the presiding officer if their serial numbers were to agree with those issued to the polling station, though often ballot papers not in the series were used. In many cases the presiding officers and

---

3. *Onyedibe & Others v. Offia-Nwali*, FCA/E/182/83 of 3/11/83.
4. *Odumegwu-Ojukwu v. Onwudiwe & Others*, HN/1EP/83 of 17/9/83, High Court, Nwewi; *Alli & Another v. Ogbemudia & Others*, ibid.

poll clerks went beyond merely supplying ballot papers and allowing them to be dumped or allowing ballot boxes to be exchanged, and actually took part in the thumb-marking of ballot papers at a fixed rate for a given number of ballot papers so thumb-marked. The number of ballot papers a poll clerk was able to thumb-mark determined, in part, the size of his purse at the end of each election. It was necessary to bribe the presiding officers and poll clerks to co-operate in this illegal practice because of the decision to count the votes at the polling stations, which made it impossible for ballot boxes stuffed with thumb-marked ballot papers to be exchanged for those used at the polling stations in the course of their being carried from there to the counting stations.

A common complaint in the election petitions was that the petitioner's duly accredited agents were chased away from the polling stations by the police, party thugs, and the FEDECO officials (presiding officers and poll clerks), and thereby prevented from being present during the voting and the counting of votes, the aim being to enable illegal voting, especially dumping or swapping, and other malpractices, to be done unnoticed by such agents. Where, however, the party agents could not be kept away in this way, then dumping or swapping became well-nigh impossible.

Bribery, treating and intimidation of, and the exertion of undue influence on, voters were widely and brazenly practised by the political parties and the candidates or their agents or supporters, with the object of inducing them to vote or not to vote for a particular candidate. The bribe was usually in the form of cash payment, loan, patronages, valuable articles like vehicles, salt, clothing materials and other benefits in kind or promises of them.

Meals, drinks and other forms of entertainment were commonly provided as a treat for voters. Undue influence took the form of priests, family, clan or district heads and other group leaders directing their members how to vote or whom to vote for, some even attending at the polling stations to direct their members where on the ballot paper to put their thumb-mark. Electoral officials and party agents had also been reported to direct voters to vote for particular candidates.

Intimidation of voters was usually in the form of violence or a threat of it by party thugs, harassment and application of force or threat of it by the police, returning officers and presiding officers. Each political party maintained an army of thugs, who scared or chased away and generally terrorised supporters of other parties. Cases were reported of voters being beaten up by party thugs, and of road blocks being mounted in front of some polling stations where prospective voters were screened in order to keep out non-supporters.

Illegal voting and the bribery, treating, intimidation etc. of voters do not guarantee victory at an election because at the level of the more than 200,000 poll clerks and presiding officers deployed in the polling stations scattered all over the country's vast expanse of territory, every political party has a good chance of securing the co-operation of a fair number of them while the voter is equally accessible to all for the exertion of influence by means of bribery, treating and so on. However, at the level of the returning officer and his deputy, where the results from the polling stations are collated, recorded and forwarded to the Electoral Commission, only the party in control of the federal government and the police is in a position to effectively exert corrupt influence, and to affect the results decisively.

Just as the presiding officer and the poll clerks were the instruments for rigging at the voting stage of the electoral process, the returning officer and his deputy served as the effective instrument for falsifying the results sent from the polling stations. In the Ondo State gubernatorial election, for example, the National Party of Nigeria (NPN) candidate, Chief Akin Omoboriowo, was declared elected by the Electoral Commission with 1,228,891 votes as against 1,015,385 votes credited to the Unity Party of Nigeria (UPN) candidate, Chief Michael Ajasin, whereas the true scores, as found by the election court, the Federal Court of Appeal and the Supreme Court from the certificates of results signed by the assisting returning officers and by the party agents as well as from the oral testimony of those assistant returning officers and party agents, were 1,563,327 votes for Chief Ajasin and 703,592 for Chief Omoboriowo. Chief Omoboriowo's score was thus inflated by 525,389 votes while that of Chief Ajasin was decreased by 547,942 votes. The evidence showed that the falsification was done at the level of the deputy returning officer. Chief Ajasin was accordingly declared by the court to have been duly elected.[5] A similar technique was employed in several other states and constituencies.

Such, then, is the measure of the danger and challenge facing democracy and democratisation in Africa.

Disastrous Consequences for Democracy of Wholesale Election Rigging

Wholesale election rigging has disastrous consequences for democracy in that it deprives elections of their essential purpose. In the first place, a government which, by electoral malpractices, keeps itself in office against the votes of the majority of the electorate lacks the legitimacy of the moral authority that popular mandate bestows. An election does not of course completely lose its legitimising effect on government because it is rigged. The very fact of an election and the processes through which it takes place have by themselves an inherently legitimising effect, apart altogether from the votes of those, albeit a minority, supporting the party that rigged itself into power. This at once distinguishes such a government from one which comes into office purely by force, appointment or inheritance. Although, however, a minority government does not lack a popular basis as completely as does a military, appointed or hereditary government, yet, without the mandate of a majority of the electors, its legitimacy or moral authority is tainted and greatly weakened.

In the second place, election rigging undermines another cardinal principle of democracy: the principle that the welfare of the people being the object of government, victory at an election must be related and linked to ability to secure and promote the people's welfare, and that a government which has not performed well in this respect forfeits all claims to have its mandate renewed. This principle postulates elections as the people's ultimate and most effective weapon for enforcing a

---

5.   *Ajasin v. Omoboriowo & Another*, AK/EP.1/83; of 10/9/83; *Omoboriowo & Another v. Ajasin.* FCA/8/127/EP.2/83 of 27/9/83; *Omoboriowo & Another v. Ajasin*, SC.98/1983 of 15/10/83.

government's responsibility and accountability to it. If, through election rigging, government can be assumed against the votes of the majority of the electors, then ability to perform or a record of achievement counts for nothing in an election. A government can neglect the people's welfare as much as it likes; it can loot the nation's wealth and ruin its economy and still rig itself back to power at the election against the votes of a majority of the electors. Such elections would have lost all relevance and efficacy as a means of making government responsive to the welfare of the people and of enforcing upon it an awareness that the power it exercises belongs to the people and should be exercised only for their benefit. No matter how much the people disapprove of a government's performance and however much they desire a change, rigging can be used to subvert their wishes as expressed in their votes at an election. The responsibility and accountability of the government to the people would have been rendered largely nugatory.

In the third place, from the standpoint of the political parties and their candidates, rigging deprives election of its character as a competition in which all the contestants can equally aspire to win. Where the capacity of the contestants to rig is vastly unequal because one of them is in a position of irresistible influence over the electoral body and has power of control and direction over the organised coercive force of the country represented by the police as well as vastly greater resources of money and patronage, then the other contestants have no real chance of winning. An election in these circumstances cannot be a competition in any meaningful sense of the word. An election contest in which the result is not determined by the votes lawfully cast for the contestants but by fraudulent manipulation is a mockery of the very idea of a competition. And without a free competition for power politics loses its essence. It is part of the terrible thing about election rigging that, once successfully employed by a political party to get itself into power the tendency is for the party, rather than give it up and thereby risk defeat at future elections, to try to perfect its forms and techniques to a point where it becomes entrenched as part of the political culture, thereby excluding altogether the chances of elections ever being conducted in a free and fair manner. Election rigging is a tragic aberration more for what it portends for the future than for the harm it has done in the past and present.

From this, two further implications follow. First, a political party which has no chance of ever winning an election will have lost the *raison d'etre* for its existence. Sooner or later it will fade away through its members defecting to the ruling party as the hazards of opposition weigh more and more heavily upon them. In the process, the ruling party will eventually emerge as the only party for all practical purposes.

A far more serious implication is that when, because of rigging, elections become unavailing as a means of changing a government, violence, with a possible breakdown of law and order, might result. Wholesale and brazen election rigging seems to attract violent disturbances almost as an inevitable reaction. The two are clearly correlated.

From the point of view of their implications for democracy it does not matter whether the disturbances are spontaneous or are incited by leaders of some political parties. However they might have started, they simply demonstrate the kind of danger which election rigging poses for law and order and the rule of law. And a breakdown of law and order might well attract intervention by the military. Even without a breakdown of law and order, intervention by the military might be provoked where, by election rigging, the ballot box is made unavailing as a means of changing the government. A government which, by election rigging, makes itself irremovable, is definitely inviting its own overthrow by the military as the only possible means of change in the circumstances. In the oft-quoted words of President J F Kennedy, "those who make peaceful change impossible make violent change possible" — one might say, inevitable.

The Reality of Public Opinion as a Means of Popular Participation

The limitations of elections and referenda as mechanisms for popular participation create a need for additional mechanisms capable of making good part, at least, of those limitations. If the aggregate of the views held by people or a majority of them on matters affecting the affairs of the community as they arise from time to time, otherwise called public opinion, could be ascertained, then, that would provide an authentic and admirable medium of popular participation on a continuous basis and free from the influence of corruption, passion, ignorance, etc. "In the formation of opinion, knowledge and thought tell. The clash and conflict of argument bring out the strength and weakness of every case, and that which is sound tends to prevail."[6] The power of public opinion informed by the good sense of the community, its love of freedom and equality, and its sense of justice, is the greatest restraint on governmental autocracy and tyranny.

The problem, however, is how to ascertain public opinion on any matter, since it is often "confused, incoherent, amorphous, varying from day to day and week to week."[7] Difficult as it is, public opinion is nevertheless often discernible on many issues of government, although its formation in the first place presupposes, to a considerable extent, the existence of a civil society, i.e. a society bound together by common outlook and shared sentiments as citizens of one country with a common destiny.[8] And, while it is entitled to be taken into account in framing government measures when it can be reliably ascertained, public opinion carries less authority because of the fact that it is not expressed in a formal, institutionalised manner like the vote at an election or referendum.

Public opinion, to be an effective and meaningful mechanism of popular participation, presupposes freedom on the part of the people to express themselves on matters of government. Only through the instrumentality of free expression of views on such matters would the public be enabled to be informed and educated about them, to think about them, to discover the truth about them, to examine them critically in order to assess their relative merits and demerits and to form opinion thereon. It follows that a people denied of free expression of views on matters of public affairs is hardly a self-governing community; it is like a colonised people.

In particular, a free press is indispensable to the formation

---

6. James Bryce op. cit. Vol. 2, p. 180.
7. James Bryce, op. cit. Vol. 2, p. 173.
8. See Chap. 5 infra where the point is fully examined.

and ascertainment of public opinion in a large country. An opinion privately held by the generality of the people does not become public opinion until it is ascertained and held out to be such. The press is the most effective medium for crystalising and publicising the views held by people on public affairs; indeed, public opinion can be said to be, to a considerable extent, the creation of the press. Nothing, it has been said, "can drop the same thought into a thousand minds at the same moment"[9] and also represent it as the thought of all of them. What is carried in a newspaper, both as news and comments, is "like the voice of a great multitude,"[10] and commands belief and acceptance among large numbers of people because of the fascination and the hypnotic appeal of the printed word on the pages of a newspaper. "It speaks *ex cathedra* with a pontifical authority which imposes deference."[11] It causes political life to circulate throughout the country, enabling intercourse of ideas and opinions among people in different parts of it without ever coming into physical contact. It creates public opinion by rallying the interests of the community around certain principles. The press in a democracy is thus rightly regarded as "second only to the people" in terms of power and influence over the conduct of public affairs; it is also rightly regarded as "the constitutive element of liberty."[12] But to be able to discharge its unique role properly and effectively, the press needs to be truly free, independent, upright, vigorous and courageous, and its members well-educated and informed.

The opinion and feelings of the public on matters of government often find expression in public meetings, processions and assemblies staged or organised to agitate for the satisfaction of some social wants or to petition for the redress or amelioration of any government actions or policies considered obnoxious or oppressive. Because they involve action of a somewhat dramatic, though peaceful, character, public meetings, processions and assemblies have reality and

---

9.   Alexis de Tocqueville, *Democracy in America* (1835) ed. Richard Heffner (1956), p. 202.
10.   James Bryce, op. cit. Vol. 1, p. 116.
11.   James Bryce, loc. cit.
12.   de Tocqueville, op. cit. p. 95.

meaning as mechanisms of public participation in government, especially in matters of great public concern where it may be thought that public feelings on them cannot be impressed forcefully enough on government by the published word alone.

When all is said and done, however, public opinion is, as John Stuart Mill remarked, often the opinion or feelings of "a collective mediocrity," of a small, articulate and vociferous minority of the population. Particularly is this the case in the conditions of mass ignorance and illiteracy prevailing in Africa and most other developing parts of the world. The mass of the people, who form the overwhelming majority, are ignorant of state affairs, and have no opinion on them. Public opinion in these countries is formed by a handful of persons among the elite, especially those in control of the mass media, the proprietors of newspapers and magazines, the editors and other journalists.

Chapter 5

A Virile Civil Society

A concept that played a central role in opposition thinking in the
1980s was that of 'civil society'. 1989 was the springtime of society
aspiring to be civil.

— Timothy Garton Ash

In the former communist countries of Eastern Europe and the
former Soviet Union, democratisation must involve, as among
the first steps, the re-activation and re-energisation of civil
society after its emancipation from the jaws of the totalitarian
state following the collapse of communism. The notion of civil
society conceives of society as a collection of people bound
together by a feeling of common nationality or citizenship and
comprising various organisations, associations, interests and
classes, which may be national, regional, local, ethnic,
professional or occupational, and which above all, are
independent of the state and function as autonomous centres
of power.[1] It connotes the existence of a "tight network of
autonomous institutions and organisations which has not one
but a thousand centres,"[2] and is able to act as a check against
any usurpation of power and violation of individual liberty by
government, thus providing an anchorage for the individuality
of each person. The entire society too, as a single national body,
must be able to act autonomously, and must not be tied to the
apron-string of the state. The control of the rulers by the people
is possible and meaningful only if the society and its various

---

1. Timothy G. Ash, *We the People* (1990), pp. 147-149; Peter P. Ekeh, "The
    Constitution of Civil Society in African History and Politics," in Caron *et al,
    Democratic Transition in Africa* (1992), pp. 187-212, where the vast
    literature on the topic is catalogued.
2. Ralf Dahrendorf, *Reflections on the Revolution in Europe* (1990), p. 95.

organisations, associations and groups are independent of the state. And, as noted in the last chapter, democracy is not so much about institutional forms, important though they are, as about the ability of the people to control and remove the rulers.

Communist totalitarianism affects civil society in two ways. Whereas in an absolute government, the individual and society remain separate and distinct from the state, and the separation provides the context within which the government exercises its absolute powers, operating to limit those powers, under communist totalitarianism on the other hand, the separation and the limitation upon governmental powers which it implies practically disappear, with civil society and its variegated institutions being integrated into the state. Secondly, the objective of the communist social order of eliminating the division of society into classes, the replacement of class divisions by a classless society with the communist party as the "vanguard and guiding force," the "effacement of ... the essential differences between town and country, and between mental and physical labour"[3] seem to spell the virtual destruction of society as an autonomous force capable of acting as a check on government. A society which has been absorbed in the state for so long would need, upon its emancipation, to be re-energised and to learn anew the ways of independent existence and action.

The African one-party state differs from communist totalitarianism in that, unlike the latter which recasts and remoulds the society and the economy, integrating them into the state and the monopolist party, it maintains the separation between them (society and the economy) and the state (social organisation of political significance are of course integrated into the party-state) and the limitation which the separation imposes on state power, merely superimposing the monopolist party upon them. The problem about civil society in Africa is thus not one of reactivating and re-energising civil society after the collapse of the one-party state; it is rather that, never having come into existence in the first place, it has to be created anew and then nurtured for effective action as an

---

3.   S. 19 USSR Constitution (1977).

independent mechanism for checking the government.

Therein lies an important difference between African states and the nation-states in the developed countries. In the United States, Ralf Dahrendorf has remarked, "civil society was there first, and the state came later, by the grace of civil society, as it were ... Similarly in England absolute rulers never prevailed over the barons and other sources of local power to the extent they did on the Continent. Switzerland is even today more a civil society, if highly organised one, than a state. On the other hand, countries which had to create civil societies after the event were and are in trouble. Hence citizens have to borrow power from those whom they want to keep in check."[4]

The new African countries belong to the category of those who have to try to create civil society after the establishment of the state. The state in these countries was superimposed upon an agglomeration of hitherto separate and independent nationalities, the societies of which are traditional and primitive while the state is modern. These traditional societies, separated as they are by differences in values and norms of behaviour, are yet to coalesce into one national civil society animated by a common spirit and a feeling of a common nationality and identity, and propelled by common social dynamics, so as to be able to form a common public opinion in matters of government and to act together as one people against governmental abuses and mismanagement or against the seizure of the state by the military. No doubt, certain autonomous national institutions of civil society, such as religious bodies, professional, business and trade associations, trade unions, students union, media organisations, etc. have been created, yet they exert but limited influence and, in any case, are only meant to reinforce the power of the national civil society which as yet does not exist.

These countries do not yet have citizens, only people, different peoples, that is — Hausas, Igbos and Yorubas (Nigeria); Amharas, Tigreans, Oromos and Eritreans (Ethiopia); Kikuyus, Luos and Kambas (Kenya), etc.; or, in the words of de Tocqueville, they only have men, but no social body. "Colonialism was the glue that struck these human units

---

4.   Dahrendorf op. cit. p. 97.

together into a shape recognisable in an atlas." How to transform these disparate units into a nation, into one national civil society bound together by the feeling of a common citizenship, by a bond of fellow-feeling, is one of the major problems of democracy and liberty in Africa.

I agree with the former President of Nigeria, Dr Nnamdi Azikiwe, that no indigenous human society "can thrive without an ideology of its own rooted in its past,"[5] and that the various social groups comprised in the modern African state are not, and cannot be, an exception, but I disagree with him that the ideologies of the component social groups, even those common to them, necessarily characterise the conglomerate that constitutes the modern African state. The "society" of the modern African state is an entity separate and different from the sum total of the different groups that make it up, and the social values or norms that characterise these groups, even those common to them, may not necessarily characterise the "society" of the modern African state. The latter has its own dynamics that may militate against the emergence of a commitment to any one set of values or norms as a national ideology.

Since the main power of a civil society lies in a united public opinion, such a power is impossible among a people without fellow-feeling. "The influences which form opinions and decide political acts," writes John Stuart Mill, "are different in different sections of the country." Their mutual antipathies, he says, "are generally much stronger than jealousy of the government. That any of them feels aggrieved by the policy of the common ruler is sufficient to determine another to support that policy. Even if all are aggrieved, none feel that they can rely on the others for fidelity in a joint resistance; the strength of none is sufficient to resist alone, and each may reasonably think that it consults its own advantage most by bidding for the favour of the government against the rest."[6] The Igbos in Nigeria can

---

5.   Nnamdi Azikiwe, *Ideology for Nigeria*, Macmillan (Lagos), 1980, pp. x and 121.
6.   J. S. Mill, *Representative Government*; reprinted in *Unitarianism, Liberty and Representative Government* (1910), Everyman's Library, pp. 392-393.

hardly be expected to join in a common action against a government or a successful military take-over headed by an Iboman any more than the Yorubas or the Hausa/Fulanis can be expected to do so against a government (civilian or military) headed by their fellow tribesmen.

The notion of civil society is thus more or less synonymous with that of a nation (or national unity), and its creation raises the same question as, in many plural societies of the world, is generally referred to as the "national question,"[7] i.e., the welding together of disparate ethnic, racial or religious groups comprised in the state into one social body or nation. The problem is essentially one of nurturing mutual understanding and accommodation among the different groups; as experience in Africa has shown, the problem lies outside what can be accomplished through structural or institutional arrangements alone, whether of the unitary or federal brand. A properly structured federal arrangement under a constitution that guarantees to all the groups equal access to the headship of the federal government can of course contribute to this, but only to a limited extent. No amount of structural balancing will make the groups not to distrust or to be jealous of each other.

The way to inter-group understanding and accommodation lies principally in the minds and hearts of the people. The bridges to be constructed have therefore to be, not only structural bridges, but also ones that cut across people's mental attitudes and the emotions of their hearts — the sort of bridge afforded by inter-group marriages; mixed business enterprises; free mobility of people across ethnic boundaries, full residence and citizenship rights for every citizen in any part of the country; federally-operated educational institutions where children in their impressionable years are made to share life together and cultivate emotional and attitudinal intimacies; a scheme of national service that compels youths of different ethnic groups to work as a corps outside their ethnic areas with the object of developing among them common ties, as well as enabling them to understand the character and way of life of

---

7.   See J. F. Ade Ajayi, "The National Question in Historical Perspective," Fifth Guardian Newspapers Lecture delivered on Wednesday, Nov. 4, 1992.

their host communities; and by a scheme of general public enlightenment aimed at removing ethnic distrust, prejudices and fear. In addition the administration of government must be based on justice and fair play, and must accord to every citizen and every group due recognition, a due share of the national wealth and equal opportunity for advancement. On the part of the individual citizen there must be a conscious effort to rise above the disposition to champion the interest of one's ethnic group at the expense of others. All these may not provide a complete panacea for the problem of unity, but it will go a long way to nurture it.

One is not of course denouncing ethnicism. Far from it. Ethnicism is a reality, a fact of life, which can no more be wished away or banished than we can disregard our own individuality. "For most of us", said Claude Ake, "these social formations and group identities are not externalities but the core of our being; it is by these identities that most of us define our individuality."[8]

Until recent events in Europe, Africans had been led to believe that ethnicity was a peculiarly African phenomenon, but we now know that it is as much a dominant feature of Eastern European society, and that ethnic nationalism is perhaps even more a dominant feature of politics there than it is in Africa. Even the pygmies, scattered in several countries in Europe, are now in ferment, and are everywhere asserting their separate identity. It is a great eye-opener to read the numerous books that have recently appeared on current political happenings in Eastern Europe. What is bad and needs to be guarded against is not ethnicism as such but its tendency towards nepotism, towards the championing of ethnic interests in total disregard of those of others and of the nation itself. So long as we try to keep a proper balance, ethnicism is a fact of life with which we must come to terms, and to try to harness to better advantage as the foundation of national unity in a multi-ethnic society.

---

8.   Claude Ake, "The Feasibility of Democracy in Africa", Keynote Address at a symposium on Democratic Transition in Africa organised by the Centre for Research, Documentation and University Exchange, University of Ibadan, 16-19 June, 1992, p. 7.

National loyalty in such a society can only be built on top of ethnic loyalty; it cannot stand or survive hanging in the air without a foundation of ethnic loyalty. "Rather than consider ethnicity and nationalism as contradictory and opposed, it is better to think of a gradation of loyalties from family to community, to linguistic group or state, and to the nation."[9] Denied recognition or emasculated to the point of destruction, ethnicity would "soon find expression in anomic interest articulation, communal violence and centrifugal tendencies including secessionist movements — manifestations which do not serve the cause of democracy."[10]

9.   J F Ade Ajayi, op. cit. p. 13.
10.   Claude Ake, op. cit. p. 6.

Chapter 6

A Democratic Society

> Democracy is supposed to be the product and the guardian both of
> Equality and of Liberty, being so consecrated by its relationship to
> both these precious possessions as to be almost above criticism.
>
> – Lord Bryce.

Social Equality

In one sense, democracy connotes a state of society.[1] It implies
a "republican condition of society".[2] There can be no democracy
truly so-called unless the condition of society itself is
democratic, by which is meant that it should be nearly equal
among all the people. Equality of condition implies in turn a
society in which the members are independent of each other,
none being subservient to another, as in an aristocratic society,
where every wealthy aristocrat "constitutes the head of a
permanent and compulsory association, composed of all those
who are dependent upon him, or whom he makes subservient
to the execution of his designs."[3] The independence of the
members in a democratic society characterises even the social
relation of an employer and his employees, which is no longer,
as in the past, marked by the dependence and subservience of
the one to the other, the two having become social partners in a
joint enterprise built upon the capital/entrepreneurship of the
employer and the labour of the workman, and regulated, as
regards wages and other conditions of service, by forces outside
the sole control of either. The steady rise in the wages of the

---

1.   James Bryce, *Modern Democracies* (1920), Vol. 1, p. viii.
2.   Alexis de Tocqueville, *Democracy in America* (1835) ed. Richard Heffner
     (1956), p. 129.
3.   Alexis de Tocqueville, op. cit. p. 199.

workman in relation to the profit of the employer has narrowed the gap between them, resulting in social conditions becoming more equal between them, although a lot more still needs to be done to bring the relationship into fuller accord with the requirements of social justice. (This is discussed in chapter 8).

Nor does the disparity in wealth and income between the rich and the poor in a democratic society stratify the society in the same sense as an aristocratic society is, since "these rich individuals have no feelings or purposes in common, no mutual traditions or mutual hopes."[4] Moreover there is no subordinating bond between the rich and the poor, as there is between the lord to protect and the commoner to be loyal and to defend.

Modern democracy is said to have taken its rise from the general equality of condition of American society in its early days. For Alexis de Tocqueville, writing in 1835 on democracy in America, it is this general equality of condition among the people that constitutes the real essence of democracy, and he equates the one with the other. "Amongst the novel objects that attracted my attention during my stay in the United States," he wrote, "nothing struck me more forcibly than the general equality of condition among the people... The more I advanced in the study of American society, the more I perceived that this equality of condition is the fundamental fact from which all others seems to be derived, and the central point at which all my observations constantly terminated."[5]

Not only the government, but the entire course of society and relations within it were characterised by this fundamental fact. It conditioned public opinion as well as the attitudes and habits of both rulers and the ruled. Even the social relations of the country's highest office, the presidency, were also characterised by it. In the balanced words of Lord Bryce describing the social relations of the American presidency in his study, *The American Commonwealth:*

> The President is simply the first citizen of a free nation, depending for his dignity on no title, no official dress, no insignia of state... To

4.   de Tocqueville, ibid at p. 219.
5.   Alexis de Tocqueville op. cit. p. 26.

a European observer, weary of the slavish obsequiousness and lip-deep adulation with which the members of the reigning families are treated on the eastern side of the Atlantic, fawned on in public and carped at in private, the social relations of an American President to his people are eminently refreshing. There is a great respect for the office and a corresponding respect for the man as the holder of the office, if he has done nothing to degrade it. There is no servility, no fictitious self-abasement on the part of the citizen but a simple and hearty deference to one who represents the majesty of the nation... He is followed about and feted, and in every way treated as the first man in the company but the spirit of equality which rules the country has sunk too deep into every American nature for him to be expected to be addressed with bated and whispering reverence. He has no military guard, no chamberlains or grooms-in-waiting; his everyday life is simple; ... he is surrounded by no such pomp and enforces no such etiquette as that which belongs to the governors even of second class English colonies, not to speak of the Viceroys of India and Ireland.[6]

Social equality as a condition of democracy does not however mean the absolute equality of all individuals in all respects, wealth, income, social position, etc., nor does it require a general levelling down of society, the reduction of all to the same level or class. A classless society and democracy are mutually exclusive objects, since social inequality or class differentiations are indeed inevitable in a democracy founded upon individual liberty. Social inequality results in the main from the freedom of individuals to freely engage in whatever lawful occupations or activities they like and from the fact that they differ widely in the innate abilities and talents which they apply to such occupations or activities, as, for example, differences in aptitude, skill, resourcefulness, initiative, perceptiveness, strength and determination which result from differences in physical, intellectual and will power. "The gifts of intellect proceed directly from God, and man cannot prevent their unequal distribution."[7]

This is not to say that social inequalities between individuals are entirely in harmony with democracy. On the contrary, they undermine, and may even in extreme cases stultify, the democratic principle of equal participation in government. "Disparity in wealth and income produces disparity in political influence" among individuals.[8] Economic power conferred by

6.   *The American Commonwealth*, ed. Hacker, Vol. 1 (1959), p. 26.
7.   Alexis de Tocqueville op. cit. p. 54.
8.   Fred E. Harris, *America's Democracy*, 1989, p. 148.

wealth enables those who have it to exercise, by means of contributions to the election campaigns of candidates, advertising on public issues, lobbying, etc., disproportionate influence on the electoral process and on government decisions. And in cases of extreme concentration of wealth in the hands of a few, the influence exerted may indeed be so great as almost to put the control of the entire political process in the hands of the privileged few. Karl Marx was thus prompted, as a way of removing the threat posed to democracy by social and economic inequalities, to advocate the abolition of private ownership of property and its replacement by public ownership.

What the principle of social equality connotes and requires is rather the non-polarisation or non-dichotomisation of society into *only* an hereditary aristocracy or the nobility (with special privileges) and the common people or into *only* extremes of the very rich and the very poor, the educated and the ignorant and illiterate, the elite and the peasantry, the one separated from the other by a wide disparity in opportunities open to them and in living standards, and by an attitude of subservience, inferiority and servility, often accompanied by social scorn on the one side and social resentment on the other, and which necessarily exclude a spirit of equality between them. It is the absence of such a polarisation that is referred to as the general equality of condition which characterised early American society, and from which modern democracy took its rise. "In democratic America", writes Richard Heffner, "enterprise and the love of wealth will produce a few massive fortunes. But the very poor will also be few in number and the immense neither-rich nor poor majority of the nation will always hold the balance between them."[9] Thus, American society, whilst not egalitarian, is essentially republican and therefore democratic.

The one blot on the democratic nature of American society is the position of the descendants of former slaves taken from Africa. A bloody civil war had had to be fought over it, resulting in the abolition of the status of slavery in 1865 and the emancipation of slaves by constitutional amendments,[10]

9.   Introduction to Tocqueville's *Democracy in America*, op. cit. pp. 17-18.
10.   Thirteenth and Fourteenth Amendments.

although racial discrimination by some state governments persisted until the 1960's and still persists today among private individuals and organisations.

A democratic society is essential to democracy both in its rise and also in ensuring its stability and survival. For between the few very rich and the few very poor "stand an innumerable multitude of men almost alike, who, without being exactly either rich or poor, are possessed of sufficient property to desire the maintenance of order, yet not enough to excite envy. Such men are the natural enemies of violent commotions; their stillness keeps all beneath them and above them still, and secures the balance of the fabric of society."[11] This, says de Tocqueville, accounts for violent revolutions being unknown in the U.S. "If ever America undergoes great revolutions", he maintains, "they will be brought about by .. the inequality of condition" of the black population in its midst.[12]

Unlike the American, African societies are markedly undemocratic. Social inequality is indeed a conspicuous feature of an African society. It is an incident of the prevailing poverty and illiteracy. In comparison with the peasant farmer or urban labourer in Africa who form the majority of the population, the factory worker in the United States or Western Europe has a fairly good income and good living, medical, water, transport, housing, electric and educational facilities as well as facilities for leisure in the form of television, parks, holiday resorts, etc. These amenities have improved his conditions of life to an extent where the gap between him and the rich millionaire has become narrowed. He can therefore afford to regard the latter with an attitude, if not of equality, then certainly not of servility. For he has no reason to feel humbled by any sense of inferiority. To him the President or Prime Minister is just another member of the community like himself, elevated no doubt by the power and perquisites of his office, but not basically different from himself. On the part of the President or Prime Minister too, there is little ground for that feeling of arrogance which social superiority induces in the human mind.

---

11. Alexis de Tocqueville, op. cit. p. 264.
12. op. cit. p. 268.

The match of economic progress, in particular social re-distributive measures, higher wages, lower levels of unemployment, social services and general improvement in living conditions, which has almost obliterated the distinction between the haves and the have-nots, has sobered the arrogance of power so that the President or Prime Minister does not now feel himself different from the rest of the community. Equality is basically an attitude of mind, which in turn depends upon social conditions.

On the other hand, the poverty and ignorance of the masses in Africa create in them a different kind of attitude. A modern, well-furnished house excites wonderment, and a car even more so, its owner is regarded with equal curiosity, as though he were a being from another planet. His world is indeed different from theirs, because of the fantastic gap in their respective living conditions. Poverty degrades the human personality and deprives it of its self-respect. Now, if we remember that the President represents the highest point in magnificent living in the society, the contrast between him and the masses becomes glaring, excluding at once any attitude of equality on either side. In these circumstances it can only border upon the ridiculous to speak at all of equality between them. The masses, sunk deep in poverty and never having experienced anything better or more elevating than life in a thatched hut, barren of any kind of furnishing, not to mention other modern comforts, can hardly be expected to develop any attitude of equality with the President. If anything, he is to them like a demi-god who occasionally comes down from his high pedestal to visit them during a tour of inspection or what is sometimes called a meet-the-people tour, in the course of which he addresses huge crowds, tells them nice, seductive things about what the government plans to do for them in the next planning period — promises which as often as not remain unfulfilled. Such meetings are an occasion for adulation and the display of slavish obsequiousness. The President is hailed, feted and entertained with traditional dances, and showered with gifts. A modest president may take the opportunity of such meetings to demonstrate to the people that he is one of themselves, as President Kaunda of Zambia did when, during a tour of the southern province in 1971, he told the crowd that "for anyone to say that President Kaunda is not a common man because he is President is rubbish. Kaunda is a common man just like you."[13] On another occasion during a tour of the northern province he spoke of the equality of the masses with himself and his ministers. This is good politics, and coming from a professed humanist, it was probably sincerely meant. More than any African President with the exception of Julius Nyerere, Kenneth Kaunda lived a life of Christian simplicity, without the kind of ostentatious display of wealth which characterises Presidents and ministers elsewhere. Yet, while this may mitigate, it cannot remove the stark reality of the economic and social gap between him and the huge peasant and labouring masses. The President's style of living, though simple, was none the less too far removed from their common experience for them to be able to regard him in terms of equality.

Splendour is indeed part of the social pre-eminence of African Presidents. "Personifying the state", writes Arthur Lewis, "they dress themselves up in uniforms, build themselves palaces, bring all other traffic to a standstill when they drive, hold fancy parades and generally demand to be treated like Egyptian Pharaohs."[14] One is not of course condemning ceremonies of any kind nor is there any suggestion that the president should move with the traffic on a busy street. Ceremonies may indeed have quite a useful role in the life of a nation, provided that they are limited to appropriate state occasions and not made to attend the everyday life of the President. It gives expression to a nation's past and culture, and in Africa there is a special need for salvaging African traditional forms of ceremony from years of neglect and suppression under colonialism. It was this desire for cultural revival, a desire to demonstrate that the African has a past, that lay behind the elaborate and somewhat extravagant pomp and pageantry that marked ceremonial occasions in Ghana under Nkrumah. It was a desire to recreate in the institutions of the present the glory and splendour of ancient African

---

13. Times of Zambia, October 13, 1971.
14. Arthur Lewis, *Politics in West Africa*, 1965, p. 31.

kingdoms, like that of ancient Ghana, whose king was said, when holding audience, to sit "in a pavilion around which stand his horses caparisoned in cloth of gold; behind him stand the pages holding shields and gold-mouthed sword..."[15] This is a desire in which every African should feel a nationalistic pride. George Washington too tried to create ceremony and pomp for the new American nation. For the state opening of Congress he drove to Capitol Hill in "his coach and six, with outriders and footmen in livery."[16] As it happened, however, his taste for ceremony and pomp on state occasions was not shared by his successors. And so, as Lord Bryce wrote, "after oscillating between the ceremonious state of George Washington ... and the ostentatious plainness of Citizen Jefferson, who rode up alone and hitched his horse to the post at the gate, the President has settled down into an attitude between that of the mayor of a great English town on a public occasion, and that of a European cabinet minister on a political tour."[17] Yet, granted the need for ceremony, a desire for African cultural revival might be only a cover for indulging personal vanity and a desire to assume the style and attributes of a king. "The adulation of ancient monarchs might overspill and help to create modern equivalents. Ancient kings and modern presidents are then forced to share royal characteristics."[18] Some of the African presidents, Nkrumah in particular, cannot be acquitted of this charge.

One particular exception deserves to be specially noticed, namely President Julius Nyerere. An almost ascetic figure, he found State House too much of a palace, and not easily compatible with his idea of equality which is a central theme in his philosophy of socialism. He preferred therefore to live in his own modest private house of four bedrooms. He had forbidden roads, buildings, etc., to be named after him, and had asked not to be addressed as "Excellency" except on very formal occasions. He appeared genuinely embarrassed by the gap in

15. Stephen Dzirasa, *Political Thought of Dr Kwame Nkrumah* (Accra Guinea Press Ltd.) pp. 19-20.
16. James Bryce, op. cit. p. 26.
17. loc. cit.
18. Ali Mazrui, "Nkrumah: the Leninist Czar" (1966), Transition 26, p. 16.

the standard of living between himself and the masses. But he passionately pleaded that his extra comforts should be regarded as a necessary aid to the carrying out of his duties, as a "tool" entrusted to him for the benefit of the people.[19]

It can be said therefore that there is as yet no true democracy anywhere in Africa, because of the thoroughly undemocratic nature of African societies, which are markedly polarised by the mocking disparity in wealth, income, opportunities and living standards between, on the one hand, "the huge mass of family farmers, living very like the English peasant of the middle ages, illiterate, superstitious, handling very little money, their world bounded by the family or clan; the wage-earners and urban proletariat, living like their counterparts in nineteenth century Britain, semi-literate, under-paid, badly housed", and on the other, "the top professional and business men, whose material and often professional standards equal or exceed those of the Western world."[20] These words by Wraith and Simpkins portray a graphic imagery of the polarised condition of African societies. "It is," they added in a telling comment, "metaphorically possible ... to span the centuries in the course of a short walk." They omitted to mention the large and growing army of the unemployed and beggars. A society so polarised between the very poor and the very rich is not a democratic society, from which it follows that the first condition for a true democracy is yet to be created.

One last point needs to be emphasised. Not only does the principle of social equality not mean absolute equality of wealth, income, education and social standing, it does not require that individuality, i.e. individual differences, the peculiar characteristics or distinctive character and disposition of each individual and his freedom of dissent, should be sacrificed for a forced uniformity in thought, opinions, tastes and manners.[21] To equate social equality with sameness and

---

19. Julius Nyerere, *Ujamaa: Essays on Socialism* 1968, p. 4.
20. Wraith and Simpkins, *Corruption in Developing Countries* (1963) p. 196.
21. J. S. Mill, *On Liberty*, chap. 3 titled "Of Individuality" reprinted in *Unitarianism, Liberty and Representative Government*, Everyman's Library ed. (1910) pp. 123-42.

uniformity is fraught with the danger of the individual being submerged, or propelled, willy-nilly, to go along with the decisions, tastes and manners of the majority or else be ostracised from society, leaving no room for the eccentric and the non-conformist. Of the tendency towards sameness and uniformity in American society, Alexis de Tocqueville has said, in rather sonorous words, that "every citizen, being assimilated to all the rest, is then lost in the crowd, and nothing stands conspicuous but the great and imposing image of the people at large."[22]

It is not America alone but, says John Stuart Mill, mankind as a whole that is threatened by a growing tendency towards forced assimilation into a uniform mould, towards a situation where "peculiarity of taste, eccentricity of conduct, are shunned equally with crimes,"[23] where custom and public opinion, which is often the opinion of a collective mediocrity, impose a despotic reign over the life of the individual, thereby endangering genius, originality and eccentricity in character. "At present," he asserts, "individuals are lost in the crowd... The only power deserving the name is that of masses, and of government while they make themselves the organ of the tendencies and instincts of masses. This is as true in the moral and social relations of private life as in public transactions."[24] It cannot be disputed that customs and public opinion are necessary and useful for orderly social life, yet conformity with them should not be carried to the point where varieties of character — individual judgments or choices based on individual desires, feeling and impulses -- are denied ample scope for self-expression.

The great problem of social equality as a condition of democracy is, then, to prevent it from succumbing to a depraved taste on the part of the masses for egalitarianism, which "impels the weak to attempt to lower the powerful to their own level."[25] Equality should not be elevated into an idol

---

22. *Democracy in America*, op. cit.
23. J. S. Mill, op. cit., p. 129.
24. op. cit., p. 134.
25. de Tocqueville, op. cit., p. 55.

on whose altar each person's individuality must, if a choice has to be made between them, be sacrificed. Both are essential and fundamental to happiness in society, but individuality, the freedom to be different, has a prior claim to primacy and pride of place in a democractic society. Democracy is meaningless without freedom of dissent and respect for the individuality of each person. For man is first and foremost an individual human being, and his individuality must come before the demand of equality with other members of society. A democratic society must therefore combine social equality with respect for each person's individuality and his freedom, within certain limits, to be different and to dissent. What this comes to is that a democratic society (as distinct from democratic government) presupposes a free society, a concept examined in the next chapter.

Dangers of Gross Social Inequality for Democracy: The Rise of Socialism/Communism

The notion of a democratic society as a condition of democracy and its critical relevance and importance to democratisation is perhaps best appreciated by reminding ourselves that it was gross social inequality that led, by means of violent revolutionary action, to the rise of communism, from whose dreadful evils mankind is only just escaping. (It is still in operation in Cuba, China and some other Asian countries). Moved by this gross inequality as it existed at the time, Karl Marx, writing in 1867, in his great work, *Capital*, had prophesied that such an order of society, which he styled capitalism, was bound to give rise to a social revolution because of the grievous imbalance and injustice involved in the oppression and exploitation of the working people, comprising the great majority of the population, by a small class of capitalists who owned and controlled the means of production. A social revolution, he maintained, was inevitable by reason of the tendency of the system towards an increase in the wealth and power of the numerically dwindling capitalist class as well as a corresponding increase in the misery and privation of the numerically growing class of the working people. And in proportion, as more and more wealth (capital) became concentrated in fewer and fewer hands, resentment among the workers would grow, giving rise eventually to resistance and revolt against the exploiters. In the ensuing struggle, the working people would emerge victorious, overturn the existing order of society, and establish in its place, a dictatorship of the working people (socialism).

Marx's social revolution, as Karl Popper explains, denotes, not necessarily a civil war or violent revolt (although it does not exclude violence should its use become necessary), but "the more or less rapid transition from the historical period of capitalism to that of socialism. In other words, it is the name of a transitional period of class struggle between the two main classes, down to the ultimate victory of the workers."[26] This, then, is Marx's theory of the inexorable march of history.

With the liquidation of the capitalists (bourgeoisie), the working people (proletariat) would remain the one and only social class. The society would thus have become a classless one culminating, with the eventual consolidation of the socialist system, in the emergence of communism.

This is not the place to enter into a critical analysis of Marx's theory and prediction,[27] except to say that subsequent developments in the structure of capitalism have rendered untenable the premise of the theory and the conclusion based on it. Capitalism, in the unrestrained, laissez-faire form in which it existed in Marx's day, has, as Karl Popper observed, disappeared, reformed out of recognition by a variety of interventionist measures enacted by the modern welfare state, with the object of promoting social justice between the classes. (This is discussed in detail in chapter 7). "Unrestrained capitalism," says Karl Popper, "has given way to a new historical period, to our own period of political interventionism, of the economic interference of the state."[28] Marx could not have foreseen the advent of the International Labour Organisation (comprising some 150 member states) and its standards — setting activities which have resulted in some 167

26. Karl Popper, The Open Society and Its Enemies, Vol. 2 (1966), p. 149.
27. The reader is referred to Popper, op. cit., for a detailed incisive analysis and critique.
28. Popper, op. cit., p. 140.

not sufficiently articulated as it ought to have been, his recognition of society's right of self-protection against harm in its members' conduct towards one another is discernible as the pre-supposition of the doctrine. And there are passages in the *Essay* which attest to this recognition. Thus, the word "collectively" in the first sentence of the second passage quoted above, when read together with "self-protection", could only mean self-protection of society at large. It is true that in the very next sentence and in other parts of the *Essay*, he speaks of freedom to do as one pleases in matters that do not concern *others*, yet he acknowledges that "it is far otherwise if he had infringed the rules necessary for the protection of his fellow-creatures, *individually or collectively*."[35] Later still in the *Essay*, he says that "whenever, in short, there is a definite damage, or a definite risk of damage, either to an individual *or to the public*, the case is taken out of the province of liberty, and placed in that of morality or law."[36] Nothing could be more unequivocal that Mill recognises the right of society to protect its own interests against harm that might be done to them by a person's conduct that does not concern himself alone. And in the chapter of the *Essay* in which the practical applications of the doctrine are examined, society's right to protect its interests is again recognised. "There are," he acknowledges, "many acts which, being directly injurious only to the agents themselves, ought not to be legally interdicted, but which, *if done publicly*, are a violation of good manners, and coming thus within the category of offences against others, may rightly be prohibited. Of this kind are offences against decency."[37] The criticism that may fairly be made of Mill's thesis is that his recognition of society's right of self-protection does not receive as much emphasis as it ought to have received.

Because of the somewhat passing attention given to society's right of self-protection, the question as to the types of public interests that justify interference with liberty was not considered at all. Is liberty justifiably interfered with in order to

---

35. ibid p. 148; italics supplied.
36. ibid p. 150; italics supplied.
37. ibid p. 167; italics supplied.

protect society's interest in order, security, safety, health, morality, economic well-being and general well-being? Had he considered the question, there is no doubt that Mill would have accepted these specific public interests as legitimate grounds for interference with a person's conduct in matters that do not concern himself alone.

Conduct that Concerns Oneself Alone

A person's conduct that concerns only himself can hardly harm public order, public security, safety or the economic well-being of the society. The only public interests that have any bearing on such conduct are public health, public morality and general well-being, but in Mill's doctrine even these are not legitimate grounds for interference, except where such conduct "violates any specific duty to the public". This is the really contentious aspect of Mill's doctrine, and one that has provoked a sharp division of opinion ever since. It is his thesis that, as regards a person's conduct that concerns only himself (a "conduct purely self-regarding" as he calls it), society has no right to control him either in his own interest (to protect him, as it were, against himself) or in order to secure conformance with generally accepted standards of tastes, manners, propriety, morality, health or of behaviour generally.

Mill was not of course unmindful that a person's vices and bad ways in his personal life and in the conduct of affairs that concern no one else but himself, as, for instance, drunkenness, incontinence, idleness or uncleanliness, may affect those "nearly connected with him and, in a minor degree, society at large"[38] in the way either of direct harm or of bad influence apt to corrupt or lead others astray.[39] Yet, notwithstanding that conduct purely self-regarding may cause harm to others or to society ar large, interference is still not justified except where the individual is led by such conduct to "violate a distinct and assignable obligation to any other person or persons" as in the case of obligation owned to one's dependants or to one's

---

38. ibid p. 149
39. pp. 149-150.

creditors,[40] or to fail in "the performance of some definite duty incumbent on him to the public",[41] as in the case of a policeman drunk while on duty. He insists that any harmful or prejudicial effect of a self-regarding conduct of a person which "neither violates any specific duty to the public, nor occasions perceptible hurt to an assignable individual except himself... is one which society can afford to bear, for the sake of the greater good of human freedom"[42] Not compulsion or control but rather "advice, instruction, persuasion, and avoidance by other people if thought necessary by them for their own good, are the only measures by which society can justifiably express its dislike or disapprobation of (such) conduct."[43]

In the form which the thesis is stated by Mill's present-day disciples, a man's conduct that affects no one else but himself is his private affair, notwithstanding that others may consider the conduct immoral, improper or in bad taste; and the law has no business interfering with it, since society is not, and cannot possibly be, harmed by it in a way worth bothering about. According to the Committee on Homosexual Offences and Prostitution (the Wolfenden Committee) in England, homosexuality between two consenting adults in private should not be punished as a criminal offence because "there must remain a realm of private morality and immorality which is, in brief and crude terms, not the law's business."[44] Is there, indeed, a private realm in the affairs of the individual into which the law must not (not *may* not) enter? In his delightful book, *Law, Liberty and Morality* (1963), Professor Hart, the leading present-day proponent of this thesis, while not agreeing with all that Mill said, has gone to great lengths in trying, unconvincingly in our view, to demonstrate its correctness.

The rationale on which the thesis is premised is Mill's assertion that "mankind are not infallible; that their truths, for the most part, are only half-truths..., that there should be different experiments of living; that free scope should be given

40. p. 149.
41. ibid p. 160.
42. lot cit.
43. ibid pp. 162-163.
44. *Report CMD 247 (1957) para. 61.*

to varieties of character, short of injury to others; and that the worth of different modes of life should be proved practically, when anyone thinks fit to try them."[45] This is, undeniably, true, to some extent, but, as a practical matter, society can exist and function only on the basis of certain generally accepted moral beliefs, which may well be only half-truths. As Mill himself says in a passage that answers the point so admirably:

> There is no question here (it may be said) about restricting individuality, or impeding the trial of new and original experiment in living. The only things it is sought to prevent are things which have been tried and condemned from the beginning of the world until now; things which experience has shown not to be useful or suitable to any person's individuality. There must be some length of time and amount of experience after which a moral or prudential truth may be regarded as established; and it is merely desired to prevent generation after generation from falling over the same precipice which has been fatal to their predecessors.[46]

So we are talking, not about morality imposed by the state, nor about morality based on popular prejudice, rationalisation or aversion, but about one that has passed the test of time and experience and been accepted by the society as part of its common heritage, and on which its integrity and, perhaps, its very existence as a cohesive entity, hinges. Surely, society is entitled to enforce such a morality by law, even in relation to a person's conduct that affects no one else but himself, provided that —

(i)   the conduct is an infringement of *the* morality, (infringement alone or what Professor Hart refers to as immorality *as such* would not of course justify interference).

(ii)   the offending conduct is, by its nature, injurious or prejudicial to society.[47] Since we are concerned with conduct that affects no one else but the actor, what is relevant to its enforcement by law is whether it is

---

45.   ibid.
46.   ibid p. 149.
47.   Ronald Dworkin would seem not to dispute this conclusion so long as public morality is understood in the sense defined above; see his article, "Lord Devlin and the Enforcement of Morals", (1966) 75 Yale Law Journal 986.

harmful or prejudicial to society at large, not whether it is harmful or prejudicial to others, for it cannot, from our premise, be so. Professor Hart seems clearly to have misconceived the issue by basing his opposition to legal enforcement on the ground that "immorality as such" is not harmful to others.[48]

(iii) interference with freedom is considered, having regard to the nature and extent of the harm to society, a lesser evil than letting the immorality go unpunished.

It follows, therefore, that the questions posed by Professor Hart and which form the basis of the discussion in his book are the wrong ones and irrelevant to the issue, viz "Is the fact that certain conduct is by common standards immoral sufficient to justify making that conduct punishable by law? Is it morally permissible to enforce morality as such? Ought immorality as such to be a crime?"[49] From what is said above, the answer to his questions is not in dispute, and it is an unequivocal negative. As Lord Devlin said, "what is in dispute is ... whether it is a condition of a free society that private immorality should altogether and always be immune from interference by the law. No one suggests that all private immorality should be punished by law. You can grant that private immorality is within the competence of the legislature in a free society and still advance many powerful arguments why the law should not try to punish particular vices in particular circumstances."[50] In other words, the law should punish, not every private immorality, but only such as is, by its nature, harmful or prejudicial to society at large, and even then only if punishment would be a lesser evil than letting the immorality go unpunished.

Lord Devlin has convincingly shown that certain vices (i.e. conducts that offend accepted morality) are, by their nature, injurious or prejudicial to society and may, (assuming that the right balance lies in favour of punishment rather than toleration) be rightly punished by law. Drunkenness, for example, when habitually indulged in by every one in society is

48.   ibid, particularly pp. 5, 25, 30, 33, 34 and 57.
49.   ibid p. 4.
50.   Patrick Devlin op. cit. p. 110.

harmful or prejudicial to the society because it diminishes the ability of the members to contribute to its general well-being. So also unrestricted indulgence in homosexuality is bound to undermine, if not destroy sooner or later, the institutions of marriage and the family and the breeding of children, leading, ultimately, to the weakening of the society itself; it might also create widespread emotional instability among men and women.[51] Celibacy, as a general practice, does not have quite the same effect, for, while it would destroy the institution of marriage, it would not stop co-habitation and sexual relationship between the sexes and the breeding of children as a result of that nor would the parties be less emotionally stable than under a formal marriage relationship. All the other cases cited by Professor Hart as attempts to enforce immorality *as such* — sodomy between persons of different sex, bestiality, living on the earnings of prostitutions and keeping a house for prostitution — are really conducts which, by their nature,[52] may be considered injurious or prejudicial to society at large; they are, therefore, not really cases of immorality *as such.* To these may be added one other offence connected with prostitution — pimping. It is difficult to see how the effect of these vices on the general well-being of society differs from the effect on its economic well-being, of certain economic crimes prohibited as constituting economic sabotage but not for the harm they do to any one. Treason and other subversive activities too harm no one directly but only society's interest in its safety and security. Surely it should be a proper concern of the law not only to punish conduct *directly and immediately* injurious to society (or individuals of course) but also to prohibit under penalty, acts which, if allowed unrestricted indulgence, might attain proportions that cannot but injure society's general well-being.

By far more serious is the harm unrestricted indulgence in vice may do to a society's system of moral beliefs, its collective sense of right and wrong. If everyone were free, in matters that

---

51. Ronald Dworkin thinks that these harmful effects attributed to homosexuality are speculative, not demonstrable; ibid at p. 993.
52. ibid p. 25. According to Ronald Dworkin, the error in Lord Devlin's arguments is "not his idea that the community's morality counts, but his idea of what counts as the community's morality;" ibid at p. 1001.

concern themselves alone, to indulge in vice without restriction, the ultimate result might be a general disbelief in the existing morality, without its being immediately replaced by a new morality, which will inevitably take time to establish itself and get accepted. "The old belief", says Lord Devlin, "must first be driven out by disbelief ... Whether the new belief is better or worse than the old, it is the interregnum of disbelief that is perilous,"[53] In short, no society could permit unrestricted deviations from its common morality and still retain its cohesiveness and sense of direction.

Lord Devlin has also raised the fundamental point whether it is part of the concept of liberty to be free to do things which one knows or believes to be a vice. "Freedom," he says, "is not a good in itself. We believe it to be good because out of freedom there comes more good than bad ... But no good can come from a man doing what he acknowledges to be evil. The freedom that is worth having is freedom to do what you think to be good notwithstanding that others think it to be bad. Freedom to do what you know to be bad is worthless."[54]

It should perhaps be reiterated that, while society is entitled to control a person's conduct which, though it affects only himself, offends accepted morality, its control should not extend to conduct which is a vice only by some other standard of morality. Outside socially accepted morality, it is interference with liberty for the state to impose its own ideas of morality, and use them to restrict people's freedom of action in matters that affect only themselves. To this extent, Mill is right.

On the question whether it is justifiable for the state to control people in their own interest, Mill's opposition to such control seems inconsistent with the principle on which interference to protect others against harm rests, namely, that it is morally wrong to harm others. There are cases when an act harmful to others would be morally wrong when done to oneself. To kill, maim or otherwise inflict severe physical pain or other inhuman suffering on oneself is as morally wrong as when the harm is done to another person, and should be

---

53.   ibid p. 114.
54.   ibid at p. 108.

amenable to control by the law on the same principle that justifies interference in the latter case. On the other hand, there is nothing morally wrong in a person throwing away or destroying his own property otherwise than by a method prohibited by law.

The primary duty of government is to safeguard and promote the welfare of all its citizens equally, and the duty could not stop short of protection against morally wrongful harm to oneself, whether such protection is called paternalism or whatever. Freedom to do something which one knows or believes to be morally wrong, including harming oneself in a way rightly regarded as morally wrong, is, as earlier stated, a negation of the idea of freedom.

Happily, Mill's position on this point is not shared by his disciples. In supporting the increasing interference with individual freedom on paternalistic grounds, e.g. the law compelling people to wear crash helmet when riding a motor-bicycle or a seat belt in a car, prohibiting the sale of drugs or narcotics except under medical prescription or excluding consent as a defence to a crime except in certain cases, Professor Hart thinks it "a perfectly coherent policy."[55] Mill's rationale for his opposition to it that people know their own interest best is, says Professor Hart, greatly weakened by the fact that his conception of the ability of the human being to decide what is good for himself does not now correspond to reality and by the increased awareness that people's choices or consent are often not as free as they are supposed to be. "Choices may be made or consent given without adequate reflection or appreciation of the consequences; or in pursuit of merely transitory desires; or in various predicaments when the judgment is likely to be clouded; or under inner psychological compulsion; or under pressure by others of a kind too subtle to be susceptible of proof in a law court."[56]

55. ibid pp. 31-32.
56. ibid p. 33.

Other Grounds of Criticism

Mill's doctrine may be fairly criticised on at least three other grounds. First, as regards freedom of thought and conscience, he is of course right in according them absolute, unqualified scope, free of all interference by society, since what a man thinks in his mind or feels or believes in his heart without manifesting it in some overt way cannot affect other individuals or society at large. In any case, to attempt to control the human thought and conscience is simply futile as an attempt to control what cannot be controlled; for, "nothing that law-makers and lawyers can do can fetter the mind of man, only his body."[57] However, Mill errs in classifying speech with thought and conscience and according to it the same absolute, unqualified freedom, simply on the ground of man's fallibility and the unattainability of absolute truth;[58] it cannot be disputed that a man's utterances or published words may harm other individuals or society to a grievous degree indeed, thus justifying their control by society. Absolute liberty of speech and press just cannot be squared with the equal liberty of other individuals not to be defamed or with the legitimate interest of society in the maintenance of order.

Second, the doctrine omits mention of the right to life and the death penalty. From the maxim that silence implies consent, the omission must be taken to imply that, in Mill's view, the death penalty is warranted. It may, however, be countered that the right to life falls outside the title of Mill's *Essay*, life and liberty being usually treated as separate notions.

Securing a Free Society by Means of Constitutional Protection of Liberty

Mill failed also to consider the means by which his doctrine of liberty may be realised, for this, surely, is a question crucial to the whole concept of liberty, however its scope is defined. If by

---

57. Patrick Devlin op. cit. p. 119.
58. Mill, *On Liberty*, chap. 2 titled "Of the Liberty of Thought and Discussion".

liberty is meant protection against the tyranny of both the political rulers and public opinion, then, the means of providing the needed protection becomes a critical aspect of any concept of liberty. With respect to protection against the tyranny of public opinion, Mill seems to have resigned himself to an admission of the impossibility of protection. As he wrote: "The disposition of mankind, whether as rulers or as fellow-citizens, to impose their own opinions and inclination as a rule of conduct on others, is so energetically supported by some of the best and by some of the worst feelings incident to human nature, that it is hardly ever kept under restraint by anything but want of power; and as the power is not declining, but growing, unless a strong barrier of moral conviction can be raised against the mischief, we must expect, in the present circumstances of the world, to see it increase."[59] But he nevertheless insists that "there is a limit to the legitimate interference of collective opinion with individual independence; and to find that limit, and maintain it against encroachment, is as indispensable to a good condition of human affairs, as protection against political despotism."[60] But he has nothing to say on how the limit proposed in his doctrine is to be maintained.

Whilst Mill also failed to say anything about how liberty is to be safeguarded against the tyranny of the political rulers, a means of providing the necessary protection has been found in the constitution, being the source from which government derives its existence and powers. Constitutional protection of liberty or what is known as a Bill of Rights is thus an essential mark of constitutional democracy. This is not, however, to say that a society cannot be a free society without a Bill of Rights. The test, for Mill, is whether liberty, as defined by him, is *in fact* respected or not, irrespective of how its observance is secured. Nor does the United Nations Universal Declaration of Human Rights specifically require a Bill of Rights as the only means of giving effect to its provisions; it only proclaims that respect for human rights is to be promoted through education and

59. ibid pp. 82-83.
60. ibid p. 73.

teaching, while their recognition and observance is to be secured by "progressive measures", including "law, conventions, regulations or custom." A country without a Bill of Rights may indeed respect and observe individual freedom to a very high degree based on the ordinary law and on traditions, customs, and conventions. Britain is a good example of this. "In Britain" writes Sir Ivor Jennings, "we have no Bill of Rights; we merely have liberty according to law; and we think — truly, I believe — that we do the job better than any country which has a Bill of Rights or a Declaration of the Rights of Man."[61] So also the provisions in a Bill of Rights are not exhaustive or conclusive of the scope of freedom secured or protected within a given legal and political system. The totality of the laws, customs and conventions as well as what obtains in practice has to be looked at. Yet, constitutional protection of liberty is inseparable from the concept of a constitutional democracy, and provides perhaps the most visible index of a free society.

The singular importance of the emergence of the idea of a written constitution as law antecedent and superior to government lies not so much in its function as a source of power but rather in the consequence that it necessarily operates as a limitation upon government, a consequence that flows inexorably from the fact that in constituting a government and in granting and distributing power, a constitution cannot but limit it not only as regards subject-matter and the aims to be pursued but the procedure for exercising it as well. "In any state that we may properly call constitutional," writes Professor McIlwain, "the supreme authority must be defined and defined by a law of some kind," but "there can be no definition which does not of necessity imply a limitation."[62] A constitution as a supreme law which merely grants power in all its plenitude without limitations of any kind hardly merits to be so called. To justify the name, it must be "a constitution of liberty, a constitution that would protect the individual against all arbitrary coercion."[63]

61. Ivor Jennings, *The Approach to Self-Government*, (1958) p. 20.
62. C. H. McIlwain, *Constitutionalism and the Changing World* (1939), p. 240.
63. Hayek, *The Constitution of Liberty* (1960), p. 182.

"The conception of a constitution," as Friedrich Hayek explains, "thus became closely connected with the conception of representative government, in which the powers of the representative body were strictly circumscribed by the document that conferred upon it particular powers. The formula that all power derives from the people referred not so much to the recurrent election of representatives as to the fact that the people, organised as a constitution-making body, had the exclusive right to determine the powers of the representative legislature. The constitution was thus conceived as a protection of the people against all arbitrary action on the part of the legislative as well as the other branches of government.[64] A government of the people by the people is not fully democratic unless the instrument constituting it also guarantees and protects the basic rights of the individual.

Constitutional protection of individual liberty satisfies the democractic ideal of individual participation in government by enabling the individual to intervene personally where the protection is being violated. Since they are determined by a majority, popular elections do not effectively assure individual participation. If the size and complexity of modern society make it inexpedient for every individual to participate personally in every decision which affects him, then, he must be enabled to seek redress personally by an action in court against any violation by government of the constitutional protection of his fundamental rights and freedoms. Being at the instance of an aggrieved individual, the democratic virtue of such an action is that it assures the individual's personal participation in government, thus imparting greater reality to the concept of self-government. Such an action is thus a means by which the people, as individuals, can control their elected representatives in the executive and legislature. It is, writes Professor Charles Black, "the people's institutionalised means of self- control",[65] the "self-restraint of democracy."[66] Being a practical incident of the terms and conditions upon which the majority in the

---

64.   op. cit., p. 178.
65.   Charles Black, The People and the Court (1960), p. 107.
66.   ibid p. 115.

executive and legislature holds its powers, the review by the courts at the instance of an aggrieved individual of governmental acts in terms of the constitutional protection of liberty and other limitations is indeed a constituent element of majority rule; to regard it as antithetical thereto is to misconceive the true basis of majority rule.

In a country without a firmly rooted tradition of respect for human rights, where, on the contrary, human rights violations have been part of the political culture for decades, a Bill of Rights as a legal restraint on government, enforceable at the instance of an aggrieved individual, should therefore be the starting-point in any scheme of transition from authoritarian or autocratic rule to freedom and the free society. There is no other legal mechanism known to us for ensuring that executive as well as legislative acts conform to the standards of liberty required by democracy. Without a Bill of Rights as an enforceable legal restraint, a government is inadequately limited, and is therefore, by definition, authoritarian unless the necessary restraint is supplied by firmly rooted tradition, as in the case of Britain, for example. And no matter what democratic institutions are created, e.g. elections, multi-partyism, etc., the rule of law cannot be an effective safeguard against the abuse of political power in the absence of a Bill of Rights.

It is not of course claimed for a Bill of Rights that it is a wholly effective guarantee of liberty. "No knowledgeable person has ever suggested that constitutional safeguards provide in themselves complete and indefeasible security. But they do make the way of the transgressor, of the tyrant, more difficult. They are, so to speak, the outer bulwarks of defence."[67] In equally congent language, the Nigerian Minorities Commission (1958) has said: "A government determined to abandon democratic courses, will find ways of avoiding them, but they are of great value in preventing a steady deterioration in standards of freedom and the unobstrusive encroachment of a government on individual rights."[68] They are particularly

---

67. Cowen, *The Foundations of Freedom* (1960), p. 119.
68. Report Cmnd 505 (1958), p. 97.

needed to guard against legislative encroachments.

Did, then, the one-party or socialist states in Africa, Eastern Europe and the Soviet Union, which are now embarked upon democratisation, have at the time of the revolutions in 1989-90 a Bill of Rights in the sense just stated? Certainly, none had *such* a Bill of Rights, save only Zambia, Kenya, Malawi and Uganda. (On the introduction of one-party rule in Zambia, Kenya, Malawi and Uganda, the Bill of Rights had to be modified to take account of the change.) One of them in Commonwealth Africa that had it in its independence constitution — Ghana, — jettisoned it at the time of becoming a one-party state for the obvious reason that the restraints of a Bill of Rights cannot exist together with the authoritarianism/autocracy of one-party rule; one must give way to the other, and Ghana chose to do away with the Bill of Rights in furtherance of its authoritarian ambitions.

Instead of a Bill of Rights as a legal restraint upon government, enforceable at the instance of an aggrieved individual, the one-party state or socialist constitutions of the countries in Africa, Eastern Europe and the Soviet Union purported to guarantee rights in the form either of a declaration of objectives or in terms that import no enforceable legal restraints. It is true, as noted in chapter 2 above, that the later generation of communist constitutions are framed like a Bill of Rights properly so-called, although in all of them social, economic and cultural rights were given more prominence than civil and political rights.[69] As however they were embodied in constitution that did not have the force of a supreme, overriding law, they could not have imposed a legal restraint enforceable against the state (especially the legislative organ) at the instance of the individual.

The human rights provisions in the existing constitutions of the countries previously under one-party or communist rule need therefore to be replaced by a proper Bill of Rights

---

69.   Chap. 3, arts 34-65, Bulgaria; chap. 2, arts 19-38, Czechoslovakia; Part II
   Chap. 1, arts 19-40, German Democratic Republic (GDR); chap. 7, arts 54-
   70, Hungary; chap. 8, arts 67-93, Poland; chap 2, arts 17-41, Romania;
   chap. 7, arts 39-69, USSR; chap 2, art 280-281, Yugoslavia.

A Free Society   133

enforceable against the state by an aggrieved individual. (The provisions relating to social, economic and cultural rights are unexceptionable). Romania, Bulgaria and Czechoslovakia have already done so in a most gratifying form.[70] Informed as they obviously are by the countries' bitter experience of tyranny under communist rule and by a desire to prevent a recurrent of it, (Czechoslovakia's Charter of Fundamental Rights and Freedoms recites in a preamble that its adoption is inspired by "the bitter experience of the times when human rights and basic freedoms were repressed in our country") the new provisions are truly a charter of liberty not only in the wide sweep of the rights protected but more importantly for their passionate concern for means of making the guarantee really effective in practice. Basic democratic, intellectual and religious freedoms, security of the person, other personal rights (capital punishment is prohibited in Romania and Czechoslovakia) and equality before the law are guaranteed in terms that leave it in no doubt that they are meant to have the effect of enforceable legal restraints, so are freedom of action, the right to work, free choice of occupation or profession and private enterprise generally, the right to strike (forced labour is prohibited) and the right of property. "The individual," declares the Romanian Constitution (1991), "has the right to do what he wants to do, as long as he does not violate the rights and freedoms of other persons, public order, and moral standards," or, in the words of Czechoslovakia's Charter, "everyone may do what is not forbidden by law."[71] (Both the Romanian and Bulgarian Constitutions declare the economy as a market economy and enjoin the state to ensure free trade and the protection of competition).[72] Not only are the interpretation and application of these provisions required to conform to the U.N. Universal Declaration of Human Rights (1948) and other international human rights conventions or treaties to which the countries are a party, but also the latter are accorded priority and overriding

70. Arts. 15-49 Romania (1991); Arts 25-27 Bulgaria (1991); Charter of Fundamental Rights and Freedoms of Czechoslovakia (1991).
71. Art. 2(3).
72. Arts 134 Romania; art 19 Bulgaria.

force in the event of conflict between the two. Existing laws remain in force only insofar as they are in conformity with the guaranteed rights and freedoms, and in Czechoslovakia it is expressly provided that an existing law would cease to be in force after December 31, 1991 to the extent that it is inconsistent with the guaranteed rights and freedoms.

Every person is guaranteed the right of recourse to the courts and the right to legal aid for the protection of his rights, freedoms and interests, with final appeal to the Constitutional Court whose decisions on such questions are binding on all persons and authorities. "No law can hamper the exercise of this right,"[73] or exclude the jurisdiction of the courts in the protection of fundamental rights and freedoms against interference by the public authorities.[74] Indeed, in Romania the guaranteed rights and freedoms, political pluralism and the independence of the judiciary are made altogether unalterable, even by referendum. To reinforce enforcement by the courts, a new institution, called the "People's Attorney," is established by the new Romanian Constitution, charged with the function, exercisable either on his own or at the instance of an aggrieved citizen, of defending the guaranteed rights and freedoms against violation. And all public authorities are enjoined to provide him with all necessary support for the effective discharge of his duties. In Poland too a Commission for Civil Rights Protection has been established. More significant perhaps is the provision in Czechoslovakia's Charter of Fundamental Rights and Freedoms guaranteeing to citizens "the right to rise in resistance against any person who might destroy the democratic order of human rights and basic freedoms laid down in the Charter, if the activity of constitutional organs and the effective application of legal means are rendered impossible."[75]

---

73. Art. 21(2) Romania.
74. Art 36(2) Czechoslovakia.
75. Art. 23.

Chapter 8

A Just Society

> Justice is not only the end of government, it is the end of civil society. It ever has been and ever will be pursued until it be obtained, or until liberty be lost in the pursuit.
>
> — James Madison

Social and Individual Justice

A just society is what nowadays is implied by the more popular term "social justice," although both social and individual justice must be combined in order that a society may be fully just. Unlike individual justice, however, social justice is a concept of vague and imprecise meaning. To Fredrich Hayek, it is a "mirage," "a wholly illusory ideal," and the use of the term, an abuse of language.[1] He considers the concept meaningless because the social conditions regarded as unjust are not attributable to the unjust conduct of any individual or group of persons nor are they the result of anybody's design but rather of accident or the natural inequality between people; neither individuals nor society collectively are to blame for bringing them about by any unjust conduct on their part.[2] (The addition of the adjective "social" as also in "social democracy," "social market economy," he says, makes the terms "capable of meaning almost anything one likes.")[3] But while the usage may not be entirely accurate, it seems apt enough to describe the justice or otherwise of the laws, customs, conventions, decisions, institutions, actions or lack of action of society as

---

1. *The Mirage of Social Justice* (1976), p. 62; p. 85; reprinted in *Law, Liberty and Legislation* (1982).
2. ibid pp. 68- 70.
3. ibid p. 79.

they affect or apply to its members or component groups or social relations generally, as, for instance, the distribution or allocation of benefits between individuals or groups or interventions by society in the affairs or relations of individuals or groups. The free market order is certainly governed by laws relating, e.g., to contract, property, inheritance, master and servant. Whether those laws are just in the results they produce between the parties to a transaction or in regard to social relations generally is certainly an appropriate concern of the concept of social justice.

In this connection, it is important to stress, as Frankena points out, that social justice is not simply a property or virtue of a national society "in its *formal* or legal aspect — what is called the state... Society does not consist merely of the law or the state. It has also a more *informal* aspect, comprised of its cultural institutions, conventions, moral rules and moral sanctions. In order for a society to be fully just, it must be just in its informal as well as in its formal aspects."[4] Again, it is not true as Hayek seems to think, that the demand for social justice is addressed solely or primarily to "society in the strict sense in which it must be distinguished from the apparatus of government."[5]

Social justice is thus to be distinguished from individual justice or what Honore calls the justice of private transactions and the justice of special relationships. The one concerns justice in the private dealings or relations between man and man, with the object of making "one citizen restore something to another citizen, compensate him for a wrong or pay him for goods or services rendered."[6] whilst the other concerns the justice of decisions, actions, laws or institutions of society in their bearing on individuals or component groups. As regards the distribution of benefits, for example, it is concerned with the justice of distributions made by society as a whole as distinct from "those undertaken within more limited

---

4.   W. K. Frankena, "The Concept of Social Justice," in R. B. Brandt (ed.) *Social Justice* (1962), p. 2.
5.   Hayek, op. cit., p. 64.
6.   A. M. Honore, "Social Justice", 8 McGill Law Journal, (1968), p. 81; reprinted in R.S. Summers (ed) *Essays in Legal Philosophy*, (1968).

organisations, such as firms, families or provident societies."[7]

As Honore observes, "modern social and economic developments have made it clear that individual justice, justice between wrongdoer and victim, is only a partial and incomplete form of justice."[8] This perhaps accounts for the shift in emphasis since the last century from analysis of individual justice to that of social justice. The glaring injustice of the present-day economic order, both domestic and international, the cry of the under-privileged for protection and the demands of the individual on the state for welfare services have compelled attention being increasingly focused on the need and importance of social justice and away from issues of individual justice that once dominated it and which characterised the order of society governed by classical liberalism. The concept of social justice has indeed so conquered the public imagination. "Almost every claim for government action on behalf of particular groups is advanced in its name, and if it can be made to appear that a certain measure is demanded by 'social justice', opposition to it will rapidly weaken. People may dispute whether or not the particular measure is required by 'social justice'. But that this is the standard which ought to guide political action ... is hardly ever questioned. In consequence, there are today probably no political movements or politicians who do not readily appeal to 'social justice' in support of the particular measures which they advocate."[9]

Since social justice is justice viewed in a social context, the starting point in our discussion must therefore be with justice itself, its meaning, role and importance.

Meaning and Importance of Justice

Justice is a concept that has meaning only in relations involving two or more persons as between whom a transaction or an arrangement may be characterised as either just or unjust.[10] It is a virtue that requires of a person that, in taking

---

7.   J. R. Lucas, *On Justice* (1980), p. 163.
8.   op. cit. p. 77.
9.   Hayek, op. cit., p. 65.
10.   Lucas, op. cit. p. 3.

decisions or actions affecting other persons, he should regard their interests as he would his own, and avoid any bias or partiality. It means acting *fairly* towards others without bias or partiality, and without harming their interests. It manifests a concern not so much for the other chap's faring well as for his not faring ill, an acceptance by all of each other's existence, respect for each other's interests, and rendering to one another his or her dues.[11] It is concerned to "emphasise that the other chap is not merely a human being like myself, but a separate individual, with his own point of view and his own interests" which are entitled to serious consideration just as much as mine.[12] Thus, the frame of mind in which decisions are taken (absence of bias), the way and manner in which they are taken (impartial procedure) and the result or consequences of decisions in relation to others have all a bearing on the justice of decisions.

What justice is can best be understood by considering the feelings aroused in us by injustice. Whereas justice is a cold virtue that evokes no feeling, injustice or unfairness arouses intense fury in us, as we get heated up and indignant about it. "Indignation, which is the conceptually appropriate response to injustice, expresses, as its etymology shows, a sense of not being regarded as worthy of consideration. Injustice betokens an absence of respect, and manifests a lack of concern."[13] For this reason, the occurrence of injustice, especially if it is on a wide scale, immediately puts the "unity and coherence of society under strain."[14]

Justice is thus rightly regarded as the "bond of society,"[15] the "cornerstone of human togetherness."[16] It is the condition in which the individual can feel able "to identify with society, feel at one with it, and accept its rulings."[17] An unjust society

---

11. C. A. Oputa, "Towards Justice with a Human Face" — Paper presented at the Law Week of the Nigerian Bar Association, 18-23 February, 1985.
12. Lucas, op. cit. p. 4.
13. Lucas, op. cit. p. 7.
14. Lucas, op. cit. p. 4.
15. Lucas, op. cit. p. 18.
16. Oputa, op. cit.
17. J. R. Lucas, op. cit. p. 1.

cannot maintain its unity and cohesion, because it cannot arouse in its members a strong enough feeling of loyalty and allegiance. Injustice not only alienates the individual's loyalty, what is worse, it also arouses him to disaffection. An individual or group denied recognition by society cannot but feel alienated and disaffected.

In a just society, Lucas has pertinently observed,

> it does not matter whether decisions are taken by me or by someone else — they will not conflict, because they are taken in the same frame of mind, whoever it is that takes them — and yet this absence of conflict is achieved not by some self-abnegation, some absorption in a higher whole, but by the acceptance on the part of each of the existence and legitimate interests of everybody else. If I am treating you justly, it will be all the same whether I am deciding what I should do to you, or you are deciding it, or somebody else is. It is not biased my way, so my decision will be the same as that of a third party; and above all, it is not biased *against* you, and so the decision of a third party will be no less favourable than what you would yourself decide, if you were deciding impartially and not unfairly in your own favour. And so you and I and all of us can live together in harmony and peace, each easily identifying with everyone else, because we all recognise the individuality of each, and respect his interests, and will cherish his interests as he would himself.[18]

Justice needs, however, to be reinforced by humaneness. The ideal of humaneness views government, not as a bundle of impersonal roles and processes, but rather as a human organisation motivated by a concern to ensure that the human person is to be handled with sympathy, understanding, compassion, kindness and affection. It abhors inhuman treatment of any kind. In particular, human life is to be respected as sacred and inviolate. Governmental actions should therefore be humane, which implies a benevolent, paternalistic government, a government that has for its citizens the sort of concern and sensitivity a father has for his children, a polity where, in recognition of the divinity of the human soul, the human person is accorded supreme worth and is regarded as the cardinal object by which governmental actions should be conditioned.

It follows that if an unjust society cannot maintain its cohesion and stability, much less can an inhumane one. "A

---

18. Lucas, op. cit. p. 19.

inhumane society cannot like an unjust society, escape self-destruction."[19]

A Just Society as a Principle of Democracy

A just society or social justice is the product of the emergence of modern republicanism as a concept of government. Republicanism conceives government as the exercise of power, not for its own sake or for the selfish aggrandisement of the rulers, but for the welfare of the people as a whole. In the 18th century, it became "a counter cultural ideology of protest, an intellectual means by which dissatisfied people could criticise the luxury, selfishness and corruption of monarchical culture."[20] It was a radical ideology, which in time revolutionalised the theory and practice of democracy through its insistence on justice, the public good or the welfare of the people (the two terms are often used interchangeably) as the object of government.

Popular government itself does not of course necessarily assure the public welfare. No doubt, the expectation, indeed the rationale for it, is that when the people govern, they do so for the benefit of all. Government by the people is expected to be government for the people because the people embody all of the community's wisdom, goodness, honesty, justice, its sense of right and wrong, in short all the civic virtues available in it, which should outweigh all its vices. Animated by a concern for their own good, i.e. their own safety, liberty, prosperity, well-being and happiness, which is the same as the public good or the welfare of the community, government by the people cannot but be government for the people. The people, it is said, "cannot have an interest opposed to their own advantage."[21] "Representation, as 'a substitute for a meeting of the citizens in

---

19. General Olusegun Obasanjo, former Nigerian Head of State in a 1977 Address to the Army at Jaji.
20. G. S. Wood, "The Intellectual Origins of the American Constitution" in National Forum, The Phi Kappa Phi Journal, Fall 1984, Vol. LXIV, No. 4 p. 4.
21. Alexis de Tocqueville, Democracy in America (1885), ed. Richard Heffner (1956) p. 101.

person',[22] is intended to replicate the people's concern with their own good",[23] as elected representatives are supposed to have "a communion of interests and sympathy of sentiments with the ruled".[24]

But the actual working of popular government has proved all this to be largely an idealistic picture, quite removed from reality. To begin with, "the 'self-government' spoken of is not the government of each by himself, but of each by all the rest."[25] An assemblage of the whole citizenry in a direct democracy would often be swayed by passion rather than by reason, and even when it is not, the governing interest would usually be not that of the whole people, but of the majority which may trample on the interest of the minority. In a representative democracy, the premise that representation replicates the people's concern for their own good, and that representatives have a communion of interests and sentiments with the people presupposes the capacity of the people to choose representatives animated by a spirit for the public good, which is often not the case. In reality, elected representatives are not, for the most part, persons so animated, their actions being motivated more by selfish or other private interests than by the public good. It is for these reasons that republican democracy views government for the people as an autonomous principle, an essential requirement, of democratic government existing independently, and not merely as an incident, of that of government by the people, and which must inform the conduct of government as a matter of duty.

Compatibility or Otherwise of Social Justice with Individual Liberty

Indisputably, individual liberty is inevitably restricted when the state intervenes in social and economic life in order to redress

---

22. James Madison, *The Federalist*, No. 25, ed. Clinton Rossiter (1961), p. 327.
23. David Epstein, *The Political Theory of the Federalist* (1984), p. 148.
24. James Madison, *The Federalist*, No. 57, op. cit., p. 352.
25. J. S. Mill, *Representative Government*, reprinted in *Unitarianism, Liberty and Representative Government* (1910) Everyman's Library, p. 72.

social imbalances and injustices, as by regulative legislation which fixes minimum wages or maximum working hours, prescribes compulsory methods of settling labour disputes or which controls prices and rents. There is thus a certain conflict between the demands of individual liberty and those of social justice, of which it is necessary to take due cognisance and account. But the question is whether these inevitable restrictions are really such as to make the pursuit of social justice by the state altogether incompatible or irreconcilable with individual liberty and the Rule of Law; in other words; whether the two are mutually exclusive objects which cannot co-exist or be pursued together. Will the pursuit of social justice in the full-blown form it has taken under the modern welfare state inevitably result in the complete relegation of individual liberty, will it lead to a state of affairs in which "the liberty of the individual gradually recedes into the background and the liberty of the social collective occupies the front of the stage."?[26]

In the view of a renowned modern advocate of liberalism following in the tradition of Adam Smith and John Stuart Mill, the relegation, indeed the complete destruction, of individual liberty is an inevitable consequence of the social justice objectives of the modern welfare state, from which it therefore follows that those objectives are incompatible and irreconcilable with a free society.[27] Re-distribution of income or "distributive justice," he asserts, "can never be achieved within the limits of the rule of law."[28] He rests this incompatibility on various grounds. First, measures designed to redistribute incomes, by their nature, necessarily involve the exercise of arbitrary powers, since they inevitably confer wide discretion upon the authorities. "The restrictions which the rule of law imposes upon government," he maintains, "preclude all those measures which would be necessary to insure that individuals be rewarded according to another's conception of merit or desert...

---

26. H. Kelsen, quoted in Hayek, *The Constitution of Liberty* (1960) p. 218.
27. Hayek, op. cit., pp. 259- 260; also *The Mirage of Social Justice* (1976) pp. 80-91.
28. *The Constitution of Liberty* (1960);, p. 259.

Distributive justice requires that people be told what to do and what ends to serve. Where distributive justice is the goal, the decisions as to what the different individuals must be made to do cannot be derived from general rules but must be made in the light of the particular aims and knowledge of the planning authority...[29] Thus the welfare state becomes a household state in which a paternalistic power controls most of the income of the community and allocates it to individuals in the forms and quantities which it thinks they need or deserve."[30]

Price control, for example, is said necessarily to involve *ad hoc* decisions that discriminate between persons on essentially arbitrary grounds. This is so because it "can be made effective only by quantitative controls, by decisions on the part of authority as to how much particular persons or firms are to be allowed to buy or sell. And the exercise of all controls of quantities must, of necessity, be discriminatory, determined not by rule but by the judgment of authority concerning the relative importance of particular ends... To grant such powers to authority means in effect to give it power to arbitrarily determine what is to be produced, by whom, and for whom."[31]

Rent control is equally characterised by the exercise of arbitrary power on the part of the authority. For, "whether 'an owner, with an invalid wife and three young children, who wishes to obtain occupation of his house (would) suffer more hardship if his request were refused than the tenant, with only one child, but a bed-ridden mother-in-law, would suffer if it were granted' is a problem that cannot be settled by appeal to any recognised principles of justice but only by the arbitrary intervention of authority."[32]

Progressive taxation, which is the chief instrument of income redistribution, is represented as "simply hateful arbitrariness," resting on no principle whatever, unlike proportional taxation. Furthermore it amounts to singling out a group, a minority group, (that is those in the highest income bracket), for

29. ibid p. 232.
30. pp. 260-261.
31. ibid, p. 228.
32. ibid, p. 344.

discriminatory and oppressive treatment by legislation enacted by an elected majority; it thus infringes "a principle much more fundamental than democracy itself."[33]

In the second place, state intervention in furtherance of social justice has resulted not only in the state arrogating to itself exclusive rights in fields in which it ought not legitimately to have a monopoly, as, for example, the nationalisation of education, health services and the running of certain social security schemes, but also in the use of coercion to force individuals to take certain actions either in their own interest or for the protection of others or the public at large. State monopoly in such matters as mentioned above deprives individuals of a choice in what obviously affects vital aspects of their lives, and what they get is thus made to depend entirely upon the evaluation of their needs or desert by some state official. As regards social security systems, it is said that, while some of their objectives are not incompatible with individual liberty, their pursuit by means of compulsory schemes run by unitary monopolistic state machinery and the consequent exclusion of private enterprise are. It deprives the community of the opportunity of experimenting on alternative methods from which better solutions might well emerge.

In the third place, by reducing rents to a fraction of what they would be in a free market, rent control is said to amount, in effect, to expropriation of house property, and generally undermines respect for private property.

Finally, the attempt by the welfare state to eradicate want, disease, ignorance, squalor and idleness (the "five giants," as they are called) has created the far greater problem of an ever increasing dominance of government in education, a social service bureaucracy with far-reaching arbitrary powers and of a paralysing taxation. The evil of a social service bureaucracy is accentuated by the fact that it does not lend itself to effective democratic control by the elected majority in the legislature. "It is inevitable that this sort of administration of the welfare of the people should become a self-willed and uncontrollable apparatus before which the individual is helpless."[34]

---

33. ibid, p. 314.

Thus, while renouncing the old liberal stand that the maintenance of law and order is the sole legitimate concern of government, this brand of liberalism maintains that state intervention in social and economic life in a free society should be limited to

(a)   the provision of a framework of general rules of law and of infrastructural services like roads, electricity, water, education, health care, telecommunications, a monetary system, weights and measure, statistics and other similar services designed to assist people to achieve prosperity through their own efforts provided they involve no coercion of the individual or involve it only incidentally (as with the compulsory acquisition of land needed for road construction or proportional taxation to raise money to provide such services);

(b)   the provision of other assistance and incentives to private enterprise, e.g. subsidies to agriculture, education and housing;

(c)   the relief of poverty, want and destitution among the disabled, elderly and young persons with no or inadequate means of support, the poor and other needy persons, and even the provision of an equal minimum income for all but not the guarantee to particular individuals of the standards of living to which they have been accustomed, which is objected to, because it is not based on proof of need as does the provision of a uniform minimum income for all.

In addition, state participation in economic activities is also conceded as not involving coercion or interference with individual liberty so long as it is on the same terms as economic activities carried on by private persons and does not entail state monopoly of any particular activity except where a state monopoly relates to services that can only be provided by collective action or which cannot, for economic reasons, be provided by competitive enterprise. In the main, therefore, these extensions in the functions of the state beyond the maintenance of law and order, to which the liberals are

---

34.   ibid at p. 262.

prepared to subscribe, merely conceive of the state as a purely service agency, but insofar as a service activity will involve coercion of the individual, their position that the state should not encroach upon the private domain of the individual remains substantially unchanged.

On the other hand, an ardent liberal and constitutionalist Professor Charles McIlwain, maintains that, far from being affronted by the welfare state, true liberalism must combine the guarantee of individual liberty with the security of the good of the whole people, the security of the common weal, the elimination or amelioration of wretchedness and misery among the people. A state, he says, is "not any chance aggregation of men but a multitude united in the common purpose of securing this common good, and that can mean nothing less than the individual good of all, not some, of its members."[35] "In a word," he asserts, "liberalism means a common welfare with a constitutional guarantee. I maintain that not one part, but both parts of this definition — in essence, Cicero's definition — must be translated into working fact if we mean to live in a true Commonwealth and hope to keep it in being. So-called liberals have ignored the first part of the definition and have fouled the nest by invoking the guarantee for privileges of their own, conducive only to the destruction of any true common weal," castigating them (i.e. the so-called liberals) as "reactionaries" and as 'traitors within the gates who have probably done more than all others to betray liberalism to its enemies and put it to its defence."[36] To him, the extreme doctrine of *laissez-faire*, with its "unhistorical definition of contract under which the sanction of the law could be obtained for almost any enormity to which men could be induced to agree," is "one of the strangest fantasies that ever discredited human reason,[37] "a caricature of liberalism."[38]

In the view of the present writer, the conflict between social justice and individual liberty is all a question of balance.

35.   C. H. McIlwain, *Constitutionalism and the Changing World* (1939), p. 285; see also Walter Lippman, *The Good Society* (1937).
36.   ibid, p. 286.
37.   Loc. cit.
38.   at p. 287.

Between the position of the brand of liberalism represented by Hayek and the extreme form of social justice based on the nationalisation of all means of production (socialism/ communism), there is quite ample room for the pursuit of the aims and goals of social justice within the overall framework of individual liberty and the Rule of Law. No doubt, individual liberty and the Rule of Law will suffer considerable incursions and inroads as a result but so long as they remain the general principles governing the social order, the conflict posed by the pursuit of social justice can be accommodated. It seems rather an extreme position to maintain, as does Hayek, that the conception of social justice would necessarily "lead straight to full-fledged socialism"[39] or to the total destruction of individual liberty or that it can be given meaning only at the cost of "a complete change of the whole character of the social order."[40] It cannot be disputed that individual liberty and the Rule of Law still form the framework of the social order of Britain today which, with all the extensive welfare services undertaken by the state, still remains a model of a free society.

The necessary balance seems to me to be appropriately expressed in the notion of the open society, that is to say, a society that does not enthrone either individual liberty or social and economic rights to the exclusion of the other, but is open to both. It does not, as under socialism/ communism, elevate social and economic rights into a supreme object in the pursuit of which individual liberty must be sacrificed or suppressed. It recognises man as both a human being and a social being, and that his needs for social services and amenities are entitled to be catered for by the state within the framework of a free society. While according priority to man's humanity, it also recognises that food, clothing, shelter, health care and other material conditions of a good, decent life are necessary for human existence, and indeed indispensable to make him better able to breathe, think, feel, speak, move about and act, and to realise and develop his human personality more fully. Still they are not a constituent element of man's humanity but only supplements.

---

39.   Hayek, *The Mirage of Social Justice* (1976), p. 64.
40.   ibid, p. 67.

It would of course be a contradiction if the provision of social and economic amenities by the state were to override man's humanity. In an open society, neither should override the other. They must be properly balanced, one with the other. It is the undue emphasis on social well-being at almost the total expense of individual liberty that proved part of the undoing of socialism of the communist type. A rigid, doctrinaire attachment to individual liberty is equally anthithetical to the open society. What is needed, in Sir Ralf Dahrendorf's words, is a "combination of democracy and planning, of economic freedom and demand management, of individual choice and redistribution, of liberty and justice."[41] The "social entitlements of citizenship" should be secured by the state at the same time as "the spirit of innovation and entrepreneurship" is being aroused.[42]

The appropriate balance between liberal democracy and social democracy clearly does not admit of too much state intervention in social and economic affairs which poses a real danger for both individual liberty, the Rule of Law and democracy, because it unduly increases the size, influence and importance of the state, imparting to the struggle for its control an undue importance, especially in developing countries. Politics or the struggle for the control of the state comes to loom too large in national life, to dominate it so utterly as to submerge everything else. It also gives to corruption, electoral perversion and abuse of power a greatly increased stimulus and incidence. There should therefore be only so much state intervention as is compatible with freedom and democracy.

We will now consider in some detail the elements and applications of social justice desirable and required for democracy and democratisation.

Elements and Applications of Social Justice

Social justice is predicated on the notion that organised society, as an association of people, creates in the members certain

41.   Ralf Dahrendorf, *Reflections on the Revolution in Europe* (1990) p. 50.
42.   Ralf Dahrendorf, op. cit. p. 71.

reasonable expectations or claims which it would be unfair to disappoint. It gives rise to certain claims which each member either in virtue purely of being such a member and irrespective of his conduct or choice, or in virtue of his desert, merit or need as such member can fairly make on the society as a whole, and which it would be unfair for society to deny or to fail to meet. It seems an unjustifiably narrow view of the concept to limit it, as Honore does, to just what each member is entitled to demand of society considered simply as such member and irrespective of his conduct.[43]

What, then, are the expectations or claims which it may be said a person reasonably has or should reasonably have against society?

1. Social Welfare Services and Amenities: The Welfare State

The primary claim is that arising from the purpose for which human society is formed, namely the duty of organised society, in return for the individual's obedience and fidelity, to protect his life and property and to cater for his general welfare and maintain at least the minimum standard of subsistence, in particular his need for health, food, water, shelter, clothing and other basic necessities for a decent and full life. "A just society," it is said, is that which provides "a certain minimum level of welfare for everyone," one which assures or at least has a concern for the good life of its members, and by good life is meant a happy and contented life.[44] It follows from the duty to protect or secure the good lives of members that "a society is unjust if, by its actions, laws, and mores, it unnecessarily improverishes the lives of its members materially, aesthetically or otherwise, by holding them to a level below that which some members at least might well attain by their own efforts."[45]

It has been suggested that the minimum should not be limited to the basic necessities of life but should extend to "all advantages which are commonly regarded as desirable and

---

43. Honore, op. cit. p. 95.
44. Frankena, op. cit. p. 17.
45. Frankena, op. cit. p. 14.

which are in fact conducive to human well-being," such as recreation, travel, opportunities for amusement, education and so on.[46]

The rationale for requiring that such amenities should be provided for all is "not because they are equal in any respect, but simply because they are human", with human emotions, desires and needs.[47] Every human being has a similar (not necessarily equal) desire for a good life and a capacity for enjoying it. A just society, then, is one which respects, protects, secures and promotes a minimum level of good life for its members on the basis of equality. (The general question of equal treatment of all citizens by the state, which is a principle both of social justice, liberty and of democracy, is examined in the next chapter).

Whether social justice covers within its meaning and application the notion of the welfare state to its fullest extent is, however, disputed. The welfare theorists insist that it does. Whilst conceding that social justice does require action by society in a welfare direction, Frankena maintains that it is not synonymous or co-terminous with beneficence which is what is implied in the notion of a welfare state. "It does not involve," he says, "direct action on the part of society to *promote* the good life of its members, whether this be conceived of as pleasure, happiness, self-realisation or some indefinable quality. Such direct action is beneficence, not justice," adding that the "question is what is required of society and the state if they are to be just, not what is required if they are to be good, ideal or to have virtues other than justice."[48] He concedes, nevertheless, that, "although we are speaking of a *just* society, and not of the *good* society, its concern with the goodness of the lives of its members need not be considered merely negative and protective. It seems reasonable to assign to the just society a more positive interest (though one which falls short of beneficence) by saying that it must, so far as possible, provide equally the conditions under which its members can by their

---

46.   Honore, op. cit.
47.   Frankena, op. cit. pp. 19-20.
48.   Frankena, op. cit. p. 6.

efforts (alone or in voluntary associations) achieve the best lives of which they are capable. This means that society must at least maintain some minimum standard of living, education and security for all its members."[49] It does not seem unreasonable to say with Honore and the welfarists that the notion of the welfare state is properly an application of the concept of social justice.[50]

The provision by the state of social welfare services for all involves re-distribution of wealth. It re-distributes wealth by taking money from the rich, by means of various forms of taxation, in order to provide such amenities. Intervention by the state for this purpose is justified because of the inadequacy of the principle of non-discrimination which presupposes and is built upon the preservation of the result of past malapportionment of the nation's wealth. As Honore observes, the non-discrimination principle, "though directed towards securing what is fair, is at the same time directed toward the maintenance of the *status quo* or its equivalent. In other words the non-discrimination principle seeks to retain for the various members of society the resources and assets which they already possess and to equalise opportunities and the distribution of advantages thereafter."[51]

To ensure social justice, it is not enough that existing inequalities in income should be redressed; the result of past malapportionment should also be attacked and redressed by re-distributive measures. "Each man as man has a prior claim to at least certain essential advantages, and this will involve a redistribution or equalisation of at least certain such advantages."[52] The claim for redistribution as a means of securing a measure of equalisation in the allocation of existing resources is, Honore asserts, "something which belongs to man as a member of society and is therefore part of the notion of social justice."[53] The discrimination involved is not an unfair one; it is, on the contrary, a much needed instrument in aid of social justice.

---

49.   Frankena, op. cit. p. 21.
50.   Honore, op. cit. p. 77; also Hayek, op. cit.
51.   Honore, op. cit. p. 98.
52.   Honore, loc. cit.
53.   Honore, op. cit. p. 100.

The provision of the conditions under which people can, by their own efforts (alone or in voluntary association), achieve the best lives of which they are capable clearly covers the provision by the state of assistance and incentives to private enterprise, which must therefore be considered an application of the concept of social justice. State assistance in the form of subsidies to particular economic activities, it has been suggested, "can only be explained by an appeal to social justice,"[54] not for any benefits they confer on the providers or the consumers of the subsidized services, but because of the general benefits which they are supposed to bring to the general public. But whether state assistance to private enterprise can also be rationalised as a form of redistribution is disputed.[55]

2. Social Security

Social security is concerned with the social protection of the individual against want, poverty, destitution, disease and idleness which may be thrust upon him by the varied hazards and vicissitudes of social life, notably loss or suspension of income or means of sustenance resulting from sickness, maternity, accident-injury, invalidity, old-age, death of breadwinner or unemployment. The concept is predicated upon a vision of a fairer arrangement of society in which the state assumes a general responsibility to ensure that the individual is secured by organised collective action against the risks of social and economic life. The individual's claim to social security can be rested in part on the principle of need, since "a person in need, for instance, a person who is unemployed or ill, is regarded as having a claim, derived from his need, to a contribution by his fellow men, to help relieve his lack of earnings and his ill-health respectively."[56] It is thus based on "solidarity (one of Africa's traditional fundamental values), which gives greater protection against certain social risks than

54.   Kenneth E. Boulding, "Social Justice in Social Dynamics" in R. B. Brandt (ed.) *Social Justice*, op. cit. p. 89.
55.   F. A. Hayek, *The Constitution of Liberty* (1960), p. 264.
56.   Honore, op. cit. p. 92.

individual effort to provide for the future. It works by pooling resources to provide benefits and services to the person protected when a prescribed contingency takes place."[57] It is a matter to be tackled by general policy and under a general national scheme. The least required of the state is to regulate by law the way social security is organised and administered, but its responsibility should extend beyond this to involvement in its administration and, in appropriate cases, its funding in whole or in part.

Social security should be differentiated from social welfare services (including public health services). The latter are amenities provided by the state, either free or at a fee, for the population at large as part of its social responsibility to cater for the well-being of its citizens but no individual can claim them as an entitlement or right legally due to him from the state. In a situation, such as exists in most parts of Africa, where "there is one doctor for every 43,500 inhabitants and one hospital bed for every 1,580 inhabitants,"[58] one cannot begin to talk of individual medical care under the public health system as a right. Social security, on the other hand, is founded on the notion of individual right whereby cash benefits or medical care can, in the cases covered by it, be claimed as an individual entitlement. But the fact that social welfare services cannot, for reasons of limited resources, be claimed as an entitlement suggests that the range of persons and contingencies that can be covered by social security is necessarily limited, at any rate in countries whose economy is insufficiently developed. Social security and social welfare services need, however, to be co-ordinated for them to be able to complement one another.

Modern social security seeks to fulfil at least six objectives. The foremost, and one with which it began, is income security, that is to say the maintenance of income by cash benefits in the event of its loss or suspension caused by any of the contingencies mentioned above, with the object of creating

---

57. Report of the Fifth African Regional Conference on "Improvement and Harmonisation of Social Security Systems in Africa," held in Abidjan, Sept-Oct 1977, ILO (Geneva 1977), p. 3.
58. ibid. p. 17.

among individuals and families "the confidence that their level of living and quality of life will not, in so far as possible, be greatly eroded by any social or economic eventuality."[59] The machinery of social security thus seeks, irrespective of social contingencies, to make it possible for "the entire population, or at least the great majority, to benefit progressively from the same guaranteed maintenance of their standards and ways of life," which for long had been the privilege of a small minority.[60] It seeks to ensure that those who are well-off do not become poor, that the poor do not become destitute and that generally want is alleviated. The objective covers everybody earning an income — employees as well as self-employed workers, although in Africa and other developing countries it has largely been restricted to the former. With the exception of family allowances and other social assistance schemes, all social security cash benefit schemes — sickness benefits, maternity benefits, compensation for employment injury, old-age, invalidity and survivors' pensions, and unemployment benefits — are directed toward income maintenance.

A guaranteed maintenance of the individual's standard of life must include a guaranteed access to medical care, this being a basic need for human existence. Social security seeks to satisfy this need by providing for "protected persons the right, in fact and not merely in theory,"[61] to free or inexpensive individual health care covering medical attention by a doctor, essential pharmaceutical supplies, hospitalisation and, additionally, in case of employment injury, attention by a dentist, medical, surgical or dental supplies (other than pharmaceutical supplies), including prosthetic appliances and eyeglasses.[62]

It performs this role by means largely of social insurance. By pooling the risks and resources of persons covered, it is able to generate funds to provide these services for them. It meets the

59.   *Into the Twenty-First Century: The Development of Social Security,* published by the ILO, Geneva (1986), p. 19.
60.   ibid p. ix.
61.   Report of the Fifth African Regional Conference on "Improvement and Harmonisation of Social Security Systems in Africa", op. cit. p. 16.
62.   Social Security (Minimum Standards) Convention 1952 (No. 102), Part II; Employment Injury Benefits Convention 1964 (No. 121), art. 10.

cost either by paying it direct to the source of medical care (which may be publicly or privately owned) or by reimbursing the insured person, but in some cases the services are provided directly in medical centres or clinics run by social security institutions. Thus, by means of social insurance supplemented by social assistance, social security is able to secure guaranteed medical care to most people in the industrialised countries.

Outside the industrialised countries, however, the objective is hardly being achieved, as only few people benefit from it. In many places the little that is achieved is through the employer's liability system whereby employers are required by law to provide medical care for their workers, particularly in cases of maternity and employment injury, thus making medical care a right or an entitlement for the workers covered. In a few other countries social security medical care has been introduced as a complement, extension and adjustment of the employer's liability system. This takes the form of inter-enterprises medical services organised and run by a social security body, and financed by contributions made to it by the employers.[63]

Income maintenance and guarantee of access to medical care are the two functions traditionally performed by social security. But it has other roles, which are more in the nature of aspirations, at any rate for many countries. One such objective is the relief of poverty, want and destitution among the disabled, elderly and young persons with no or inadequate means of support, the poor and other needy persons. It seeks to achieve the objective by means of family allowances and means-tested cash benefits as well as by benefits in kind in the form of medical care, the provision of food, clothing, housing, holiday or domestic help.[64] It has been suggested that "building an effective minimum income for all residents should be accepted as the major challenge of social security policy to be achieved before the year 2000."[65] Ambitious as it is, some

63. Report, op. cit. p. 20.
64. Social Security (Minimum Standards) Convention 1952 (No. 102) Part vii.
65. *Into the Twenty-First Century: The Development of Social Security*, op. cit. p. 29.

affluent industrialised countries have already embarked upon or are seriously contemplating such a scheme. For it is considered socially unjust and an affront to the collective conscience of society that in an affluent country with abundant resources, there should be poverty and destitution among large sections of it. In a country where a reasonable, effective minimum income is, by law, guaranteed to all residents as a matter of right or entitlement, then, destitution would have been eliminated, poverty largely relieved and want greatly alleviated. That should be the ultimate objective and challenge of social security.

In Africa, Asia and other developing areas of the world, the extent to which social security is able to fulfil the objective of relieving poverty, want and destitution is necessarily limited by various constraints, chief among them being finance. In the circumstances of Africa today where an estimated "239 million people or 69 per cent of the population... were very poor and 134 million of them, or 39 per cent, were destitute,"[66] where the vast majority of the people live in the rural area, mostly as self-employed workers (farmers, artisans etc), where the welfare of the rural population and rural development generally are given low rating by government, and where financial and administrative resources are very thin, relieving poverty by means of social security is indeed a far cry, almost an impossible dream. But it should nonetheless remain part of its challenge.

Income re-distribution with a view to reducing inequality and inequity is another objective of social security. The relief of poverty and destitution by means of family allowances, means-tested cash benefits and a guaranteed minimum income for all residents clearly involves a measure of re-distribution of income between the different income groups in the society, since such schemes are generally financed from the general revenue of the state. Within the category of persons covered by a social insurance scheme, re-distribution of income does take place between the healthy and the sick, the active and inactive persons (the elderly or invalid workers), persons with a job and

66. Report, op. cit. p. 24.

those who are unemployed, and to some extent between persons earning a high or moderate wage and lower-paid workers. Also in an insurance scheme involving various enterprises for protection against employment injury and disease, there is again some redistribution of income between the enterprises concerned.

The increasing transformation of social security system from an apparatus originally meant to relieve poverty into an instrument for income re-distribution, a mechanism of the welfare state aimed at bringing about "a 'just distribution' by handing out income in such proportions and forms as it sees fit,"[67] has made it the central object of liberal attack on grounds earlier noted. "Freedom," it is asserted, "is critically threatened" by the obliteration of "the line that separates a state of affairs in which the community accepts the duty of preventing destitution and of providing a minimum level of welfare from that in which it assumes the power to determine the 'just' position of everybody and allocates to each what it thinks he deserves."[68]

Social security contributes to national solidarity in two ways, depending on the method of financing. An individual secured by the state against the risks of life, as by a guaranteed minimum income even during a period of unemployment, would naturally feel that society cares for him and his interests, and may thus be able to identify with it, and to feel a sense of belonging with other members. Where protection is provided, not through direct state funding, but by workers or residents pooling their resources together to cover one another and put out cash benefit as and when any one of them is affected by a covered risk, then again a sense of inter-dependence, of community and of solidarity would thereby have been generated among them. In Africa, as the traditional security and solidarity provided by the kinship system loses its hold due to modernisation, the spread of cash incomes, changes in values, etc, modern social security is needed to fill the gap.[69]

---

67.   Hayek, *The Constitution of Liberty* (1960), p. 289.
68.   Hayek, op. cit., p. 289; also pp. 302-303.
69.   See Report, op. cit. p. 4.

Finally, the payment of cash benefits after the risks have occurred cannot provide full security. Social security also seeks to prevent the risks from arising in the first place, since in the final analysis the prevention or reduction of risks is a better way of providing security. "Preventing accidents and ill-health," it has been rightly said, "is to be preferred to the provision of curative and social services and cash benefits... Protection against unemployment by employment maintenance and promotion, by job creation and job subsidy, by retraining those with redundant skills, by assisting the mobility of the workforce and by resettling the unemployed, is to be preferred to the replacement of lost income. Prevention needs therefore to permeate virtually all departments of government, the actions of employers and employees, the activities of voluntary bodies and most important of all, the actions of individuals and families."[70]

However imperfectly or inadequately the objectives of social security are being achieved, the need for it has certainly gained near universal acceptance. Thus, the Universal Declaration of Human Rights (1948) proclaims that "every one, as a member of society, has the right to social security," to "protection against unemployment," and to "a standard of living adequate for the health and well-being of himself and his family, including food, clothing, housing and medical care and necessary social services and the right to security in the event of unemployment, sickness, disability, widowhood, old age or other lack of livelihood in circumstances beyond his control."[71] These declarations were given legal force in the International Covenant on Economic, Social and Cultural Rights (1976) by which the ratifying Member States of the United Nations assume a legal obligation to recognise "the right of everyone to social security, including social insurance."[72]

Likewise, the ratifying member states of the International Labour Organisation (ILO) have, in several international

---

70. *Into the Twenty-first Century: The Development of Social Security*, op. cit. pp. 21 & 55.
71. Arts 22, 23, and 25.
72. Art. 9.

conventions, entered into a legal obligation to implement within their territories, various schemes of social security which conform to the standards prescribed in those instruments. As at 1989, there were 26 ILO Conventions on the subject.

At the regional level, a number of social security instruments have also been adopted, notably the European Social Charter (1961) and the European Code of Social Security (1964) which have been subscribed to by the sixteen member states of the European Economic Community. In the African continent a special resolution of the Working Committee of the Organisation of African Unity (OAU) was adopted in 1976 calling for collaboration with the ILO on social security.

At the level of individual states, 141 countries have social security schemes in one form or another. It is a mark of the importance attached to social security that expenditure on it now amounts to nearly 30 per cent of GDP in many of the industrialised countries.[73] Some countries, indeed, have a whole ministry of social security as well as degree courses in it.

We need to say something, however briefly, about the method of financing for the light it sheds on what social security is. Social security is financed from three main sources, viz, contributions by workers and employers based on wages or earnings, and state financing. Usually, financing is by a combination of all three methods, a combination of workers' and employers' contributions or a combination of employers' and state financing; sometimes it is financed by the employer alone (e.g., the employer's liability scheme) or by the state alone (e.g., family allowances).

Financing by each of these methods is rationalised on different grounds. Workers' contributions is said to ground entitlement to benefits as a right and to participation in the management of a protection scheme; it forces upon workers an awareness about the uncertainty of the future and their responsibility to provide for it by compulsory saving. The employer's contribution is rationalised by reference to his part in the chain of causation of some of the risks against which

---

73. See Chantal Euzeby, "A minimum guaranteed income: Experiments and proposals," International Labour Review (1987), Vol. 126, No. 3, p. 253.

protection is needed, particularly occupational or disease, unemployment, illness or invalidity associated with exertions at work and their wear and tear on the human system, as well as his responsibility for the maintenance of the human resources that sustain his enterprise and its profitability. There is also the gain from good labour relations with the resultant improvement in the quality of work and the stability of labour.

The state's contribution is predicated on its social responsibility to ensure that the individual, in particular the needy — the aged, the invalid, the blind or mothers with dependent children — and the economically weak class, is protected against the risks of life. Moreover, its actions and policies or lack of them are often a major contributory factor in the causation of some of the risks, e.g. unemployment and sickness. Also the financial intervention of the state is viewed as "a practical necessity where funds were insufficient or where low contributive capacity of certain categories of workers had to be remedied."[74]

Tripartite financing, while it is, and remains, the usual method of financing, raises the difficult question concerning the share of the cost to be borne by each of the three social partners. The guiding principle embodied in ILO Income Security Recommendation, No. 67 of 1944 stipulates that "the cost of benefits, including the cost of administration, should be distributed among insured persons, employers and taxpayers, in such a way as to be equitable to insured persons and to avoid hardship to insured persons of small means or any disturbance to production."[75] This broad principle is then spelt out into specific stipulations which require that employers should be made to bear the entire cost of compensation for employment injury, that they should contribute not less than half the total cost of the other benefits and that the community should bear the cost of benefits which cannot be met by contributions, i.e., for example, the contribution deficits resulting from bringing persons into insurance when already

---

74. Financing Social Security: The Options —. An international analysis ILO Geneva (1984), p. 5.
75. para. 26.

elderly, the contingent liability involved in guaranteeing the payment of basic invalidity, old-age and survivors' benefits and the payment of adequate maternity benefit, the liability resulting from the extended payment of unemployment benefit when unemployment persists at a high level and subsidies to the insurance of self-employed persons of small means.[76]

The Social Security (Minimum Standards) Convention 1952 (No. 102) re-affirms the guiding principle in its article 71(1) which provides that the cost of benefits, including the cost of administration "shall be borne collectively by way of insurance contributions or taxation or both in a manner which avoids hardship to persons of small means and takes into account the economic situations of the Member and of the classes of persons protected," but without going into specifics except only to say that the total contribution borne by workers must not exceed 50 per cent of the total of the financial resources allocated to the protection of employees and their wives and children.[77] But most important of all it puts on the state the "general responsibility for the due provision of benefit," as well as responsibility to "take all measures required for this purpose."[78]

The specifications in ILO Income Security Recommendation (No. 67) have been considerably modified in the practice of different national systems. A 1984 ILO study reveals, for example, that in many countries the system imposing exclusive liability on the employer for occupational injury or disease is being replaced by joint financing from employers' and workers' contributions while in other cases workers' contribution is being reduced or altogether abolished. On the whole, payroll contributions (mainly employers') remain "globally the predominant source of social security financing."[79] At the same time, quite apart from the traditional forms of state participation "there has been a significant development of the public financing of either the entire expenditure of one or

---

76. ibid.
77. art. 71(2).
78. art. 71(3).
79. Financing Social Security: The Options — An international analysis, ILO General (1984), p. 16.

several branches or of a specific class of benefits, in particular basic pensions ... or benefits granted to certain categories of persons ... or benefits granted subject to a means test."[80] Furthermore, instead of self-employed persons paying the combined employer's and worker's contributions as is envisaged by the Income Security Recommendation (No. 67),[81] their contribution is at a much reduced rate in many countries, with the state making up the difference.

3. Social Protection of Workers Against Exploitation by Employers

Social justice for workers should be a cardinal objective of the regulation of the economy by government. Aside from the relation of a slave to his owner, there is probably in the modern world no other social or economic relationship that is fraught with so much actual or potential injustice than that between the workers and his employer. It is the modern equivalent of the relation of a serf to his lord under the feudal system of the medieval world, shorn of the latter's more subordinating and primitive incidents.

The power relation is best expressed by the term master and servant. It is a relationship which, by virtue of the enormous power which it gives to the employer over the worker, makes the latter so easily amenable to exploitation and manipulation by the former. And employers do in fact, exploit their workers to a very great extent.

Given that workers constitute a significant proportion of the population in every country, a situation in which they are left to be exploited by the employing minority is dangerous to industrial peace and consequently to the well-being and economic development of the entire community. The situation is thus one that places upon government an inescapable duty to take measures to remove or check the injustice inherent in such exploitation, and thereby promote lasting peace, economic progress and prosperity for the wider community.

---

80. ibid. p. 18.
81. see paras 21 and 26.

Social protection for workers should be a concern not only for the government of each individual country but also for the world at large. For since workers' revolt or revolution in one country may have explosive repercussion in other countries, the injustice occasioned by the exploitation of workers is a threat to the peace of the world, which therefore makes it a matter of global concern. The international community has concretised its concern by the establishment in 1919 of the International Labour Organisation (ILO) whose Constitution proclaims the provision of social justice for workers to be the central objective of its existence. In the affirmative words of the ILO Constitution:

> Whereas universal and lasting peace can be established only if it is based upon social justice;

> "And whereas conditions of labour exist involving such injustice, hardship and privation to large numbers of people as to produce unrest so great that the peace and harmony of the world are imperilled; and an improvement of those conditions is urgently required; as, for example, by the regulation of the hours of work, including the establishment of a maximum working day and week, the regulation of the labour supply, the prevention of unemployment, the provision of an adequate living wage, the protection of the worker against sickness, disease and injury arising out of his employment, the protection of children, young persons and women, provision for old age and injury, protection of the interests of workers when employed in countries other than their own, recognition of the principle of equal remuneration for work of equal value, recognition of the principle of freedom of association, the organisation of vocational and technical education and other measures;

> "Whereas also the failure of any nation to adopt humane conditions of labour is an obstacle in the way of other nations which desire to improve the conditions in their own countries;

> "The High Contracting Parties, moved by sentiments of justice and humanity as well as by the desire to secure the permanent peace of the world, and with a view to attaining the objectives set forth in this Preamble, agree to the following Constitution of the International Labour Organisation:"

In the historic Declaration of Philadelphia on 10 May, 1944, the General Conference of the ILO, convinced of the truth of the statement, as fully demonstrated by experience, that lasting peace can be established only if it is based on social justice, proclaimed that the attainment of conditions in which social justice shall be possible must constitute the central aim of national and international policy," and that "all national and international policies and measures, in particular those of an economic and financial character, should be judged in the light and accepted only in so far as they may be held to promote and not to hinder the achievement of this fundamental objective."

It is a measure of the unique importance attached to social justice for workers that workers are not only admitted into the membership of an organisation of sovereign states but are also (together with employers) given equal representation with the governments on ILO's two primary organs, the General Conference and the Governing Body. Furthermore, the president of the General Conference, which is the legislative organ of the Organisation empowered to adopt Conventions, may be elected from members representing any one of the three groups. The requirement of two-thirds majority of the votes cast for the adoption of a Convention ensures that a Convention cannot be adopted with the votes of government members alone. Also the three vice-presidents of the General Conference are elected from each of the three groups. The ILO is thus an organisation "in which the representatives of workers and employers, enjoying equal status with those of governments, join with them in free discussion and democratic decision with a view to the promotion of the common welfare."[82] The intention is to ensure that Conventions adopted by the ILO shall take into account the views and interests of governments, employers and workers.

The ILO had, as at March 1988, 150 states as members, and has, over the years since 1919, adopted some 167 conventions (only 157 have actually entered into force), all aimed at securing social justice for workers in one form or another. They cover practically the entire field of labour relations and employment — right of workers to organise, collective bargaining, forced labour, equality of opportunity and treatment in employment and occupation, labour inspection consultation, wages, particularly minimum wages, general conditions of employment, including hours of work, occupational safety and health, protection of women, children and young persons, etc. While the eradication of exploitation is the principal concern of the ILO Conventions, the demands of

---

82.   Declaration of the 26th Session of the General Conference of the ILO held in Philadelphia on 10 May, 1944.

social justice for workers go beyond that, and have inspired quite a number of Conventions, such as those on social security, unemployment and employment policies, which are not strictly predicated on the eradication of exploitation.

A state member ratifying a Convention thereby assumes an obligation to give effect to it within its territory by means of appropriate legislation and by taking appropriate enforcement measures to ensure that employers (including the government as employer) in fact comply with the stipulations and requirements of the implementing legislation; to report to the International Labour Office yearly, two-yearly or four-yearly, as may, according to the circumstances, be requested, the actions taken to give effect to the Convention, with copies of the implementing legislation and detailed information on its operation; and to furnish copies of its report to the representative organisations of employers and workers in the country. Even without ratification, the member is still under an obligation to report to the International Labour Office, at appropriate intervals as may be requested, "the position of its law and practice in regard to the matter dealt with in the Convention, showing the extent to which effect has been given, or is proposed to be given, to any of the provisions of the Convention by legislation, administrative action, collective agreement or otherwise and stating the difficulties which prevent or delay the ratification of such Convention."[83]

Africa has the lowest number of ratifications, the average for the continent being about 28 for each country. It must be admitted that the burden in policing the operation of implementing legislation in accordance with ILO requirements and the organisation's complex and demanding reporting procedures is quite an onerous one, and may well be beyond what a developing African country can afford within its limited resources of manpower, money and organisational capacity. Then there is the critical question which has been raised by many African countries as to whether the standards embodied in some of the ILO Conventions have universal validity and application considering the great diversity of social, economic,

---

83. Art 19(5) (e), ILO Constitution.

and ideological conditions and objectives of different countries, and in particular whether they are really suited or appropriate to the conditions and development objectives of African countries. African countries are also vexed by what they consider the somewhat legalistic approach of the ILO supervisory bodies, which seems not often to take fully into account national necessity. "The important thing," they maintain, "is to respect the spirit of Conventions and their objectives of social protection, rather than to adhere strictly to the letter of the text."[84]

While ratification is important, in that it more or less guarantees implementation even if it be only to a partial extent, it is not an end in itself. The end intended to be attained by ratification which is to have international labour standards given the force of law in each country and effectively enforced as such, can also be attained without ratification if the government is sufficiently motivated by its membership of the ILO to take steps to make its labour laws and practice reflect the standards embodied in the Conventions without incurring the onerous obligations implied by ratification and without the somewhat harassing pressure by ILO to secure effective implementation.

4. Social Protection Generally

In a free enterprise system, social control is necessary for a balanced economic growth, the prevention of undue concentration of wealth in a few hands, the minimisation of exploitation inherent in the system, the protection of the economically weak classes and of the general public. There is also the need to check inflation and the selfish desire for private gain at the expense of the nation.

"Economic development", it has been rightly said, "is not just a process of growth; it involves the radical reorganisation of society itself"[85] to ensure a satisfactory and acceptable balance

---

84. Report of the Sixth African Regional Conference, Tunis, October 1983, p. 11.
85. Kenneth E. Boulding, "Social Justice in Social Dynamics," in R.B. Brandt (ed.), *Social Justice* (1962), p. 91.

between the classes. In other words, it must be a balanced development. Economic development that benefits only a minority of the people is an affront to social justice. "The poor will inevitably become discontented as they observe the increasing riches of the rich. If this discontent can express itself in personal terms and the process of development is such that the poor can better their condition through individual effort, political upheaval may be avoided," otherwise the discontent may eventually lead to the poor overthrowing the rich.[86]

Given the nature of contract as the basis of all economic activity in our modern society, and the inherent inequality in the bargaining power of the parties to modern economic transactions, as, for example, between the consumer and the supplier of goods or services, the tenant and his landlord, the worker and his employer, the investor and the promoters and directors of a company, the terms of a contract should not be left to be determined by the contracting parties in every respect, but should rather be regulated by the state with the object of minimising exploitation of the weaker party by the other. The doctrine of freedom to contract on any terms mutually agreed between the parties was based, not on the modern industrial society, but on that dominated by buying and selling of basic and simple commodities.[87] The objective of minimising exploitation demands intervention by the state by appropriate measures, such as the control of prices, quality and standards, especially prices, quality and standards of basic necessities of life; control of transport fares and of incomes, both earned and unearned income, in particular fees charged by professionals like lawyers, architects, estate surveyors, locum medical doctors, engineers, quantity surveyors, accountants, auditors, etc., with a view to reducing inequalities in inter-personal incomes; control of rent, etc.

As with contracts, the corporate form of organisation and shares in it have attained universal applicability in modern business activity involving a certain number of persons or a large capital, thus creating a necessity for social control to

---

86. Boulding, op. cit. p. 92.
87. P. S. Atiyah, *An Introduction to the Law of Contract*, 2nd ed. (1971) p. 3.

check its use for the exploitation of, and fraud on, the investing public. Control is usually instituted in the form of legal requirements relating to capital structure and its maintenance, management structure, filing of annual accounts, the keeping of proper books of accounts, audit of accounts, disclosures of information, inspection, winding-up, control of share prices, even spread of ownership of shares, surveillance of the securities market to ensure orderly, fair and equitable dealings, etc.

Together with contract and the corporate form of business organisation, money and credit plays an indispensable role in economic activity, which again makes control necessary to ensure equitable disbursement among the different sectors of economic activity and its proper channelling into more productive activities with a view to increasing national output, income and employment, controlling inflation and maintaining price stability, all of which have a vital bearing on social justice.

Land is another indispensable factor of production requiring to be controlled by appropriate measures to ensure equitable distribution and avoid its concentration among a few persons through land speculation and racketeering and prohibitive land prices. In the urban areas particularly where land is scarce relatively to demand, the need to give everyone nearly equal opportunity to acquire it demands that the amount of land that anyone person can acquire should be limited or controlled. It is a negation of justice and equity that any one person should own so much land when others with comparable means have none and are unreasonably prevented from acquiring it.

Taxation is a potent instrument of social control in aid of social justice. There are at least two ways in which it is used to serve that purpose:-

(i)   To discourage actions or activities considered injurious to the well-being of those engaging in them or of others (as in the case of cigarette smoking or alcoholic consumption) or harmful to the welfare of society as a whole as with the importation of certain foreign goods. By taxing such actions or activities instead of prohibiting them outright, individual freedom of choice is respected; the individual is left to choose between not engaging in such actions or activities and suffering the burden of paying the tax as a price for engaging in them.

(ii)   To re-distribute income from certain classes to certain other classes by way of family allowances, for example, or for the benefit of society as a whole in the form of social welfare services and amenities. Such re-distributive taxation may take the form of a tax on the sale of commodities considered to be luxuries or non-necessary goods or of a tax on unearned wealth (e.g. death duty, capital gains tax, capital transfer tax) but its most general form is progressive tax on earned income.

The justice of progressive taxation is, however, disputed. It is contended, on the one hand, that the rich are better able than the poor to afford the money to pay, to absorb the pain of parting with it, and to make the sacrifice called for; secondly, that the diminishing marginal utility of money means that ₦1 paid out as tax is worth less to the rich than the poor, and to "exact contributions that were equal in monetary terms would be to impose sacrifices that were unequal as experienced by those called upon to make them;"[88] thirdly, that "the rich stand to benefit more by the preservation of civil society than the poor"[89] by reason of the protection it bestows on property rights, privileges deriving from social status, etc.

On the other hand, progressive taxation is said to be unjust, because it is a flagrant violation of the cardinal principle of justice, namely equality of treatment, which can be maintained only by exacting from individuals the same proportion or percentage of their income or of their property. The rationale of decreasing marginal utility has no validity because utility, being a purely relative concept, it is meaningless to speak of the degree of utility of a thing by itself; "we can only say that a thing has greater, equal or less utility compared with another."[90] In this view, therefore, the basis of progressive taxation is not justice but envy; it is "a mild form of robbery."[91]

---

88.   Lucas, *On Justice* (1980) p. 245.
89.   Lucas, op. cit. p. 245.
90.   Hayek, *The Constitution of Liberty* 1960), p. 309.
91.   J. S. Mill, *Principles of Political Economy* (1848), p. 353.

However this may be, it seems to be agreed on all sides that taxation should not be excessive. Desirable as it may well be, the re-distribution of income by progressive taxation does not require that private wealth should be taxed out of existence which, being a form of confiscation, is unjust. An unjust tax excites resentment. "First avoidance, then evasion, will become respectable and widespread."[92] And widespread avoidance and evasion will in turn give rise to a "collapse of confidence in the tax system, with taxes being regarded as the arbitrary imposition of rapacious tax-gatherers, which everyone should do his utmost to fend off, ending with a general collusion on the part of the public to defeat the requisition of the public fisc."[93] The justice of taxation presupposes that everyone contributes their due share, and that one is not called upon to make a sacrifice for the public good when some people successfully evade it.[94] To be just, the burden of contributions for the common good must not bear on some and not on others; it must bear on all according to their wealth or, more precisely, their ability to pay.

5. Equality of Opportunities

Equality of opportunity for all citizens is considered the very "essence of social justice," since, to quote Honore again, "we mostly believe, not that all advantages should be equally distributed to all men, but rather that, provided that all men have equal opportunities, distribution should be made according to desert. Thus, we do not generally think that social justice requires that the income of all should be equal."[95]

By equality of opportunities is meant equal starting conditions which can be assured by ensuring that all have equal opportunities for education, for medical attention, for work and for earning a living; it should also include, on a wider view of the concept, equality of opportunities for the pursuit of happiness and the enjoyment of life. Equality of opportunity for

92. Lucas, op. cit. p. 233.
93. Lucas, loc. cit.
94. Lucas, op. cit. pp. 236-237.
95. Honore, op. cit. p. 101.

education, medical attention, work and for earning a living requires that there should be equal access to the means (e.g. instructions in educational institutions, books and medical attention) of acquiring "that bodily and mental equipment," like knowledge, skill, health, etc, which, "so far as the citizen is capable of acquiring it, will enable him to compete fairly with his fellow-men" in the various activities and affairs of life, while equality of opportunities for the pursuit of happiness and the enjoyment of life requires equal access to places of amusement, parks, concert and playing grounds, television facilities, etc needed for enjoyment in the form of literature, art, music, sport and "all those advantages which are not directly relevant to an increase in the quality or quantity of one's work."[96]

Equality of access to the necessary facilities and means gives meaning and reality to equality of opportunities by putting the citizen on an equal footing with his fellow-men to profit from them, so far as he is capable of doing so. As has been pertinently observed, "it is senseless to speak of a claim to enjoy something which the citizen is incapable of enjoying or to work which he is incapable of doing. In this sense the formula of equality of opportunities serves to mark the point that no amount of social justice will do more than extend and develop the capacities of citizens to their limit, whatever those limits may turn out to be."[97] But it is said that equal access to the necessary means and facilities would be still far from creating real equality of opportunity unless all have also equal chances in the competitions of life, and that this cannot be assured unless government assumed power to "control the whole physical and human environment of all persons."[98]

Equality of opportunities for education is perhaps the most important and fundamental of all, because education is "required for the performance of our most basic public responsibilities... It is the foundation of good citizenship. Today, it is the principal instrument in awakening the child to cultural values, in preparing him for later professional training and in

---

96. Honore, op. cit. p. 102.
97. Honore, op. cit. p. 102.
98. Hayek, *The Mirage of Social Justice* (1976) pp. 84-85.

helping him to adjust normally to his environment. In these days, it is doubtful that any child may reasonably be expected to succeed in life if he is denied the opportunity for an education."[99] For education is the qualification for gainful employment, whether paid or self employment, and for nearly all economic activities.

The crucial question, however is when access to educational opportunities can be said to be equal between the rich and the poor or between members of advantaged and disadvantaged racial or ethnic groups. Opportunity for education cannot be said to be equal between the rich and the poor unless both have equal access to it, and equal access can be assured only if education is free, for there are among the poor many who cannot afford to pay school fees, even at a subsidized rate, and whose children will consequently be denied the benefit of education. Free education is thus the only guarantee for equality of education opportunities; without it equal opportunity for education is not assured for the poor. This places a heavy responsibility on the state, since it alone can finance free education; hence the indispensability of free education in assuring equal educational opportunity makes education perhaps the most important responsibility of the government in a democratic polity committed to social justice. But it is not enough that education is provided free for all, since there may be some people who, for some reasons, religious, cultural or other, may not want to avail their children of the opportunity, thereby depriving them of the opportunity to be able to compete on an equal footing with the educated ones in the various struggles of social life. In addition to being provided free, therefore, education should be made compulsory up to a certain level, and the law strictly and regularly enforced upon parents and guardians. Coercion of the individual for this purpose is justified because of the immense benefits education has for society as a whole and for democracy in particular.

The financing of free education by the state need not, and should not, however, imply that the state alone should control

---

99.   Per Chief Justice Earl Warren in *Brown v. Board of Education of Topeka*, 347 U.S. 483 (1954).

the content and management of all education to the exclusion
of private enterprise. Certainly, the state can finance free
education without at the same time taking over all educational
institutions.[100] A slightly different question has arisen in a
Nigerian case whether free education provided by the state
renders incompatible the existence of schools operated by
private individuals and organisations at a fee. In abolishing
private fee-paying schools in its area, the government of one of
the states in the country had claimed that the abolition was
required by the duty explicitly cast on it by the Constitution to
provide, so far as practicable, free education and equal
educational opportunities; it was contended that educational
opportunities could not be equal where public schools provided
free of charge by the state operated side by side with fee-paying
private schools.[101] For, with money collected as fees, the
private schools might be better able to provide better or higher
standards of education in return for such fees, and difference
in standards of education provided by them and by the public
schools meant that educational opportunities are not equal
between those who could afford to go to them and those who
could not. In rejecting this argument, the court observed that
the existence of private fee-paying schools with higher
standards along side the public schools should spur the
government to try and bring the standards in its own schools to
the level existing in the private schools. The decision is in
accord with article 13(4) of the International Covenant on
Economic, Social and Cultural Rights to the effect that the
obligation of the state to provide free education shall not be
"construed so as to interfere with the liberty of individuals and
bodies to establish and direct educational institutions." It can
also be supported on the grounds previously noted, that, while
the state may engage in economic activities in competition with
private enterprise, state monopolies are in general inimical to
individual liberty; in the field of education in particular,
diversity of education is of great importance in maintaining

---

100. See Hayek, *The Constitution of Liberty* (1960), p. 381.
101. *Archbishop Okogie & Others v. The Att-Gen of Lagos State* 1981 NCLR 218
     (High Court); 1981 2 NCLR 337 (Court of Appeal).

individuality and variety in character, opinions and modes of conduct among the people. "A general State education is a mere contrivance for moulding people to be exactly like one another; and as the mould in which it casts them is that which pleases the predominant power in government ... it establishes a despotism over the mind, leading by natural tendency to one over the body."[102] The central control and direction of all education is therefore much too dangerous to liberty to be permitted in a free society.

As concerns equality of educational opportunities between members of advantaged and disadvantaged racial or ethnic groups, it has been held that "segregation of children in public schools solely on the basis of race, even though the physical facilities and other 'tangible' factors may be equal, deprives the children of the minority group of equal educational opportunities," because the sense of inferiority generated by such segregation "affects the motivation of a child to learn," and may therefore retard his educational and mental development.[103]

While acknowledging the school segregation decision to be principled, because based on an analysis of the nature of the educational process from which a reasoned conclusion was drawn that separate educational facilities for whites and blacks are inherently unequal, Herbert Wechsler thinks that its extension to segregation in other public facilities, such as public transport, parks, golf courses, bath houses and beaches seems to have rested purely on expediency, not principle, because of the absence of a similar analysis showing that the principle of the school segregation is also applicable in those other cases. Constitutional decisions, he insists, should be "genuinely principled,"[104] in the sense that they must rest upon "reason with respect to all the issues in the case, reasons that in their generality and their neutrality transcend any immediate result that is involved," meaning that a

---

102. J. S. Mill, *On Liberty*, reprinted in *Unitarianism, Liberty and Representative Government* (1910), Everyman's Library No. 482, p. 175.

103. *Brown v. Board of Education of Topeka* ibid.

104. Herbert Wechsler, "Towards Neutral Principles in Constitutional Law," in *Selected Essays in Constitutional Law*, ed. Assn. of American Law Schools (1963), p. 475; reprinted from Harv. L. Rev., 73 (1959), p. 1.

constitutional decision should not be based on expediency but upon reason commanding a generality and neutrality of application. If, because of the nature of the educational process, separate educational facilities are inherently unequal, it does not, he maintains, follow that separate public transportation, parks, golf courses, bath houses, etc are also inherently unequal. It seems that Wechsler's rule of principle is much too rigid and neutral to be a realistic yardstick of judicial action in a complex society.

Like education, medical attention should be free, or at any rate, heavily subsidized by the state, to bring it within reach of the poor on nearly equal footing as the rich.

After education and health care, equal opportunity for work and for earning a living is the next most important, and nothing more seems to be needed to assure it than to prohibit all forms of irrational discrimination in employment by the state as well as by private individuals and organisations. The United States enacted such a prohibition in its Civil Rights Act of 1964, which makes it unlawful for an employer "to fail or refuse to hire or to discharge any individual or otherwise to discriminate against any individual with respect to his compensation, terms, conditions or privileges of employment because of such individual's race, colour, religion, sex or national origin," except "where religion, sex or national origin is a *bona fide* occupational qualification reasonably necessary to the normal operation of that particular business or enterprise."[105] An agency, the Equal Employment Opportunity Commission, was created by the Act charged with its application and administration. (The attempt to incorporate the essence of this provision into the Constitution as the Twenty Seventh Amendment failed to get the required number of ratifications in the States.)

The prohibition has been applied, for example, to invalidate as an unlawful discrimination, an enterprise's employment policy that denied employment to women with pre-school children but not to men with pre-school children.[106] In the

---

105. S. 703.
106. *Phillips v. Martin- Marietta Corp.* 400 U.S. 542 (1971).

opinion of Justice Marshall, in a separate concurring judgment, the distinction drawn between men and women could not be justified on the basis of the "ancient canards" about women having different responsibilities for the up-bringing of children which affect their performance at work. "The exception for a *bona fide* occupational qualification," he said, "was not intended to swallow the rule," and is "applicable only to job situations that require specific physical characteristics necessarily possessed by only one sex."[107] As far as is known, no doubt has been cast on the constitutional validity of the Civil Rights Act of the United States.

The Constitution as a Means of Imposing on the State a Duty to Secure the Welfare of the People

Just as the notion of government by the people is implemented in the constitution of a democratic government, so also, it is suggested, should that of the public welfare as the object of government be given constitutional force, by making a positive declaration in the constitution to the effect, coupled with a directive as to the broad lines of policy to be pursued by government in furtherance thereof. It should also give constitutional force to the notion of civic virtues by embodying the necessary civic virtues in a code of conduct for public servants. The effect of such a constitutional declaration of objectives, directive principles of state policy and a consti-tutional code for public servants will be to cast upon the legislative and executive functionaries of government a consti-tutional obligation to inform and guide their actions in accordance with such stipulations. They would also serve as a reminder to them that their position is one of trust involving powers as well as duties; a truly republican tradition and culture may thereby, hopefully, be nurtured among the leadership.

The appropriateness of the constitution for directing the state as to its duties to the citizenry and the policies and actions called for on its part should perhaps be less grudgingly conceded. It is not enough to grant powers to government and

---

107. At pages 545 and 546.

to impose limitations upon them. For power implies no obligation to exercise it at all or to exercise it in a particular direction. The legislature is under no duty to exercise its power to make law on any matter nor is the executive obliged to execute the law when it is made. Thus, although government has the constitutional power to do so, it is not legally obliged to provide medical, educational and other social amenities for the welfare of the people. Similarly, the limitation on power implied in a constitutional guarantee of individual liberties imposes no duty on the state to positively do anything to promote the material well-being of the people, but only a negative duty not to violate them.

Until the second decade of this century, constitutional-makers had been pre-occupied largely with constitutional power and limitations. In a society built upon *laissez-faire* and economic individualism, as most societies were before the twentieth century, the securing to the individual of social and economic amenities is regarded as none of the state's business. (Concern by some private individuals about the condition of the masses and how to ameliorate it dated of course back to the 19th century, and found powerful expression in the writings of Karl Marx, particularly *The Communist Manifesto* of 1848). But the economic and social consequences of the two world wars have compelled among some countries a change of attitude towards the duties of the state to the individual, with the result that increasing concern is now being shown for his claim to social and economic amenities, sometimes referred to as the "social entitlements of citizenship" or social democracy. Throughout the world today the question is agitated as to how this claim could be more effectively secured against the state. The constitution is seen by many as perhaps the most appropriate means of doing so, as witness the Constitutions of Cyprus, India, Pakistan, Nigeria (1979/1989), the French-speaking African countries, the Social Charter of the European Economic Community and the International Covenant on Economic, Social and Cultural Rights of the United Nations.

By the U.N. International Covenant on Economic, Social and Cultural Rights, which entered into force on 3 January, 1976 after securing the necessary 35 ratifications, each ratifying State "undertakes to take steps ... to the maximum of its resources, with a view to achieving progressively the full realisation of the rights recognised in the present Covenant by all appropriate means, including particularly the adoption of legislative measures". (art. 2(1)).

The benefits and amenities covered by the Covenant are: the right to work, to earn a livelihood by work freely chosen, and to the enjoyment of just and favourable condition of work, including decent minimum remuneration, safe and healthy working conditions, equal promotion opportunities, rest, leisure and reasonable limitation of working hours and periodic holidays with pay (arts. 6 & 7); the right of workers to form or join trade unions of their choice and to strike (art. 8); social security (art. 9); special protection for mothers during a reasonable period before or after childbirth; protection of children and young persons from economic and social exploitation (art. 10); adequate standard of living such as will secure freedom from hunger, in particular adequate food, clothing and housing (art. 11); the highest attainable standard of physical and mental health (art. 12); free and compulsory primary education while education at the secondary and tertiary levels should be generally accessible and be made progressively free (art. 13); and, finally, the right to take part in cultural life and to enjoy the benefits of scientific progress and its application (art. 15).

It needs to be stated that the use of the term "right" in this connection is a misnomer, a perversion of language. The so-called economic and social rights are not rights in the traditional acceptation of the word. The right to work, which is part of everyone's inherent freedom to act for himself without coercion or control by the arbitrary will of others, has, for example, been perverted to embrace a so-called right to be provided employment by the state or by others. The so-called right to be provided free medical care, education, housing, etc., is of the same type of perverted application of the term. They are not rights or liberties in the traditional sense of freedom from coercion or control by the arbitrary will of others; they are rather in the nature of privileges or amenities to be provided by the state from its resources. Hence the duty put on the state to provide them is made subject to the availability of resources. Indeed developing countries are free to determine to what extent their economy would permit guaranteeing them (art. 2(3)).

Democratisation should therefore involve the use of the constitution to impose upon the state a duty to provide for its citizen the social, economic and cultural "rights" specified in the International Covenant. Nigeria did that in the Directive Principles of State Policy enshrined in its Constitutions for transition from military rule to democracy in 1979 and 1989 which represent perhaps the best attempt to give constitutional force to the democratic principle of government for the people.

A duty is laid upon the government to provide adequate facilities for, and to encourage free mobility of, people, goods and services throughout the country; to secure full residence rights for every citizen in all parts of the country, and to direct its policy towards ensuring for all Nigerians suitable and adequate shelter, food, medical and health facilities, and facilities for leisure and for social, religious and cultural life, and free education at all levels. On the economic side, the state is required to direct its policy towards ensuring that all citizens have the opportunity for securing adequate means of livelihood and suitable employment; that for all Nigerians there should be a minimum living wage, unemployment benefits, old age care and pensions, just and humane conditions of work, and equal pay for equal work without discrimination on account of sex; that the health, safety and welfare of all persons in employment be safeguarded and not endangered or abused; that children, young persons and the aged be protected against any exploitation whatever, and against moral and material neglect; that provision be made for public assistance in deserving cases or other conditions of need; that the national economy be controlled in such a way as to secure the maximum welfare, freedom and happiness of every citizen on the basis of social justice and quality of status and opportunity; that the material resources of the community be harnessed and distributed as best as possible to serve the common good; that the economic system should not be operated in such a way as to permit the concentration of wealth or the means of production and exchange in the hands of few individuals or of a group; and that planned and balanced economic development be promoted.

All organs of government and all persons or authorities exercising executive, legislative or judicial functions are required, as a matter of constitutional duty, to conform to, observe and apply these principles. It must be emphasised that the duty thus cast on the state is only to pursue a policy that is geared towards securing the amenities specified; it does not confer on any individual a corresponding entitlement to demand such amenities as a right. Regrettably, however, the Constitution provides no machinery for ensuring such compliance, and expressly excludes the use of the courts for the purpose, even to the limited extent of a mere declaration by a court that the government is or is not complying with the principles. This exclusion is predicated on the danger of a confrontation between the court and the political organs and on the alleged incompetence of lawyers to decide such matters. The danger of confrontation hardly justifies the complete exclusion of judicial intervention, and judges are no less competent than politicians to assess the performance of a government. However, the National Assembly is given power to provide for a machinery to promote and enforce the directive principles of the Constitution.

Political parties also are required to conform their aims and objectives and programmes to the declared principles and to the fundamental objectives and ideals of the nation.

As noted in chapter 2, a declaration of social, economic and cultural rights has, conformably with the socio-economic objectives of the communist order of society, been a conspicuous feature of communist constitutions. This feature is largely retained in the new constitutions of Bulgaria and Romania (1991) and in Czechoslovakia's Charter of Fundamental Rights and Freedoms, adopted after the democratic revolutions of 1989-90. They guarantee the right to free education provided by the state, to health care, social protection of labour (including safety and hygiene, working conditions for women and youth, minimum wage, weekly time off, paid vacation time, equal pay for equal work for men and women and collective bargaining), decent standard of living, pension, unemployment benefit and other forms of social assistance, social protection of children, the youth and the handicapped.[108]

---

108. Arts 32, 33, 38, 43, 45 and 46 Romania; arts 48(5), 51, 52, 53, 54 and 55 Bulgaria; arts 26-35 Czechoslovakia.

The Constitution as a Means of Securing Social Justice for Disadvantaged Ethnic, Racial or Religious Groups in a Plural Society

Having regard to its duty to treat equally all citizens whose circumstances are the same, the state is not competent to try to redress inequalities in wealth, income, standard of living or social status between racial or ethnic groups by means of preferential measures designed for the exclusive benefit of disadvantaged groups. But the constitution itself can, in order to secure or promote social justice, institute such measures directly or authorise the government to do so.

The constitution of India affords an example of this. It provides that the guarantee of non-discrimination shall not "prevent the state from making any special provision for the advancement of any socially and educationally backward classes of citizens or for the scheduled castes and scheduled tribes" (s.15(3)) or from "making any provision for the reservation of appointments or posts in favour of any backward class of citizens" (s.16(4)). In even more affirmative terms, it provides for the reservation of appointments for scheduled castes and scheduled tribes in the administrative services as well as in Parliament and the State Assemblies (s. 335). We need not concern ourselves with the elaborate quota reservations in the Cyprus Constitution which simply caricature reason.

Preferential measures designed avowedly for the exclusive benefit of a disadvantaged group are open to objection because it is unjustifiable to give a benefit to an individual in preference to more deserving, more meritorious or more needy individuals, simply because he belongs to a disadvantaged group. Clearly, in the distribution of benefits, the depressed social and economic circumstances of a group should not be a justifiable basis for preferring an individual member thereof to someone else from a privileged group, even though the former, considered as an individual, may not personally be disadvantaged or otherwise deserve, merit or need such preferential treatment. Preferential treatment of an individual based on his membership of a disadvantaged group rather than on his individual desert, merit or need is objectionable because it sacrifices individual rights to group rights; it runs counter to the whole concept of a right as something inhering in, or pertaining to, a person, not a racial or ethnic group.

Fixed quota reservations are objectionable on still other grounds. There is, first, the danger that acceptable minimum requirements in public appointments and admissions to universities and colleges might be abandoned. They are also over-laid with the notion of proportionality of representation. Once conceded, it should not, logically, stop short of being made to bear a statistical proportionality to the numerical strength of the group. For, since it implies that the group in question is under-represented, full redress demands proportionality of representation or at least a representation that bears an equitable relation to its numerical strength, not an arbitrary, concessionary quota totally unrelated to its population. But once we begin to talk in terms of the reservation of statistically proportionate quota for a disadvantaged group(s), then, merit would have been compromised to an unacceptable extent.

The experience of India shows that the system of quota reservations is a veritable source of endless controversies about the criteria for choosing groups to be given preferences, the choice of groups in accordance with the criteria so determined and about the kinds of preferences to be provided. The years since the introduction of the system have witnessed a vast extension of groups covered by preferences and of preferences provided. The process seems a never-ending one as agitations by groups for inclusion continue to mount, marked by "struggles in the streets, at the polls, within the government bureaucracy and in state legislatures. Concessions granted to one group then become the basis for demands by another."[109]

Yet, while inherently objectionable for the reasons above stated, preferential measures are necessary for democracy and social justice in a multi-racial or multi-ethnic society. In such a society, a right to govern, or participation in government based solely on individual merit, is no less unacceptable than one based on birth or wealth. Participation by group representation

---

109. Myron Weiner, "The pursuit of ethnic equality through preferential policies: A comparative public policy perspective," in Goldmann and Wilson, ed., *From Independence to Statehood* (1948), p. 76.

in a plural society should not be confined to elective offices in the legislature and other bodies. Group representation must be carried to the non-elective offices in the executive council, civil service, the armed forces, police force, parastatals, etc. The problem of social justice and democracy in a multi-racial or multi-ethnic society is about how to give all the component groups the opportunity to participate in both the elective and non-elective organs, arms and agencies of government, since only thus can each feel that it is a full member of the nation, bound to the others by a common feeling of belonging together. "National loyalty," Prof Arthur Lewis has said, "cannot immediately supplant tribal loyalty; it has to be built on top of tribal loyalty by creating a systems in which all the tribes feel that there is room for self-expression"[110] and participation in the government.

The provision in the Nigerian Constitution (1979) seems quite apt to answer the need for constitutional protection. It avoids the inflexibility of fixed quota reservations and the dangers with which it is fraught. It simply says that "the composition of the Government of the Federation or any of its agencies and the conduct of its affairs shall be carried out in such manner as to reflect the federal character of Nigeria and the need to promote national unity, and also to command national loyalty thereby ensuring that there shall be no predominance of persons from a few states or from a few ethnic or other sectional groups in that government or in any of its agencies" (s.14(3)).

As articulated in this provision, the federal character principle is not a rigid formula, but only a broad guide for action. As a guide, it needs to be applied, not with the mathematical exactitude of fixed quota reservations, but only with a due sense of equitable balance. This requires that public appointments, in particular appointments in the strategic departments and functions of government, should be equitably distributed among the component groups, and to be equitable the distribution should reflect, in some *rough or approximate* way, the respective numerical strengths of the groups but

---

110. Arthur Lewis, *Politics in West Africa* (1965), p. 68.

without adhering rigidly to fixed quota reservations. Obviously, the application of such a broad guide calls for a high degree of statesmanship.

Properly applied, it should not require the appointment or promotion of anyone who does not possess the qualification prescribed for an office or the admission to a university or college of anyone who did not score the minimum pass mark in an entrance examination. All it does is to permit a person with the requisite qualification to be appointed or admitted to represent his group, although he may not be the best man available in a nation-wide competition. Admittedly, he may not perform as well as the best man. Yet, so long as acceptable standard determined by prescribed minimum qualification or experience are not lowered to unacceptable level simply to accommodate the disadvantaged groups, his appointment or admission to represent his group fulfils a higher societal need than that of the highest standards of performance which may be expected from the best man.

But it is not enough merely that the "federal character" of the country is reflected, in the way suggested, in the composition of the government and its agencies and in the conduct of their affairs unless the application of the principle results in "ensuring that there shall be no predominance of persons from a few states or from a few ethnic or other sectional groups in that government or in any of its agencies." It is not enough that each group is represented in the organs, councils and departments of the government if the government is permanently dominated by one group or a combination of the same groups. The prevention of domination, more than mere participation by representation, is the central objective of the federal character principle in the Nigerian Constitution.

Now, domination arises not so much from numbers as from control of the key positions where vital decisions regarding policy, financial disbursements, appointments, award of contracts, etc are made, where, in short, the business of governing takes place. The messengers, artisans, clerks, the technicians, executive officers and the middle cadre officers are undoubtedly an indispensable part of the machinery for the administration of government. They all contribute vital inputs to the total material on which decisions about government are based. They are even more vital in the execution of decisions. Yet they are no more than supports with very little real power to affect the conduct of government. They cannot dominate, whatever their number. Domination is material at the level of the director-general and his deputy, minister and head of government. It is at these levels that the actual governing takes place. In terms of representational value, the director-general or minister counts for almost as much as the rest of the staff in a ministry put together. Indeed, under the presidential Constitution of the Second Republic, the President was, to all intents and purposes, the executive government. So is the Head of the Federal Military Government (FMG) in the military administration. It is such key positions particularly that the federal character principle requires not to be dominated by any one group.

The principle requires therefore, above all else, that the headship of the government should move round, and that *ordinarily* no two persons from the same group should hold it successively when the other groups have not held it. It is predicated upon the view of a multi-ethnic society as a house on many pillars, and that the edifice will begin to wobble and its stability imperilled if the headship of the government is not made to move round the groups. That is the national question in all multi-ethnic societies. It is also the lesson of the impending break-up of the Czechoslavak Federation.[111] The question can be constitutionally resolved, not by an elaborate formula for rotating the office, but by a simple provision to the effect that no one ethnic group shall hold the office twice when other groups, qualified by a criterion or criteria prescribed in the constitution for the purpose, have not held it.

---

111. See the Editorial in *The Guardian*, Wednesday, August 5, 1992, p. 8.

Chapter 9

Equal Treatment of all Citizens by the State

> But though Natural Equality triumphed as a doctrine, Natural Inequality remained as a fact... To reconcile this Natural Inequality as a Fact with the principle of Natural Equality as a Doctrine is one of the chief problems which every government has to solve.
>
> — Lord Bryce.

Rationale and Applications of Equality Before the Law as a Principle Both of Liberty and of Democracy

Ever since the French revolutionaries popularised it in 1789, "Liberty and Equality" has everywhere been the rallying cry, the watchword, of revolutionaries agitating or fighting for democracy. Earlier in their Declaration of Independence from British monarchical autocracy in 1776, the American revolutionaries had also proclaimed that "all men are created equal, and are endowed by their creator with certain inalienable Rights." Liberty and equality always go together in the aspirations of revolutionaries just as they do in the thoughts of liberal philosophers. Liberty cannot exist unless the rulers and the governed, the high and the low, are equal before the law, unless all are equally protected by the law and equally obligated to obey its rules — without exemption based on official position held or social status. "It is this fact that all rules apply equally to all, including those who govern, which makes it improbable that any oppressive rules will be adopted."[1] Nor can democracy exist unless political rights are equal for all citizens. Political liberty enjoyed by the minority

---

1. F. A. Hayek, *The Constitution of Liberty* (1960), p. 210.

but denied to the majority or *vice versa* cannot found democracy. It must be enjoyed by all equally to create democracy.

Equality as a principle of liberty and democracy has two aspects viz; social equality which has already been considered in chapter 6, and equality of all citizens in relation to the state.

Constitutional democracy does indisputably require that basic human rights should be constitutionally guaranteed to all on the basis of equality. The principle is predicated upon our common human nature,[2] which consists of body and soul for everybody. Every human being is characterised by the ability to breathe, think, speak, move about and to act; he has emotions and sensations, he feels pain, anguish and happiness, he has a conscience and beliefs just like everyone else; in addition every human being is endowed by nature with the faculties of sight, hearing, smell, taste and touch. No doubt, there are differences between individuals but such differences do not affect our basic common human nature; they are differences of degree, not of essential nature.

The fact of a common human nature therefore gives to every one equal claim to the fundamental right of life and personal liberty, to freedom of thought, conscience and religion, freedom of expression, including freedom to receive and impart ideas and information, freedom of association and movement. Given also the common humanity of all, everyone has equal right not to be subjected to torture or to inhuman or degrading treatment, not to be held in slavery or servitude and not to be required to perform forced or compulsory labour. These rights must be protected for all individuals without any distinction whatsoever.

As regards participation in government and politics, however, it was argued that considerations of a common humanity should not be determinative, and the wealth, ability and knowledge (or education) which are the product of innate or natural inequality in intelligence, strength, skill, etc., should determine eligibility for participation. According to this

---

2.   Hayek seems to disagree with what he calls "the widely held uniformity theory of human nature" op. cit., p. 86.

argument, "ignorance should disqualify for the suffrage, and one who has not enough property to give him a permanent interest in the country, or who contributes nothing in taxes, should not be placed on a level with the man of education possessed of at least some taxable property."[3] This ignores the fact that the poor, uneducated person has also a vital interest in the country and its fortunes or misfortunes, and that he also makes an invaluable contribution through his labour, which is perhaps more indispensable to the country's prosperity and wealth than the richman's property. Whilst education serves to ensure that the franchise is intelligently exercised, it should not deny those without it, the right to participate in choosing who should take decisions on their behalf on matters which affect their lives. Whatever the relative plausibility of the competing arguments, the equalitarian view prevailed in the end, and rightly so, as it is supported and demanded by justice.

And so it has come to be almost universally accepted as a principle of democracy that all citizens have equal rights of participation in government and politics without any distinction whatsoever, whether on the ground of race, colour, ethnicity, sex, religion or political opinion. In particular, participation in elections for the choice of rulers or representatives must be based on the principle of one person one vote, and is not to be enjoyed by "the rich, more than the poor; not the learned, more than the ignorant; not the haughty heirs of distinguished names, more than the humble sons of obscure and unpropitious fortune."[4]

Participation in the choice of rulers or representatives should be equal not only in the sense of one person one vote but also in the weight given to the votes. Thus, a disparity ranging from 2,340 to 33,990 voters between rural and urban constituencies in Tennessee (U.S.) was held to be void as an unconstitutional discrimination.[5] In the view of the U.S. Supreme Court in another case, the Constitution requires that "as nearly as is practicable one man's vote in a congressional election is to be

---

3.   James Bryce, *Modern Democracies* (1920), Vol. 1, p. 71.
4.   James Madison, *The Federalist No 57*, ed. Clinton Rossiter (1961), p. 35.
5.   *Baker v. Carr*, 369 U.S. 186.

worth as much as another."[6]

Also the privilege to stand for election and be elected shall be open, on a footing of equality, to every citizen, and "no qualification of wealth, of birth, of religious faith, or of civil profession" shall be a bar.[7]

Equality of participation in government requires further that the minority as well as the majority must have equal freedom of self-expression, however abhorrent their views may be, and equal freedom to associate and organise together in order to make the advocacy of their views more effective with a view ultimately to securing the mandate to run the government.

Democracy is not satisfied simply because participation in government and politics and the basic human rights are constitutionally guaranteed to all on equal basis. Equality of treatment by the state in all matters is what is required, that is to say, rights, privileges or obligations created or dispensed by the state (as distinct from purely private rights having no connection at all with the state, e.g., succession or contractual rights) should be equal for all citizens without distinction. If the state is the product of a social contract, then, no citizen should rank higher or lower nor count more or less than any other citizen in relation to it. In this view, a democratic state is an organisation in which the relationship of all members to it is on equal terms whether it pertains to rights, obligations, the security of lives and property, the administration of justice or the exercise of legislative and executive power generally. The formulation used for this in the Commonwealth Bills of Rights is that a citizen "shall not, either expressly by, or in the practical application of, any law or any executive or administrative action of government, be subjected to any disabilities or restrictions or be accorded any privilege or advantage" by reason "solely" of sex, ethnicity, place of origin, religion or political opinion.

Laws should accordingly be made for the generality of the people, and not for named persons or groups. Singling out a person or group for individualised treatment by legislation may

6.   *Wesberry v. Sanders*, 376 U.S. 1 at p. 7.
7.   James Madison loc. cit.

not only be arbitrary, it can easily lend itself to oppression, favouritism or other kinds of discriminatory uses. The greatest protection against legislative arbitrariness and discrimination lies therefore in its generality and equality of application to all persons. "Although the fact that a general measure has been adopted is not conclusive evidence that it is good or wise, it is strong presumptive evidence of its being so. In order to show that it is unfair in its bearing on any one individual, it is necessary to show that it is a measure which is quite unjustifiable, and which society could not have any good reason for imposing on itself."[8] *Ad hominem* legislation becomes singularly oppressive and unjust when it inflicts punishment or disability on the individual affected without the benefit of trial by a court of law.

Ex post facto legislation, like *ad hominem* one, has a potentiality for discriminatory or oppressive use, for though ostensibly general in form, it is often in reality aimed at particular persons. It may, for instance, be used to reverse a particular court decision in favour of a particular person and against the government or to take away accrued or vested rights of identifiable persons, which may be rights arising under a contract or other transaction or rights arising from a public appointment, as where a public office is vacated retrospectively in order to disentitle its incumbent to the benefits of the office or where an act of a public functionary, agency or individual, which was valid when done, is invalidated by a retrospective repeal statute. But the most oppressive or discriminatory use of retrospective legislation is to make a criminal offence of an act that was not such when it took place, or to increase retrospectively the punishment for an offence.

Apart from the discriminatory use that can be made of it, retrospective criminal legislation is inherently unjust because "it puts a man in jeopardy of punishment without his having had a chance to avoid it. If Parliament makes it a crime to drive at more than 70 m.p.h., then I can keep out of trouble by keeping to the speed limit. But if it enacts that it shall have been a crime, then, I did not know in time to avoid incurring the penalty."[9]

---

8.   J. R. Lucas, *On Justice* (1980), p. 159.

Prohibitions backed by criminal sanctions (punishment) should also be imposed and enforced on citizens on an equal footing with no exemption based on official or social rank, what Dicey calls "the universal subjection of all classes to one law administered by the ordinary courts."[10] In words that have become classic, Dicey explains this "idea of legal equality" as meaning that "no man is above the law but (what is a different thing) that ... every man, whatever be his rank or condition, is subject to the ordinary law of the realm and amenable to the jurisdiction of the ordinary tribunals."[11]

Under the U.S. Constitution, equality in relation to the state is further protected by an absolute prohibition of titles of nobility,[12] a prohibition regarded by Hamilton as "the cornerstone of republican government,"[13] because it precludes the creation by the state of a class with special privileges, especially a superior right to rule or to choose those to rule. By reason of this prohibition, no titles of distinction, such as Highness, Lord or Sir, are recognised or used. Everyone is plain Mr, Mrs or Miss except of course for academic, professional or ecclesiastical titles. The absence of titles labelling or identifying people by status or rank shows the United States as truly a democratic republic in name and in fact, and the example has been followed by later democratic republics in Europe, America and some parts of Asia. Africans, on the other hand, are greatly enamoured of titles symbolising high social status or rank, particularly chieftaincy titles, which suggest that they are yet to imbibe truly republican habits and attitudes.

The rationale for the state treating all citizens the same is that all have more or less the same need for the security of their person and property, for justice in their dispute with others, for peace and order, for happiness and the good life, for obedience to the laws on the part of all, etc., which therefore makes it unfair to discriminate between them, specially where the discrimination is based *solely* and *entirely* on factors like race,

---

9.   J. R. Lucas, op. cit. pp. 115-116.
10. A. V. Dicey, *The Law of the Constitution*, 10th ed. p. 193.
11. loc. cit.
12. Art. 1 Sec. 9.
13. *The Federalist* No. 84, op. cit. p. 512.

colour, ethnicity, place of origin, sex, religion or political opinion. Yet, on the other hand, it would also be unfair to carry equal treatment to the point of ignoring the innate inequalities between people, Natural Inequalities, as they are called — "natural" because of "the differences in the gifts which Nature has bestowed on some and denied to others."[14] As Lord Bryce has observed, "the fact that the progress of mankind in arts and sciences and letters and every form of thought has been due to the efforts of a comparatively small number of highly gifted minds rising out of the common mass speaks for itself. Natural Inequality has been, and must continue to be one of the most potent and effective factors in human society."[15]

Accordingly, it is universally recognised that differences based on Natural Inequalities or other real and substantial differences provide a rational basis for the state treating persons unequally; and provided that it is reasonably related to such differences, unequal treatment, far from being unfair, is perfectly justified and permissible. As the U.S. Supreme Court said in interpreting the provision in the country's Constitution guaranteeing to all persons "the equal protection of the laws", the Constitution does not require "things which are different in fact or opinion to be treated in law as though they were the same;"[16] it does not intend to create "a fictitious equality where there is a real difference."[17] Treatment or protection is not unequal merely because real and substantial differences between individuals, classes or groups are recognised by law for purposes of special protection or treatment reasonably related to such differences. Provided therefore that such special protection or treatment is reasonable, and not arbitrary, oppressive or capricious, there is no discrimination and no denial of equal treatment or protection.[18] "The mere production of inequality", said the U.S. Supreme Court in another case, "is

---

14.   James Bryce, op. cit. p. 70.
15.   op. cit., p. 70; also J.S. Mill, *On Liberty*, reprinted in *Unitarianism, Liberty and Representative Government* (1910), Everyman Library ed. pp. 123-142.
16.   *Tiner v. Texas*, 310 U.S. 141, 147 (1940).
17.   *Quong Wing v. Kirkendall*, 223 U.S. 59, 63 (1912).
18.   *Ferguson v. Skrup*, 372 U.S. 762, (1963); *Lindsley v. Natural Carbolic Gas Co*, 220 U.S. 61, 78-9 (1911).

not enough. Every selection of persons for regulation so results, in some degree. The inequality produced, in order to encounter the challenge of the Constitution must be actually and palpably unreasonable and arbitrary."[19]

The problem, then, is to determine when differences between people, classes or groups are real and substantial enough to justify unequal treatment or protection, and as Lord Bryce said in the statement quoted at the opening of this chapter "to reconcile this Natural Inequality as a fact with the principle of Natural Equality as a Doctrine is one of the chief problems which every government has to solve."[20]

Differences Justifying Unequal Treatment

1. Differences Between the Advantaged and Disadvantaged Members of Society

There are real and substantial differences in economic and bargaining power between the consumer and the supplier of goods or services, the tenant and his landlord, the worker and his employer, the investor and the promoters and directors of companies, as there are disparities in wealth, income, opportunities and living standards between the rich and the poor, the educated and the illiterate, urban and rural dwellers, the able-bodied and the disabled and handicapped. It is justified and permissible for the state to intervene to redress such differences by appropriate measures, such as the control of the prices and quality of goods or services; rent control; control of the prices of, and dealings in, shares; the fixing of minimum wages and the regulation of other aspects of the employer/worker relationship; progressive or differential taxations and other taxes to raise revenue for social services; measures designed to equalise opportunities; social security benefit schemes for the poor, the needy, the disabled and the handicapped; control of the ownership of business and property, particularly land.

---

19. *Radice v. New York*, 264 U.S. 292, 296; quoting *Arkansas Natural Gas Co v. Arkansas R. Commission* 261 U.S. 379, 384.
20. op. cit. p. 70.

2. Differences in Individual Desert, Merit and Need

It is universally accepted that, in the distribution of benefits, society can, quite justifiably, discriminate or differentiate between its members on the basis of desert, merit or need. Discrimination or differentiation based on these grounds is not irrational or arbitrary, and is not therefore unfair. Frankena puts it admirably thus:-

> The demand for equality is built into the very concept of justice. The just society, then, must consider and protect the good life of each man equally with that of any other, no matter how different these men may be, and so it must allow them equal consideration, equal opportunity, and equality before the law. The equal concern for the good lives of its members also requires society to treat them differently, for no matter how much one believes in a common human nature, individual needs and capacities differ, and what constitutes the good life for one individual may not do so for another.[21]

Not only is it not unfair, it has become a necessity in modern government. "The progress of physical science, involving special training for the purposes of production, and the enlarged sphere of governmental action, which increases the value of skill and knowledge, have been making the recognition of Natural Inequality in the selection of administrative officials more and more inevitable. A country which should fail to recognise this cannot but fall behind its competitors."[22]

Thus, the principles of desert, merit or need do constitute an exception to, or a qualification on, that of equality, which may operate to exclude it in certain circumstances. By the principle of desert, benefits should be allocated, not on the basis of equality but rather according to people's contribution to society. Merit and need can be subsumed under desert, although they are not exactly synonymous with it. In their strict meaning, merit refers to a person's personal qualities, such as ability, promise, intelligence or skill, while desert refers to the deeds he has done, i.e., performance (actual or potential) and other conduct.[23] But in a general sense, merit and need

---

21.   W. K. Frankena, "The Concept of Social Justice", in R.B. Brandt (ed.), *Social Justice* (1962), p. 21.
22.   James Bryce, op. cit., pp. 73-74.

are an index of desert. The meritorious and the needy are both deserving of reward or protection because of their merit and need. The notion of need connotes, not every conceivable kind of need, but only such things as are necessary for a decent existence, like food, shelter, clothing, etc.

According to these principles, the person who has made the most contribution or who has the greatest merit or the greatest need is entitled to preference. The problem, however, is how to measure one man's contribution, merit or need against those of others, and how to resolve conflicts that may arise between the principles of desert and need. Because of this, the appearance is often created that distributive justice is "an inherently confused and self-contradictory concept."[24]

The things which may be the subject of distribution by society according to these principles embrace not only material goods or other property but also "interests which are not legally regarded as property but which are legally protected, like medical care, honour, reputation as well as opportunities or facilities such as the right to free education, etc."[25]

Now, if the desert principle applies to such a wide variety of benefits or advantages, it may be wondered what place, if any, is still left for the principle of equality. There is obviously a dilemma here. For, whilst the principle of equality conceives society as but "a great family from whose table not even the humblest of her members shall be excluded," that of desert does entail that "if everyone gets his desert, some may be driven from the table; and if everyone comes to the table, some may not get their deserts."[26] Boulding has suggested that an accommodation between the two principles may be found in the principle of a social minimum, as reflected, for instance, in the poor law, in social security, and in various welfare services. "The principle of desert", he suggests, "may come into play above the social minimum. That is to say, society lays a modest table at which all can sup and a high table at which the

23. Lucas, *On Justice* (1980), p. 166.
24. Lucas, op. cit. p. 168.
25. A. M. Honore, "Social Justice", 8 McGill Law Journal (1968) p. 81.
26. Kenneth E. Boulding, "Social Justice in Social Dynamics" in R. B. Brandt. op. cit., p. 83.

deserving can feast." He maintains that this principle "can be traced in almost all practical efforts to solve the problem."[27]

In Ross's analysis, however, the principles of desert, merit and need are accommodated within that of equality although they operate to empty quality, as a general principle, of much practical content, reducing it to a mere formal requirement, that is, as far as the distribution of benefits and burdens are concerned. From the premise that the principle of equality is only a demand that like shall be treated in a like manner, Ross maintains that desert, merit and need are criteria for determining the different classes whose members are to be considered as equals because they have equal desert, merit or need. They are criteria for determining the classes or categories in which people should be placed before the principle of equality can be applied to them in the distribution of benefits or burdens. "In other words, the demand for equality contained in the idea of justice is not directed absolutely at each and all, but at all members within a class as determined by certain relevant criteria."[28]

Thus, remuneration should be equal among persons who have made the same or equal contribution or done equal amount of work, as in the case of the demand for equal pay for men and women for equal work. Similarly, people who have the same needs are to be treated alike regardless of their contribution. "The principle of needs", he asserts, "is the basis for the idea that the unemployed, the sick, the invalid, the defectively equipped or the family breadwinner have a claim to the supplying of those needs which are the consequence of his particular position."[29] And ability to pay determines the assessment of income tax with regard to minimum tax-free incomes, progressive scales, allowance for children, and so on.

Ross's explanation, though valid to an extent, seems inadequate. First, not all benefits in society are distributed on the basis of desert, merit or need. Boulding's idea of a certain

---

27. loc. cit.
28. A. Ross, *On Law and Justice* (English translation 1974) p. 270.
29. Ross, op. cit. p. 271.

social minimum provided for *all* on the basis of equality and on top of which distribution based on desert, merit or need is then superimposed, appears more satisfactory. Secondly, equality of treatment has a wider application than the distribution of benefits, as, for instance, equality as respects fundamental human rights, equality of obligations, equality as respects the administration of justice and equality as respects the physical security of life and property.

3. Differences Between the Sexes

While men and women share a common human nature characterised by a common basic physical and spiritual constitution and the ability to breathe, think, speak, feel and act, there are real and substantial biological and emotional differences between them. We know as a fact of our humanity that women are weaker than men in physical strength, and are tender, soft and feeble in their emotional make-up. Hence they are called the weaker sex. We also know as a fact of our humanity that women conceive and give birth to children and become nursing mothers whereas men cannot. Men are of course needed to fertilise the egg that women produce in their wombs. And we do know too that the sex organ of women is different from that of men, and that for this and other reasons a woman can be a wife to a man, and a man a husband to a woman but not conversely. The word "wife" does not connote just the status of marriage; it connotes a married female, and a female is defined by the attribute of being able to lay egg which, upon fertilisation, forms and develops into a human being, which in due time is born.

These are real and substantial differences which constitutionally justify unequal treatment of the sexes by the state. It is therefore not unconstitutional for the state to provide by law, as is done in most countries, that a woman employed in any industrial, commercial and agricultural undertaking "shall not be permitted to work during the six weeks following her confinement"; that she is entitled to be paid not less than 50 per cent of her wages during any period of absence on maternity leave; that, while nursing a child, she shall be allowed half an hour twice a day during working hours for that purpose.[30] These special privileges are accorded to women, not by reason *solely* of sex, but for reasons connected with childbirth or the status of a nursing mother.

Although this is today being vehemently protested by women, and has been abolished in many countries, the prohibition of night and underground work by women is based on the fact that their weak physical strength, tenderness and delicacy unfits them for that kind of strenuous work. The injurious consequences of the loss of restful night's sleep were thought to "bear more heavily against women than men." In upholding the constitutionality of the prohibition, the U.S. Supreme Court has observed that "the two sexes differ in structure of body, in the functions to be performed by each, in the amount of physical strength, in the capacity for long-continued labour, particularly when done standing ... and in the capacity to maintain the struggle for subsistence. This difference justifies a difference in legislation."[31]

The decision upholding the constitutionality of a statute which prescribed maximum working hours for women is, however, more difficult to accept. The Court's opinion rested it on a woman's physical structure and performance of maternal functions. "By abundant testimony of the medical fraternity" said the Court, "continuance for a long time on her feet at work, repeating this from day to day, tends to injurious effects upon the body, and, as healthy mothers are essential to vigorous offspring, the physical well-being of women becomes an object of public interest and care in order to preserve the strength and vigour of the race."[32] But, surely, these considerations do not justify the Court in affirming the constitutionality of a statute which fixed minimum wages for women but not for men.[33]

In consonance with this, the International Labour Organisation Convention on Equality of opportunity and treatment in Employment and Occupation 1958 (No. 111) permits a ratifying state to make exceptions "designed to meet

---

30. See, e.g. s.53 Labour Act 1974 (Nigeria).
31. *Radice v. New York,* 264 U.S. 292 at p. 295 (1923).
32. *Muller v. Oregon* 208 U.S. 412, at p. 421 (1908).
33. *West Coast Hotel Co. v. Parrish* 300 U.S. 379 (1937).

the particular requirements of persons who, for reasons such as sex, age, disablement, family responsibilities or social or cultural status, are generally recognised to require special protection or assistance."

Today, we would regard as out-moded and unacceptably undemocratic the rather quaint statement by the U.S. Supreme Court in a 1873 case in which the Court upheld the constitutionality of the refusal by the State of Illinois to license a woman to practice law; interestingly, old-fashioned as it is, the statement had dominated the thinking of the Court on the subject for a long time, being indeed a true reflection of the opinion prevailing among the public in the United States at the time on the position of women, as attested by Alexis de Tocqueville's description of it in 1835.[34] Said the Court:

> The civil law, as well as nature itself, has always recognised a wide difference in the respective spheres and destinies of man and woman. Man is, or should be, woman's protection and defender. The natural and proper timidity and delicacy which belongs to the female sex evidently unfits it for many of the occupations of civil life. The constitution of the family organisation, which is founded in the divine ordinance, as well as in the nature of things, indicates the domestic sphere as that which properly belongs to the domain and functions of womanhood. The harmony, not to say identity, of interests and views which belongs or should belong to the family institution is repugnant to the idea of a woman adopting a distinct and independent career from that of her husband.[35]

Also out-moded and unacceptable to our present-day thinking are the decision of the Court in 1875 sustaining the constitutionality of a statute which restricted the franchise to men[36] and another in 1948 sustaining, on the ground that it was necessary for the protection of the health and morality of women, a state law which forbade the licensing of women as bartenders.[37] A majority of the Court held that the line drawn by the statute between men and women is "not without a basis

---

34. Alexis de Tocqueville, *Democracy in America*, ed. Richard Heffner (1956) pp. 233-237; 243-247. "In the United States," he wrote, "the inexorable opinion of the public carefully circumscribes woman within the narrow circle of domestic interests and duties, and forbids her to step beyond it." at p. 236.

35. *Bradwell v. Illinois* 16 Wall (83 U.S.) 130 at p. 141 (1873).

36. *Minor v. Happersett* 21 Wall (88 U.S.) 162 (1875).

37. *Goesaert v. Cleary* 335 U.S. 464 (1948).

in reason", since bartending by women may give rise to moral and social problems which the legislature is entitled to try to prevent by protective legislation of the sort challenged, and this despite the vast changes in the social and legal position of women. The words of Justice Frankfurter, delivering the opinion of the majority, have a quaint ring to our modern ears. "The fact," he said, "that women may not have achieved the virtues that men have long claimed as their prerogatives and now indulge in vices that men have long practised, does not preclude the States from drawing a sharp line between the sexes, certainly in such matters as the regulation of the liquor traffic."[38] A minority of three thought the distinction to be invidious, arbitrary and without any justifiable basis in the protection of "the moral and physical and well-being of women."[39]

On the other hand, the great Oliver Wendell Holmes seems to have shown undue favouritism towards women when, in upholding the constitutionality of a law which imposed a fee upon all persons engaged in the laundry business but excepted women where not more than two of them were so employed, he said: "If Montana deems it advisable to put a lighter burden upon women than upon men with regard to an employment that our people commonly regard as more appropriate for the former, the Fourteenth Amendment does not interfere."[40] That was in 1912, nearly 80 years ago. I am sure that not even women will support this kind of favouritism today.

Apart from biological and emotional differences, it cannot be denied that disparities do exist between the sexes in the social, economic and political fields; they are indeed a global fact of life. Except in the case of hereditary offices not barred to women by law, political power has been the preserve of men, and it is only in the last 40 years or so that women began to make incursions into the preserve, particularly with the emergence of first women presidents and prime ministers. The economic field has been and continues to be dominated by men

---

38.   ibid at p. 466.
39.   ibid at p. 468.
40.   *Quong Wing v. Kirkendell* 223 U.S. 59, 63 (1912).

as leaders of industry, entrepreneurs, financial giants, economic policy makers, chief executives and other top executives of industrial, commercial and financial enterprises, etc. So are the professions of law, medicine, engineering, accountancy, journalism, etc., although here the dominance of men is being increasingly threatened. Socially, women occupy a lower status than men, both in the home and in society at large.

Social disparities among *individuals* are normally the result of circumstances of birth, of the fact that people may be born into royalty, a nobility, a wealthy class, a superior or inferior caste, into serfdom or into a free or unfree class. Aside from inherited wealth, disparities in wealth and income among *individuals* are, in general, the product of innate differences in ability and talents, for example, differences in aptitude, skill, resourcefulness, initiative, perceptiveness, persuasiveness and personal disposition.

But the social and economic inequalities between the sexes are accounted for neither by circumstances of birth nor by innate differences in talents or ability. Certainly, men are not superior to women in intellect, insights, instinct, resourcefulness, initiative, skill, aptitude or personal charm. The inequalities are simply the product of cultural factors like customs, conventions, taboos and other cultural factors which, aided by suppression and discrimination by men, have operated to relegate women to a subordinate position in the social, economic and political scheme of things, and to keep them there. Not resting on innate differences in talents and ability, these inequalities are unfair and contrary to the principles of social justice and democracy.

Depending on the type of measures instituted, it is again justified and permissible as consistent with democracy for the state to take appropriate measures to reduce or remove these inequalities. But it may be noted that re-distributive measures and those aimed at equalising opportunities have a generality of application to all citizens; accordingly, as they are not specifically directed to the reduction or removal of social or economic disparities between the sexes, their impact on the problem is necessarily limited.

4. Differences Between Ethnic or Racial Groups.

Race, colour, ethnicity or place of origin do not give rise to real and substantial physical, intellectual or emotional differences between persons as does sex; accordingly, unequal treatment by the state of citizens based on their race, colour, ethnicity or place of origin is in general unjustified and impermissible. Thus, in the United States, state-backed discrimination against blacks in public education and in the use of public facilities has been held to violate the right to equal protection of the laws guaranteed by the U.S. Constitution.[41] The provision of separate schools for blacks, even when the physical facilities and other tangible factors can be shown to be equal to those for whites, was held to be nonetheless a violation, on the ground that the psychological inferiority which segregated accommodation engendered among negroes made it inherently unequal. All forms of segregation by the state in its schools, swimming pools, railroad stations, parks, golf courses, bath houses, beaches, courtrooms etc. were accordingly struck down.[42] "The principle thus finally emerged free of more particularised rationalisation that state enforced segregation, whatever the circumstances, whatever the context, violates the equal protection clause."[43] The fact of enforcement by the state court in private litigation, it was held, gave an otherwise private discrimination the character of state-backed discrimination, thus bringing it within the constitutional prohibition.[44]

The truth, however, is that there do exist inequalities or disparities in wealth, income, education, opportunities, standards of living, social standing, etc. between racial or ethnic groups in a plural society. Such inequalities or

---

41. *Missouri ex rel. Gaines v. Canada* 305 U.S. 337 (1938) *Sipuel v. Board of Regents*, 332 U.S. 631 (1948) (exclusion from educational opportunities furnished by the state); *Bouchanan v. Warley*, 245 U.S. 60 (1917) (exclusion from certain residential areas).
42. *Sweat v. Painter*, 339 U.S. 629 (1950); *Brown v. Topeka*, 347 U.S. 483 (1954); *Brown v. Board of Education*, 349 U.S. 294 (1955); overruling *Plessy v. Ferguson* 163 U.S. 537 (1896).
43. Jaffe, *English and American Judges as Lawmakers* (1969) p. 41.
44. *Shelley v. Kraemer* 334 U.S. 1 (1948). For a critical examination, see Jaffe, op. cit. pp. 40-1; Archibold Cox, *The Warren Court* (1968) chs. 2 and 3.

disparities are indeed a universal feature of all societies comprising peoples of different races, colours, tribes, religions and cultures just as they are among individuals in all societies. Racial or ethnic inequalities are, to a large extent, a consequence of differences in cultural characteristics between the groups, of the fact, for example, that "one group may have little regard for education, whereas another values education highly. One group may prefer entrepreneurial activities, another the professions, and still another physical labour. One group consists of high achievers who seek to move up to whatever occupation are most valued or best paid, while members of another group have less ambition, prefer to live as they have in the past and are less willing to venture forth from the community or into new occupations."[45] They may also result from the domination by some group(s) of political and/or economic power, and its use to advance their members and hold back others.

Inequality between individuals differs from group inequality not only in its cause but also in the fact that it only divides society into classes cutting across the entire society. But the division of society into racial or ethnic groups marked by wide disparities in wealth, income, education, opportunities, social status and living standards, whether the division be horizontal or vertical, poses a far graver danger because of its tendency to generate greater bitter resentment and to provoke more violent social conflicts than inequality between classes.

Granted the prevalence of racial or ethnic inequalities in all multi-racial or multi-ethnic communities and its tendency to generate violent social conflicts, whether unequal treatment by the state of citizens based on these considerations is justified as being required by social justice and democracy is a question the answer to which must depend on the measures employed by the state for redressing such inequalities. Redistributive measures aimed at benefiting disadvantaged racial or ethnic groups raise no problem of justification, as, for example, the

---

45. Myron Weiner, "The Pursuit of Ethnic Equality through preferential Policies: A comparative public policy perspective" in R. B. Goldmann and A. J. Wilson, *From Independence to Statehood* (1984), p. 65.

siting of development projects in their areas with a view, among other things, of providing more jobs for their members; government aid for selected occupations or trades in which disadvantaged groups predominate; social service programmes for improving their health, education and housing; etc. Redistributive measures of this type are not open to objection because they are not really based on race or ethnicity. But, since they are not specifically directed to the problem of reducing racial or ethnic inequalities, their impact on the problem is necessarily limited.

But affirmative measures that confer positive preferences on members of disadvantaged groups, such as quota reservations and other preferential measures are beyond the power of the state to institute because they run counter to its duty to treat equally all citizens whose circumstances are the same. This was the issue in the celebrated *Bakke Case, Regents of the University of California v. Bakke,*[46] where a white applicant who failed to gain admission into the University of California Medical School challenged the University's admission policy of reserving 16 admission places for educationally disadvantaged blacks, American Indians and Asian-Americans who, though qualified, would not have been admitted on strict merit. The trial court and a majority of the California Supreme Court and of the U.S. Supreme Court were agreed in holding that the University's quota reservation programme violated the equal protection clause of the Fourteenth Amendment which clearly predicates "individual, not group-based, attributes as the only permissible factors to be counted." "Only in individual accomplishment," said the trial judge, "can equality be achieved." (Whether the constitution should, in order to secure or promote social justice, authorise such preferential measures is considered in the immediately preceding chapter).

---

46.   438 U.S. 265 (1978). For an illuminating article supporting the University of California's position, see Timothy J. O'Neill, "The Language of Equality in a Constitutional Order," American Science Review Vol. 75, No. 3 (September 1981) pp. 626-35.

5. Protection of the Head of State from Suit and Compulsory Process

This much disputed question will be more appropriately discussed in the next chapter.

Chapter 10

The Rule of Law

> The rule of law means the freedom of men under government to
> have a standing rule to live by...; a liberty to follow my own will in
> all things, where that rule prescribes not: and not to be subject to
> the inconstant, uncertain, arbitrary will of another man.
>
> — John Locke.

Essence of the Rule of Law

The Rule of Law embraces within its ambit particular
application of the concepts of a free society and equality before
the law discussed in chapters 7 and 9. But it is wider than
those two concepts. For, it enjoins not only unwarranted
coercion of the individual by law but, more importantly,
coercion not backed by law at all. Its essence is thus the
principle that law, rather than the arbitrary will or the
momentary and changing whims and caprices of the rulers,
should govern or rule the affairs, actions and rights of the
individual. It means, in the words of John Locke quoted above,
the "freedom of men under government to have a standing rule
to live by...; a liberty to follow my own will in all things, where
that rule prescribes not: and not to be subject to the
inconstant, uncertain, arbitrary will of another man."[1] And by
arbitrary government is meant a government whose coercive or
interfering actions against the individual, whether such actions
be legislative or executive, are not subject to law or to
fundamental rules accepted by the society as the basis of its
togetherness.

The crucial question in the doctrine of the Rule of Law, then,

---

1.   J. Locke, *The Second Treatise of Civil Government*, ed. J. W. Gough (1946)
     sec. 22, p. 13.

is as to the characteristics or attributes of the law which it requires should be the only power to govern the affairs, actions and interests of men in society. Is it just anything that goes by the name law? First, the power to make law governing the affairs, actions and interests of the individual, which is the greatest of all governmental discretions, must itself be subject to a higher law or to fundamental rules accepted by the society as the basis of its togetherness, a higher law or fundamental rules which oblige the lawmaker not to exercise his law-making power by extemporary, arbitrary decrees and, above all, to respect the basic rights of the individual. For, a legislator not limited in his law-making powers by the fundamental principle of respect for individual liberty necessarily tantamounts to an arbitrary government, and all arbitrary law-making is inherently tyrannical and antithetical to the Rule of Law.

To ensure that law-making is not to be arbitrary, it is necessary that its exercise should be by an organ separate, in terms of structure and personnel, from that which executes the law after it is made. And to put it beyond the power of the law-making organ to decide whether or not, in making laws, it should be bound to respect the basic rights of the individual, the constitution, as the source from which government derives its very existence and powers, should be, and nowadays often is, used to subject it to that principle. In other words, respect for individual liberty by the law-maker should not rest entirely upon the willingness of an elected majority to accept it as a matter of self-limitation or mere convention; it should be imposed upon it by the higher law of a constitution adopted by a more all-embracing majority of the people, with the consequence of rendering void, any law made by it in violation of the individual's basic rights.

A written constitution as a supreme, overriding law enshrining a guarantee of individual liberty and the separation of the legislative from the executive power is thus an essential attribute of the Rule of Law. It is also an essential attribute of the Rule of Law that the application of the law in disputes between persons or between a person and the government must be done impartially through a judicial mode of proceeding by an organ separate from, and independent of, that which makes the laws. The Rule of Law does not exist where the law-maker could, by means of a law made by it, pronounce a person guilty of an offence and inflict punishment on him therefor. The power to adjudicate disputes between persons must therefore be enshrined in the constitution as a separate power and the independence of the adjudicators must likewise be constitutionally guaranteed.

But respect for individual liberty is not the only principle of law-making which the Rule of Law requires the law-making organ to observe in making laws governing the affairs and actions of men in society. The Rule of Law is not just a doctrine about legality; it is not just a requirement that all law-making must be subject to a higher law which enshrines the principle of respect for individual liberty, or that all executive actions of government affecting the individual must be backed by, and be strictly in accordance with, law. While government must have power to govern effectively and while power implies discretion, the Rule of Law requires that, within the limits of the law-making power allowed by the higher law of the constitution, the law must circumscribe the discretion it grants to government in matters affecting the interests of the individual, so as to curtail as much as possible the scope of governmental arbitrariness. If, for example, the law authorises government to act in all matters as it thinks fit, then, all acts of government, however capricious or oppressive, would be legal as being authorised by law, yet the unlimited discretion thereby conferred upon the government by law negates the idea of the Rule of Law almost as completely as where an act of government interfering with the individual is not backed by law at all. Thus the existence of the Rule of Law is not determined by "whether all actions of government are legal in the juridical sense. They may well be and yet not conform to the Rule of Law. The fact that somebody has full legal authority to act in the way he does gives no answer to the question whether the law gives him power to act arbitrarily or whether the law prescribes unequivocally how he has to act."[2]

In this sense, as Hayek observes, the Rule of Law is only a guide for law-making, directing the legislature as to the form its

2.   F. A. Hayek, *The Road to Serfdom* (1944), p. 61.

laws should take in order to be effective in curbing the arbitrariness incident to discretionary powers. As a mere directive principle of law-making therefore, it is "not a rule of the law, but a rule concerning what the law ought to be, a meta-legal doctrine or a political ideal. It will be effective only in so far as the legislator feels bound by it. In a democracy this means that it will not prevail unless it forms part of the moral tradition of the community, a common ideal shared and unquestioningly accepted by the majority."[3]

The Rule of Law requires in the second place that laws must be made, not by one man or a junta of men, but by a representative body mandated in that behalf by popular consent.[4] Law-making, not by a popularly elected body, but by a hereditary monarch, a usurping, self-appointed dictator or a military junta provides no basis for the Rule of Law. Nor is it enough that laws are made by a popularly elected body. The Rule of Law requires that law-making by such a body must follow a process pre-determined by laid-down rules of procedure, requiring legislative proposals to be presented in the form of a bill, with the precise wording of its provisions fully set out, and then to be put through a ponderous process of long-drawn-out debates in the assembly and its committees, during which the substance of the proposed law and the meaning and implications, of its wording are examined in detail. The procedure of committees, hearings, and long debates which characterises the legislative process of a democratic government may well be cumbersome, time-consuming and even inefficient, but it has the important merit of minimising the incidence of arbitrary and ill-thought-out legislation. It serves to "prevent those inroads upon the law of the land which a despot... might effect by ordinances and decrees... or by sudden resolutions."[5] It also helps to enhance the fixity of the law. Above all, it is perhaps the best guarantee of regularity in the conduct of the affairs of the society, enabling its members to know in advance when the government is planning to

---

3.   F. A. Hayek, *The Constitution of Liberty* (1960), p. 206.
4.   F. H. Hayek, *The Constitution of Liberty* (1960), p. 174.
5.   A. V. Dicey, *The Law of the Constitution*, 10th ed. (1960), p. 407.

interfere with the course of their lives, and to mobilise in opposition.

The laws by which alone men in society are to be governed in their affairs and actions in the sense required by the Rule of Law must, in the third place, be standing, fixed laws, not extemporary or *ad hoc* decrees. And they must be certain and known laws which apply only with respect to the future, and not retrospectively. The necessity for requiring that the law be known and certain is so that the individual will know in advance how he stands in relation to the coercive power of government and the extent it can be used to interfere with the course of his life and activities. There is no Rule of Law if laws are made separately for specific, named persons, or with respect to specific acts or transactions which have already taken place in the past, with the object of invalidating them or otherwise prejudicing the rights of the individuals concerned or making criminal, acts which were not so when they were done or increasing retrospectively the punishment for prohibited acts. "It is this fact that all rules apply equally to all, including those who govern, which makes it improbable that any oppressive rules will be adopted."[6]

The equal subjection of rulers and the ruled alike to the law and the implied prohibition of any exemptions based on official position held is indeed cardinal to the Rule of Law. What it means is that no one should be above the law, the government and its officials included. All acts or omissions by government and its officials must be subject to the same laws as govern the acts or omissions of private persons, and must attract the same consequences, whether they be breach of contract, tort or a criminal offence. For, any exemption allowed to the rulers would enable them to commit breaches of contract, torts, criminal offences etc. with impunity knowing that they are not answerable to the law for their misdeeds, and leaving the injured individual without any remedy.

It is, however, a much-disputed point whether this principle should apply to the Head of State to the fullest extent. In the United States where no immunity from liability or from suit is

6.   F. A. Hayek, *The Constitution of Liberty* (1960), p. 210.

granted to him explicitly by the Constitution, it is argued that any concession of it would amount to placing him above the Constitution and thereby violating the cornerstone of American constitutionalism that the government is one of laws, and not of men. "Under our system of government," said Chief Justice Bartley in granting a *mandamus* against a state governor, "no officer is placed above the restraining authority, which is truly said to be universal in its behests, all paying it homage, the least as feeling its care, and the greatest as not being exempt from its power."[7] These observations, it is argued, should apply with equal, if not greater , force to the president of the United States. The argument was indeed accepted by Chief Justice Marshall when he sustained an application for a *subpoena duces tecum* against President Jefferson. Rejecting the president's contention that he could not be drawn from the discharge of his duties at the seat of government and made to attend the court sitting at Richmond, the chief justice drew a distinction between the president and the king of England, and held that all officers in the United States were subordinate to the law and must obey its mandate. In 1973 an action was allowed against President Nixon personally.[8]

Unlike their American counterpart, the Nigerian and some other Commonwealth Constitutions grant to an incumbent president immunity from court action, both civil and criminal, arrest or imprisonment in pursuance of a court process, and from any court process requiring or compelling his appearance. The immunity prevails only during his period of office. A civil action against the president in his official capacity as well as a civil or criminal action in which he is only a nominal party, is not affected by the immunity.

It seems that the procedural immunity from suit and from court process granted to an incumbent president can be defended. The protection is essentially for the office, not for the individual incumbent as such. It is the majesty and dignity of the nation that is at stake. To drag an incumbent president to court and expose him to the process of examination and

---

7.   State of Ohio v. Salmon P. Chase, Governor, 5 Ohio St. 529.
8.   See *United States v. Nixon* (1973), 41 L.Ed. 2nd 1039.

cross-examination cannot but degrade the office. The interest of the nation in the preservation of the integrity of its highest office should outweigh any objections to the immunity. After all, members of the national assembly are also granted some immunity from legal process for the very same reason that it is necessary for the protection of their office and for the unhindered discharge of its functions.

But it is necessary to emphasise that the protection is against suit and compulsory process. It does not extend to liability. The Constitution does not say that an incumbent president shall, during his tenure of office, be immune from civil and criminal liability for his acts; only that "no civil or criminal proceedings shall be instituted or continued" against him during that period. The institution of proceedings or their continuation is a procedural matter, which presupposes the existence of a cause of action, i.e. an antecedent liability for the violation of a right or criminal prohibition. A president who, before or during his tenure of office, commits a criminal offence, a tort or breach of contract is as fully liable therefore as any other person. The office affords him no immunity from liability for acts done during his tenure any more than it wipes out liability for acts done before. The only effect of the immunity is to suspend enforcement of the liability by civil or criminal proceedings until the time when the office is vacated. Equally any such proceedings already instituted and pending at the time of assumption of office are suspended. But since liability is not affected, the incumbent becomes amenable to civil or criminal action after he ceases to hold office. The Constitution confirms this by providing that the period covered by his tenure of office shall be discounted in calculating the period prescribed by law for instituting civil actions.

The immunity from civil or criminal process has also only a procedural significance. The fact that legal process cannot be issued for the arrest or imprisonment of an incumbent president or to compel his appearance before any tribunal or body does not imply that he is unanswerable for his actions, nor does it take away his competence as a witness. It leaves unaffected his obligation to answer for his acts or omissions and his competence as a witness. Thus, while he cannot be compelled to appear before any tribunal or body, he is not precluded from volunteering to do so. His freedom to volunteer appearance is not taken away by the fact that he cannot waive his immunity from suit or from compulsory process. If the position were that he is unanswerable for his acts or incompetent as a witness, then impeachment before the national assembly for gross misconduct committed in office, and his appearance to defend himself at an impeachment trial, would have been a manifest contradiction. His answerability for his official acts is affirmed not only by the impeachment procedure but also by the fact that he may be sued in his official capacity in civil proceedings.

Had the immunity from suit conferred by the provision extended beyond the time when the office has been vacated, its effect would be the same as an exemption from liability; in other words, if acts done during incumbency are immuned from suit during and after the incumbency, then the immunity ceases to be procedural only and becomes, for all practical purposes, immunity from liability. If, after leaving office as president, a person can never be sued at all for acts done while in office, then, he is as good as exempted from liability for those acts. There is no practical difference between a perpetual immunity from suit and an exemption from liability; in both cases the right to sue is completely and forever destroyed. And the extension of the immunity from suit beyond the time when the office is vacated would have absolutely nothing to justify it. For, after the office is vacated, the only justification for it disappears. The need to protect the majesty and dignity of the nation in its highest office ceases to apply when the office is vacated and the incumbent becomes a private citizen. To continue the immunity after that would amount to a purely arbitrary exemption from the law, and a blatant negation of the Rule of Law.

Factors Limiting the Operation of the Rule of Law

The operation of the Rule of Law is limited by two main practical factors. There is, first, the rise and growth of social and economic legislation of the modern welfare state, which entrusts to the executive wide discretionary power to interfere, untrammelled by judicial control, with the individual as he may think expedient in the implementation of schemes of social improvement or other social welfare programmes, a development once described by Lord Hewart as "the new despotism".[9]

Then there is the conception of the Rule of Law on the part of the courts as being concerned solely with constitutionality or legality, and their role in its application as being limited to testing the constitutionality or legality of government acts in a formal sense, so that if the act is within the formal limits of the power granted by law (the constitution or other law), the court cannot enquire further. The substantive merits of the act, whether it is just or oppressive, or otherwise arbitrary, is, by and large, no concern of the guardians of the law.

This unduly formalistic view of the Rule of Law is only slightly mitigated by the concept of the *purpose* of a statutory power, which views the legality of an administrative act as resting upon its conformance not only with the letters of the law but also with the purpose for which the power is given. Accordingly, if a statutory power, given for one purpose, is used for another, then, although the purpose of the power is not explicitly stated in the grant, its use for a different purpose is illegal just as when the formal limits of the power are exceeded. The concept of the purpose of a statutory power thus enables the court to control administrative acts motivated by bad faith or by extraneous considerations or which are arrived at without regard to relevant factors. The purpose of a power also determines what could reasonably be within its contemplation. It is here that the notion of reasonableness affects legality. If a power is used for a purpose which no one could ever reasonably suppose to be within its object, then its exercise for that purpose is unauthorised and illegal, and is amenable to control by the court.

But this is the farthest the court is prepared to go in controlling the arbitrary use or other abuses of statutory power by the executive. Subject to this, the rule is that the reasonableness or fairness of an administrative act done within

---

9.   Hewart, *The New Despotism* (1929); Hayek, *The Constitution of Liberty* (1960), pp. 234-249.

power is outside the court's concern. It is noteworthy too that the court has evolved no substantive natural justice. The rules of natural justice which it applies are limited to the procedural one that no one should be condemned unheard or be a judge in his own cause. It is thus not concerned with other causes of bias besides self-interest and a denial of a hearing — causes such as perversion or arbitrariness which may not easily be dissipated by anything an aggrieved person may say in his own defence.

The limitation imposed on the Rule of Law by the court's inability to review the merits of administrative acts (except to the extent indicated above) seems indeed to trivialise the concept, for by far the largest number of grievances that the individual has against the administration result not so much from failure to keep within the formal limits of power as from the arbitrary, oppressive or unjust manner of exercising it. By disclaiming concern with such grievances, the courts create the impression that they are abandoning the individual to the administration in a critical area, where the intervention of an impartial and independent arbiter is most needed. A distinguished English judge, Lord Devlin, has been moved by this to lament that "the common law has now...no longer the strength to provide any satisfactory solution to the problem of keeping the executive ... under proper control."[10]

The judicial approach stands indeed in dire need of revitalisation if the Rule of Law is to become or remain a really effective principle of government. Judicial law-making should be openly acknowledged, and its scope purposefully expanded. The Rule of Law cannot be made effective by a rigid, doctrinaire insistence on the so-called declaratory theory of the judicial function, which asserts that, in adjudicating a case before it, the court is simply to act according to law supposed to exist and to be well-known; its role is to be the somewhat mechanical and passive one of merely declaring the law and applying it to the determination of the case; whatever the issue, it is not to exercise any creativity by invoking any ethical notions of a just or wise decision. The doctrinal basis of the

---

10. Patrick Devlin, *Samples of Lawmaking*, 1966, p. 119.

declaratory theory is analytical positivism whose central thesis is the view that only rules forming a logically consistent system, and not any ethical notions of a just or wise result, are to be the sole guide for a judicial decision.

Such a view of the judicial function is utterly out-moded today. The maintenance of the Rule of Law demands of the court a positive role. It demands that they should look beyond the formal letters of the law, and engage themselves in a purposeful effort to try to distil principles of fairness and justice from the moral, ethical and other fundamental values of the society. It is not suggested that expediency or the judge's subjective notions of a right or wrong decision should form the basis of judicial decision. That would itself be a negation of the Rule of Law, which requires that justice be administered according to law, not according to any and every one's notions of what justice requires.

The point being made here is that the law should embody reason and the moral, ethical and other fundamental values of the community, which are an expression of the community's collective sense of right and wrong. They are values which underlie the community, and on the basis of which it is organised. While the letters of the law are and must remain the core of the Rule of Law, their interpretation and application by the court should be informed by reason and by the fundamental values of the community. A narrowly positivist view of the law could only make it sterile, devoid of a proper moral content. And judges are eminently well placed to instil into it the necessary moral content based on the notions of reasonableness, fairness, justice and respect for individual liberty.

From the application of the community's fundamental values in judicial review of administrative action will eventually grow a body of specific rules to enrich the corpus of the law. After all, a considerable part of English law, the so-called rules of equity, was evolved in just this fashion.

Enshrining The Rule of Law Explicitly in the Constitution

The Rule of Law is seldom enshrined in the constitution explicitly by name as a specific doctrine of government, although most of its principles are so enshrined, notably the supremacy of the law of the constitution, constitutional guarantee of basic rights and freedoms, popularly elected legislature and its separation from the executive, procedure for law-making, the separation of judicial power and the independence of the judiciary, judicial review of legislative and executive action, the prohibition of *ex post facto* criminal legislation and the principle of non-discrimination by the state. The new Constitutions of Romania and Bulgaria and Czechoslovakia's Chapter of Fundamental Rights and Freedoms, adopted in 1991 after the collapse of communism in the 1989-90 revolutions, have gone further to enshrine the rule of Law explicitly, thus introducing a new feature hitherto lacking in the constitutions of our modern democracies.

After affirming the doctrine as a fundamental principle of the nation,[11] Romania's new Constitution (1991) goes on to proclaim the country as "a social and democratic state of law in which human dignity, the rights and liberties of citizens, the free development of the human personality, justice and political pluralism represent supreme values and are guaranteed."[12] It further ordains that the law shall provide only for the future,[13] that "citizens are equal before the law,[14] and "no one is above the law."[15] Likewise, Bulgaria's new Constitution (1991) proclaims the country "a law-governed state," and that it is to be "governed only by the Constitution and the laws of the country," enjoining the state to "create conditions conducive to the free development of the individual and the civil society."[16] It also proclaims that "all citizens shall be equal before the law."[17] In equally explicit terms, Czechoslovakia's Charter of Fundamental Rights and Freedoms declares that "state power may be exerted only in the cases and within the limits laid down by law, and in the way laid down by law," that "no person

---

11. Art 8 (2).
12. Art 1 (3).
13. Art 15 (2).
14. Art 16 (1).
15. Art 16 (2).
16. Art 4 (1) and (2); also the preamble.
17. Art 6 (2).

may be compelled to do anything which the law does not impose on him;[18] that "obligations may be imposed only on the basis of a law and within its limits, and only on condition that basic rights and freedoms are preserved;"[19] and that "legal restrictions on basic rights and freedoms must apply equally to all cases which meet the conditions specified."[20]

---

18. Art 2 (2) and (3).
19. Art 4 (1).
20. Art 4 (3).

Chapter 11

An Ordered, Stable Society

A first force which works against constitutional government is war. In times of war or rumours of war, the government claims full freedom of action; it does not want to be bound by limitations .... Obviously government on these lines is opposed to the limited government which we call constitutional.

— Sir Kenneth Wheare

Frequent Incidence of Emergency Situations and its Dangers for Democratisation

Frequent, prolonged breakdowns in public order and public safety and the situation of emergency to which they give rise are, together with electoral malpractices (discussed in chapter 3), perhaps the greatest dangers and challenges facing democracy and democratisation in Third World countries. They constitute a real danger to liberty and democracy in the modern world partly because of the extraordinary powers exercisable by government while the situation lasts but even more so because of the frequency of their occurrence, the tendency to abuse the emergency powers, and the probable emergence of a dictatorship in the course of the emergency situation.

The emergent countries are having indeed to live under an almost continual state of emergency. Their societies are not only plural, but are often riven by deep-seated division between the component groups. Tribal or racial division has been deepened still further by the action of unscrupulous politicians who,in order to achieve political ends,have exploited group sentiments, creating thereby an atmosphere charged with tension and unrest. The process of transforming a primitive, traditional society into a modern one has also imposed its own strain. The society is in a state of flux, and change, especially rapid change such as these countries are undergoing, creates tension. The forces of change, urbanisation, industrialisation, vast increases in literacy and education all have to be reconciled within the society, and they inevitably operate to undermine the traditional bases of authority and established values. On the other hand, the new political organisation, the modern state, is as yet not sufficiently rooted or legitimised to provide the alternative base of authority needed to contain the pressure of these forces, and the struggle between the various groups for the right to administer the state has weakened it still further. All these factors react upon one another to make the society of the new nations into a kind of cauldron,which continually gives off vapours of conflict and instability. Now and again the uneasy equilibrium breaks down, giving way to violence. This violence has generally taken one of three forms, or a combination of all three, viz. traditional tribal feuds and warfare, riots and revolts against constituted authority including revolts by the military, and civil war.[1] Thus Nigeria, Guyana, Morocco, Iraq, Somalia, Uganda, the Congo, Ruanda, Burundi, the Sudan, Cyprus, India, Pakistan, Ceylon, Burma, Laos and South Vietnam have all experienced the disruption of tribal, racial or communal violence, while revolutionary violence, insurrection, and guerrilla warfare have become almost a way of life in most parts of Latin America and in many parts of the Middle East and Asia. There has been a steady progression in the incidence of organised violence in the new states, and the statistics indicate that there were 34 incidents in 1958, 36 in 1959, 42 in 1960, 43 in 1961, 47 in 1962, 59 in 1963, 56 in 1964 and 57 in 1965.[2]

Indeed, in many parts of Latin America, the Middle East, Asia and Africa, emergencies of one kind or another have tended to become the normal order of things, thus replacing constitutional democracy with emergency administration as the normal system of rule. In Africa all the countries at one time under authoritarian colonial rule came to independence under some form of constitutional democracy. But most of them have

---

1.   Burke, *Africa's Quest for Order* (1965), pp 14-16.
2.   U.S. Dept of Defence, quoted in Huntington, *Political Order in Changing Societies*, p. 4.

since, following a military *coup d'etat*, passed into military despotism (the majority of them more than once), which is still in control or has terminated itself and returned the country to democratic rule again. Even those countries which had not been under colonial rule have not escaped the scourge.

The tally as at August 1992 is 30 countries out of 53 and 74 coups (exclusive of open and publicly acknowledged attempted coups), viz Algeria (2 coups), Benin (5), Burkina Faso (6), Burundi (3), Central African Republic (3), Chad (1), Comoros (3), Congo (1), Egypt (2), Equatorial Guinea (1), Ethiopia (2), Ghana (5), Guinea (1), Guinea Bissau (1), Lesotho (2), Liberia (1), Libya (1) Madagascar (2), Mali (4), Mauritania (5), Niger (1), Nigeria (5), Rwanda (1), Seychelles (1), Sierra Leone (3), Somalia (1), Sudan (4), Togo (1), Uganda (5) and Zaire (1).

Foreign wars are comparatively infrequent, and may become more so in an age of weapons of mass destruction and long-range means of delivering them. The twentieth century has of course experienced two world wars and a few localised wars, localised, that is, in terms of the areas and the countries involved. By far more frequent are civil wars, usually the product of the act of a section of a state seeking to establish itself as a separate independent state by secession; sometimes, however, a civil war arises from a struggle between two groups for the control of the state, as in Angola, Somalia and Chad. In the last 25 years or so, there have been wars of secession in Zaire (formerly the Congo), Nigeria, Ethiopia, Sudan,Pakistan and Yugoslavia.

Secession invariably leads to the establishment of a secessionist government, and to a military confrontation to crush the rebellion. Quite often the secession is crushed, but only after a period (which may extend over some years) of illegal government in the secessionist area, and of war. Now constitutionalism presupposes legality; it is government according to law, but a rebel government is essentially a government in opposition to law, and is therefore anti-constitutionalism. And war, too, is antithetical to constitutionalism. "A first force which works against constitutional government," writes Wheare, "is war. In times of war or rumours of war, the government claims full freedom of action; it does not want to be bound by limitations ... obviously government on these lines is opposed to the limited government which we call constitutional."[3]

Extraordinary Power in Situations of Emergency Formally Declared Under the Constitution not in itself Altogether Subversive of Liberty and Democracy

It is usual in modern constitutions to confer extraordinary powers, including power to curtail guaranteed rights and suspend democratic processes, in situations of emergency formally declared in accordance with the provisions of the constitution. Even the most constitutional of constitutional regimes finds it necessary to arm itself, under the constitution, with special powers to deal with an emergency. In all countries,it is recognised that constitutionalism has to be limited by the exigencies of an emergency, since an emergency implies a state of danger to public order and public safety, which cannot adequately be met within the framework of governmental restraints imposed by the constitution. There is a good justification for this. The preservation of the state and society is an imperative necessity, which should override the need for limited government. In such situations, it is said "men care more for order than for liberty."[4] Accordingly, all constitutions which impose limitations upon government authorise the limitations to be over-stepped in times of emergency. But emergency power can be accommodated with constitutionalism if emergency situations are conceived of as an ephemeral aberration occurring once in a long while, and provided that the extraordinary powers for dealing with them are not so sweeping as to destroy or suspend the restraints of constitutional government completely.

It follows, therefore, that constitutionalism and the Rule of Law can no more forbid the grant and exercise of extraordinary power in situations of declared emergency than they can

---

3.   K. C. Wheare, *Modern Constitutions* (1966), p. 138, Carl Friedrich, *Constitutional Government and Democracy,* revised ed., pp. 12-13.
4.   C. H. McIlwain, *Constitutionalism and the Changing World* (1939) p. 276.

prevent their occurrence. The most they can do is to define in explicit terms in the constitution the kinds of situation to constitute an emergency and which must actually exist in an objective, factual sense, and either to vest in the legislative assembly the power to declare an emergency or to require a declaration made initially by the executive to be laid before it for its approval cr disaffirmation within a prescribed time. Thus, the 1960 Constitution of Cyprus authorised the proclamation of an emergency only "in the case of war or other public danger threatening the life of the Republic."[5] In line with the Constitution of the Fifth French Republic 1958, the constitutions of the ex-French African countries also define an emergency to be "a clear and present danger" threatening the institutions or independence of the nation, the integrity of its territory, or the carrying out of its international undertakings or other situation "when the regular functioning of the governmental authorities is interrupted." The danger or threat must be an imminent one, and the event giving rise to it must involve a considerable section of the public, since only so can public order or public safety be said to be in jeopardy.

The definition in the 1979/89 Constitution of Nigeria is perhaps the most comprehensive.[6] A state of emergency exists only when the country is at war or in imminent danger of invasion or involvement in a war, or there is —

(a) actual breakdown of public order and public safety in the country or any part thereof to such extent as to require extraordinary measures to restore peace and security;

(b) a clear and present danger of an actual breakdown of public order and public safety requiring extraordinary measures to avert it;

(c) an occurrence of imminent danger, or the occurrence of any disaster or natural calamity, affecting the community or a section of the community; and

(d) any other public danger which clearly constitutes a threat to the existence of the country.

---

5. Art. 183. 1.
6. SS. 41 and 265, 1979; SS. 43 and 317, 1989.

A provision, such as that contained in the Constitutions of Nigeria 1960 and 1963,[7] that an emergency shall be any period during which there was in force a resolution by parliament declaring that a state of emergency exists or that democratic institutions in the country are threatened by subversion merely sacrifices the nation and the liberty of the individual to the whims and caprices of parliament.

The usual practice of course is to vest in the executive (i.e. President or Head of Government) the power to declare an emergency but subject to the safeguards as in the 1979/89 Constitution of Nigeria, that the declaration shall cease to have effect if within 2 days when the National Assembly is in session, or within 10 days when it is not in session, after the publication of the declaration there is no resolution supported by two-thirds majority of all members of each House of the National Assembly approving it. In any event, the maximum period during which a declaration shall be in force is 6 months unless before the expiration of the period, the National Assembly shall, by resolution passed in like manner, resolve that it shall remain in force from time to time for successive periods of 6 months at a time. The only safeguard in the Constitution of the Fifth French Republic and those of the ex-French African countries is the varying requirement to consult certain authorities such as the president of the National Assembly and of the Constitutional Council, and the requirement that the National Assembly shall meet automatically by right and remain in session throughout the period of the emergency.

But what is the extent to which government may justifiably interfere with liberty and democratic processes during a declared emergency?

Extent of Justifiable Interference with Liberty and Democracy During a Declared Emergency

The extent to which declared emergencies may justify interference with liberty and democratic processes depends

---

7.   S. 70 1963 Constitution of Nigeria.

upon the kind of situation giving rise to them, but the interference must be reasonably necessary and justifiable for the purpose of dealing with the situation. War actually involving the territory of a country is perhaps the most serious emergency situation justifying far-reaching interference. The constitution in most countries usually authorises elections to be postponed for successive periods of six months at a time where the term of office of members of the legislature and the executive expires during a war involving the territory of the country making it impracticable to hold elections.

Yet the mere existence of such a war is not by itself alone such a situation of grave and extreme danger to public safety to justify the exercise of extraordinary powers by the executive. Interference with individual rights in time of war without statutory authorisation is justified only if it is necessary in connection with military operations, as where "property taken is imperatively needed in time of war to construct defences for the preservation of a military post at the moment of an impending attack by the enemy, or for food or medicine for a sick and famishing army utterly destitute and without other means of such supplies, or to transport troops, munitions of war or clothing to reinforce or supply an army."[8]

The decision of the U.S. Supreme Court in 1951 in a case arising out of a threatened nation-wide strike in the steel industry also illustrates the extent of permissible interference by the executive unbacked by statutory authorisation.[9] The strike call had occurred at a time of national emergency formally proclaimed by the president because of a full-scale war in Korea in which the United States was involved. On the premise that steel, being an indispensable component of substantially all of the weapons and materials needed for the war, a work stoppage in the steel industry would immediately jeopardise and imperil national defence, and endanger the armed forces fighting in the theatre of war in Korea, the President, without express statutory authorisation, but solely on his own independent authority under the constitution to

8.   *United States v. Russell* 13 Wall (80 U.S.) 623.
9.   *Youngstown Sheet & Tube Co v. Sawyer*, 343 U.S. 579

preserve the security and safety of the nation, ordered the steel factories to be seized and operated by government agents in order to avert a national catastrophe. But he immediately sent a message to Congress informing it of his action, and inviting it to approve or revoke it as it thought fit. In an action by the owners of the factories challenging the constitutionality of the seizure and praying that they by returned to them, the U.S. Supreme Court, by a majority of six to three, held that, without express statutory authorisation, the President had, in the particular circumstances of the case, no independent power under the constitution to take possession of the steel mills and operate them by his agents, on the ground that seizure of private property requires legislative authorisation by Congress, to which alone the Constitution has entrusted the law-making power in both good and bad times.

It rejected the argument of the President based on his authority as Commander-in-Chief, saying that "even though 'theatre of war' be an expanding concept, we cannot with faithfulness to our constitutional system hold that the Commander-in-Chief of the Armed Forces has the ultimate power as such to take possession of private property in order to keep labour dispute from stopping production."[10] "No doctrine that the court would promulgate," said Mr. Justice Jackson in a separate concurring judgment, "would seem to me more sinister and alarming than that a president ... can vastly enlarge his mastery over the internal affairs of the country by his own commitment of the Nation's armed forces to some foreign venture. The constitution did not contemplate that the title Commander-in-Chief of the Army and Navy will constitute him also Commander-in-Chief of the country, its industries and its inhabitants."[11]

How much power the executive can, without statutory authorisation, assume over individual rights during a war was again in issue in the series of cases involving Japanese living on the west coast of the United States during the second world war. The United States had gone to war against Japan on 8

10. ibid at p. 587 per Justice Black delivering the opinion of the court.
11. At p. 642-4.

December 1941, following the Japanese attack on Pearl Harbour the previous day. The existence of a state of belligerence between the two countries and the likelihood of a further Japanese attack created a necessity for safeguarding the west coast. Espionage and sabotage were particularly feared, a danger which was aggravated by the presence on the west coast of some 112,000 persons of Japanese origin of whom about 70,000 were American citizens by birth. The protective measures which the military authorities, with the approval of the executive and the legislature, instituted to combat the danger were, first, to impose a night curfew on all Japanese on the west coast, and eventually, when a curfew was thought inadequate, to have them segregated at various so-called assembly or relocation centres, which they were not to leave without military permission. These centres were a kind of concentration camp. Neither the curfew nor the segregation order differentiated between various classes of Japanese; both citizens and aliens, the loyal and the disloyal were alike incarcerated. Unquestionably these orders were an invasion of the constitutional rights of the Japanese Americans, and the question was whether this was legally justified by the danger against which it was meant to be a protection. The supreme court sustained the validity of the curfew order on the ground that it was necessary "to meet the threat of sabotage and espionage which would substantially affect the war effort and might reasonably be expected to aid a threatened enemy invasion."[12] For the same reason, too, the court upheld the validity of the segregation order.[13]

Although the decisions were based upon the war power expressly vested in the president by the constitution, the premise was clearly the doctrine that the "state must have every facility and the widest latitude in defending itself against destruction."[14] While affirming the inviolability of the individual's civil liberties,the court nevertheless conceded that

12. *Hirabayashi v. United States* and *Yasui v. United States* (1943) 320 U.S. 81 and 115.
13. *Korematsu v. United States*, 323 U.S. 214.
14. Eugene Rostow, "The Japanese American Cases — a Disaster," 54 Yale L.J. (1945) 489-505.

"pressing public necessity may sometimes justify the existence of such restrictions" on them.[15] The decisions in these cases have provoked much criticism,[16] particularly as regards the segregation order, which could hardly have been warranted by the exigency of the occasion. The curfew alone, it has been argued, would have met the danger adequately, especially in view of the fact that the danger of further attack seemed to have receded in the interval of five months between Pearl Harbour and the proclamation of the orders. And even if the segregation order was considered really necessary, an effort should have been made to separate the loyal from the disloyal Japanese,and to confine the order to the latter.[17] It seemed that the action of the military authorities was dictated more by the pressure of racial prejudice exerted by certain groups on the west coast. However that may be,the cases do give recognition to the doctrine of necessity as a legal justification for action otherwise contrary to the express provisions of the constitution, but which is necessary to save the nation from destruction.

The right of the individual not to be deprived of his liberty or life in pursuance of the judgment of a military court is more jealously guarded. The U.S. Supreme Court has rejected the argument that in time of war state necessity justifies the assumption by a military commander of absolute power to suspend all civil rights and their remedies, and to subject civilians as well as soldiers to the rule of his will. In pursuance of this alleged power, one Milligan had been tried, convicted and sentenced to death by a military commission, with the approval of the president, for alleged conspiracy against the government in giving aid and comfort to the rebels during the American civil war while in the loyal state of Indiana, whose citizen and resident he had been for twenty years. The court

---

15. *Korematsu v. United States*, 323 U.S. 214 at p. 216 — per Justice Black delivering the opinion of the court.
16. Rostow, op. cit; Nanette Dembitz, "Racial Discrimination and the Military Judgment: The Supreme Court's Korematsu and Endo Decisions," 45 Columbia L.R. 175 (1945).
17. In *ex parte Endo* (1944) 323 U.S. 283, the Supreme Court held that a loyal Japanese was entitled to be released unconditionally from a relocation centre.

held unanimously that the trial, conviction and sentence were illegal as being unauthorised by the constitution and the laws. The majority rested its decision on the ground that trial of civilians by a military court cannot be authorised,whether by the president or congress, except when, as a result of military operations, the ordinary courts have ceased to function or can no longer function. But so long as they continue to function, then, notwithstanding the existence of war, the independent and impartial administration of the law by them with the assistance of an impartial jury cannot be suspended or superseded, not even by the authority of an act of congress. The court observed:

> "Martial law cannot arise from a threatened invasion. The necessity must be actual and present; the invasion real, such as effectually closes the courts and deposes the civil administration... if, in foreign invasion or civil war,the courts are actually closed, and it is impossible to administer criminal justice according to law then, on the theatre of actual military operations where war really prevails, there is a necessity to furnish a substitute for the civil authority, thus overthrown, to preserve the safety of the army and society, and as no power is left but the military, it is allowed to govern by martial rule until the laws can have their free course. As necessity creates the rule, so it limits its duration; for if this government is continued after the courts are reinstated, it is a gross usurpation of power. Martial law can never exist where the courts are open, and in the proper and unobstructed exercise of their jurisdiction."[18]

The implication of the view taken by the majority is that since congress could not have authorised the trial of Milligan by the military tribunal, it could not indemnify the tribunal's members from the legal consequences of the illegal trial. A minority of the court took the view that only the power of the president to declare martial law was limited in the way suggested. As far as Congress was concerned, however, it was, in the view of the minority, competent,by virtue of its power to provide for the government of the national forces,to declare war and to provide for its prosecution, to authorise martial law in districts where the threat of invasion was such as to justify it. The fact that the ordinary courts are open might have been sufficient reason for its not exercising the power, but could not affect its existence.

---

18. *Ex parte Milligan*, 4 Wall 2 at p. 127.

The "open court" rule of the majority was substantially affirmed by the court in1945 in a series of cases arising out of the Second World War.[19] After the surprise Japanese air attack on Pearl Harbor, the governor of Hawaii (the island group in which Pearl Harbor lay), with the approval of the president, placed the territory under martial law and handed over the entire administration to the military authorities. The military government then closed down all the civil courts and established military tribunals in their place. The two appellants in this case were respectively convicted of embezzlement and assault by the military tribunals seven months and two-and-a-half years after the attack on Pearl Harbor, at a time when any threat of further attack or invasion had completely disappeared. The court held that, in view of the fact that the Constitution had the same force and effect in Hawaii as in other parts of the United States, the provision of the territory's organic law authorising the governor, with the approval of the president, to declare martial law "in case of rebellion or invasion or imminent danger thereof,when the public safety requires it" did not include power to supplant civilian laws and courts by military orders and tribunals where conditions were not such as to prevent the enforcement of the laws by the civilian courts; the provision was only intended to authorise the military to act vigorously for the maintenance of an orderly civil government and for the defence of the Territory against actual or threatened rebellion or invasion. The court reiterated what it had said in the earlier case of *ex parte Milligan*[20] that "civil liberty and this kind of martial law cannot endure together; the antagonism is irreconcilable, and, in the conflict, one or the other must perish."[21] It rejected the argument that, however adequate the "open court" rule might have been in 1864, it was distinctly unsuited to modern warfare conditions where all the territories of a warring nation might be in combat zones or imminently threatened by long-range attack even while civil courts were operating. The trials were accordingly declared

---

19.   *Duncan v. Kahanamoku*, 327 U.S. 304.
20.   4 Wall 2 at p. 127.
21.   327 U.S. 304 at p. 324.

illegal as an unjustified interference with the constitutional guarantee of a fair trial. "Those who founded this nation," said Justice Murphy, "knew full well that the arbitrary power of conviction and punishment for pretended offences is the hallmark of despotism. From time immemorial despots have used real or imagined threats to the public welfare as an excuse for needlessly abrogating human rights. That excuse is no less unworthy of our traditions when used in this day of atomic warfare or at a future time when other types of warfare may be devised. There must be some overpowering factor that makes a recognition of those rights incompatible with the public safety before we should consent to their temporary suspension."[22]

The fact that martial law has been validly declared does not therefore by itself confer unlimited power on the executive. It may enable it to do no more than to effect summary arrests and detentions and the forcible entry and searching of private houses. Thus, when a revolutionary group, dissatisfied with the old charter government of the state of Rhode Island, established a new constitution and government, and raised an army which attempted by force to seize possession of the state arsenal, the supreme court held that the legislature of the old government was, in the circumstances, entitled to declare martial law, and to use extraordinary powers of arbitrary arrest and detention and the forcible entry into private houses of persons reasonably believed to be engaged in the insurrection in order to maintain itself and overcome the unlawful and armed opposition.[23] The decision, as the court explained in the subsequent cases[24] did no more than approve the specific action taken in that case, namely forcible entry into the plaintiff's house for the purpose of effecting his arrest. But it did not decide that every lawful declaration of martial law, by the fact of having been lawfully made, authorises any conceivable kind of power. The extent of power it justifies depends upon the gravity of the situation, and in particular upon whether the civil authorities have been incapacitated by military operations.

---

22. ibid at p. 325, 330.
23. *Lurther v. Borden* (1849) 7 How. 1.
24. *Ex parte Milligan*, ibid.

A decision in 1972 of the Pakistan Supreme Court follows upon the same prinoiple. The court held that the martial law declared in March 1959 did not justify the military in assuming complete power to govern by military decrees and ordinances,and that the military regime so established from 1959 to 1971 was illegal with the consequence that all the laws made by that regime were void except to the extent that any of them might be saved under the doctrine of necessity.[25]

Abuse of Emergency Powers Under the Constitution

As earlier stated,emergencies formally declared under the provisions of the constitution constitute a danger to liberty and democracy more because of their frequency and their susceptibility to abuse. The abuse of emergency powers under the constitution is well illustrated by the experience in Nigeria where they were used to suspend constitutional government altogether in Western Nigeria (the emergency area), albeit for a period of six months only. The abuse in this case involved also the power to declare an emergency. (The federal government in Malaysia had also used its emergency power to declare an emergency in Sarawak in 1966 in circumstances similar to those in Western Nigeria in 1962). The events which gave rise to the declaration of an emergency in Western Nigeria in 1962 may be briefly recapitulated. Owing to factional squabbles within the ruling party in Western Nigeria, the Action Group, the regional governor dismissed the Premier,Chief Akintola, and appointed another in his place. Chief Akintola, refusing to accept his dismissal, promptly commenced a court action to determine its validity. Subsequently the House of Assembly met to approve the new government,but the meeting was unable to transact any business, because of violent clashes within the chamber of the house between members of the two factions. From this the Federal Government concluded that it had become impossible to carry on the government of the region,

---

25. *Malik Gbulan Jilami and Alter Gauhar v. The Province of Sind and Others,* Cr. Appeals nos. 19 and K2 of 20 April, 1972.

and so proceeded to declare a state of emergency. It must be noted, first, that the disturbances in the chamber of the House were caused by only ten supporters of Chief Akintola out of a house of 117, and, secondly, that apart from the event in the House the entire region outside it remained peaceful and unaffected by the rather uncivilised behaviour of the parliamentarians. When the House was cleared and locked up by the police, the members returned to their respective homes, and there was no sign of any attempt or intention to carry the affray outside the chamber. The trouble-makers were apparently satisfied that they had achieved their object, which was to prevent the House from approving the new government.

All that could reasonably be inferred from the inability of the House to transact any business was that the legislative arm of the government had been temporarily incapacitated, but surely the government of the region could have been lawfully carried on by the new executive until the legality of Akintola's dismissal had been determined by the court. Even if it be assumed that the governor acted unlawfully in dismissing him, still it was the act of a competent authority, and Chief Akintola had no justification whatever in taking the law into his own hands by refusing to accept his dismissal. The contention that there were two executives is completely untenable. From the moment of his dismissal, Chief Akintola ceased to be premier and had no right to claim to be so. It was not as if the governor acted entirely without any colour of right in dismissing him. The only question was whether he had properly exercised his lawful power by acting on a declaration of lack of confidence in the premier contained in a letter signed by the majority of the members, instead of on a formal vote on the floor of the House. The irresponsibility of his taking the law into his own hands was amply demonstrated by the decision of the court which confirmed that the governor had acted rightly after all. One would have expected that what the federal government would have done, had it been disinterested, would have been to support the authority of the new premier, pending the determination by the court of Chief Akintola's action. It cannot be seriously doubted that the declaration of a state of emergency upon the strength of the situation prevailing in Western Nigeria at the time was ill-motivated, and that it was made for a purpose other than that envisaged by the Constitution.

The next question concerns the manner in which the emergency powers were used. In pursuance of the power granted to it to legislate outside its normal sphere of competence for 'the purpose of maintaining or securing peace, order and good government during any period of emergency,' Parliament enacted the Emergency Power Act, 1961, authorising the President in Council to make 'such regulations as appear to him to be necessary or expedient for the purpose of maintaining or securing peace, order and good government in Nigeria or any part thereof.' It is almost unprecedented in the established constitutional orders,even in time of war, for the legislature to delegate the full amplitude of its power to the executive. For it was the entirety of its emergency powers that parliament passed on to the executive, in effect allowing itself to be supplanted by the executive for this purpose. A delegation of powers in these terms not only destroyed the already attenuated foundation of the separation of powers under the constitution but also impaired that aspect of the Rule of Law which requires that executive acts be justified by law and that the executive should not be the body to confer the necessary legal authority upon itself. Indeed the Emergency Power Act, 1961, went even further in relegating the legislature. It also empowered the President in Council to amend, suspend, or modify a law enacted by any legislature in the country; furthermore any regulation made by him had effect notwithstanding anything inconsistent therewith contained in any law; and any provision of a law which is inconsistent with any such regulation ... shall ... to the extent of such inconsistency have no effect so long as such regulation ... remains in force. It is true that a regulation made under the Act became void if it was not approved by the resolution of both Houses of Parliament within four months, and that both Houses could at any time by resolution amend or revoke it. Yet so long as a regulation remained unrevoked, Parliament could not legislate inconsistently with it, except by first repealing or amending the Emergency Power Act itself.

Even more destructive of constitutional government was the manner in which the unlimited powers thus delegated to the executive were used in Western Nigeria (the emergency area). Altogether twelve regulations were made by the President in Council under the Act. Of these the most far-reaching was the Emergency Power (General) Regulations, 1962. Its provisions proceeded upon the view that the government of Western Nigeria could no longer be carried on by the representative political institutions established by the constitution of the region, a view which, as already submitted, is untenable, and appeared to have been motivated by a desire to oust the Action Group from its power base as part of a grand plan to liquidate it as a political force in the country. The regulation provided for the appointment in Western Nigeria of an administrator who was to administer the government of the region. As the government of the region, the administrator was given full executive and legislative powers. He was empowered to legislate by means of orders for the peace, order, and good government of Western Nigeria; and when so legislating, he could amend any law in force in the region or suspend its operation, whether it be an Act of Parliament, a law of the regional legislature or an ordinance. The regional governor, premier, ministers, president, speaker and members of the regional Houses were forbidden to exercise their functions except to such extent and during such period (if any) as the administrator might direct. The administrator was responsible only to the Prime Minister for the exercise of his functions.

Was the suspension of the government of Western Nigeria warranted by the constitution either in letter or in spirit? The most that could be said of the power given to parliament to "make such laws for Nigeria or any part thereof with respect to matters not included in the Legislative Lists as may appear to parliament to be necessary or expedient for the purpose of maintaining or securing peace,order and good government during any period of emergency is that it brought within the sphere of concurrent powers matters ordinarily exclusive to the region. If that be the case,does the notion of concurrent powers in a federal set-up enable the unit of government with the overriding power to suspend the other completely? To admit that would be to turn concurrent power into exclusive power, and so abolish the distinction between them. Even the so-called doctrine of "covering the field" according to which the federal legislature can, by dealing completely and exhaustively with a particular matter, exclude the regional legislatures therefrom is limited to the specific subject-matter of a particular legislation. It does not enable the federal legislature to make a general legislative declaration excluding the regions completely from the concurrent field of power. Such a declaration would be manifestly subversive of the constitution, and, given the extension of the concurrent power to the whole sphere of regional exclusive competence during an emergency, would convert the constitution from a federal to a unitary one, thereby destroying the restraining role of federalism. The doctrine of covering the field is of doubtful validity, anyway. Although under the Constitution of Nigeria a federal law on a concurrent matter prevailed over an inconsistent regional law, one could not invoke the doctrine of inconsistency unless there was actual legislation in being. Only then could a comparison be made to see if one conflicted with the other. It is even doubtful whether the emergency power of parliament extended to the whole sphere of regional exclusive competence. Surely, there is a difference, however difficult it may be to define, between a power to legislate to maintain or secure peace, order and good government, and a power to legislate generally for peace, order and good government. The former assumes the existence of peace, order and good government, which only needs to be maintained or secured. It is a supplemental power. In other words, parliament could only lawfully have assumed a supplementary power in support of the government of Western Nigeria to maintain or secure peace, order and good government during the emergency. And assuming that parliament had the power which it purported to exercise, suspension of the government of Western Nigeria could only be said to be necessary or expedient on the erroneous view that the government had been rendered inoperative.

It should also be added that all the leading politicians in the region were either detained or had their movements or residence restricted,and public meetings and processions were banned.

Extraordinary Powers Under the Doctrine of State Necessity

The extent to which liberty and democracy may be curtailed or even abrogated is wider under the doctrine of state necessity, which has witnessed the most remarkable applications in recent years. In private law necessity is well-established as a legal defence for an action which would have been otherwise unlawful and actionable. Thus, where life is in danger, the necessity of saving it may justify action which will ordinarily be unlawful, such as throwing cargo overboard from a sinking boat in order to save the lives of the passengers and crew, or a doctor performing an abortion (where abortion is an offence) to save the life of a pregnant woman. A situation creating a necessity to take action to save life is the clearest example of the application of the doctrine in private law, but it does not follow that it is limited to such cases. It is also applicable where it is necessary to avert danger to property or physical injury or to escape from unlawful imprisonment or confinement. The doctrine is also recognised in public law as a justification for an action otherwise unlawful but necessary to preserve the life of the state or society.

On the face of it, the doctrine would appear to be inconsistent with the law. Glanville Williams has put the point cogently:

> What it comes to is this, that the defence of necessity involves a choice of the lesser evil. It requires a judgment of value, an adjudication between competing "goods" and a sacrifice of one to the other. The language of necessity disguises the selection of values that is really involved. If this is so, is there any legal basis for the defence? The law itself enshrines values, and the judge is sworn to uphold the law. By what right can the judge declare some value, not expressed in the law, to be superior to the law? How, in particular, can he do this in the face of the words of a statute? Does not the defence of necessity wear the appearance of an appeal to the judge against the law?[26]

The inconsistency is, however, only apparent, for the doctrine does not operate from outside the law, but is implied

---

26. "The Defence of Necessity," *Current Legal Problems*, 1953, 6, p. 216.

in it as an integral part thereof. "The Law," said Glanville Williams in answer to the questions he posed, '... includes the doctrine of necessity; the defence of necessity is an implied exception to particular rules of law." Furthermore, when applicable, it operates parallel to the express letters of the law; it does not abrogate express law, but can only qualify it for the purpose of averting the threatening danger.

The rationale of the doctrine is that, in an emergency imperilling public order or public security, the safety of the people is the supreme law — *salus populi est suprema lex*. By this supreme law of necessity, therefore, the organs of the state are entitled, in the face of such an emergency, to take all appropriate actions, even in deviation from the express provisions of the constitution, in order to safeguard law and order and preserve the state and society. Its application is, however, subject to the following conditions:

(i)   an imperative necessity arising from an imminent and extreme danger affecting the safety of the state or society;

(ii)   action taken to meet the exigency must be inevitable in the sense of being the only remedy;

(iii) it must be proportionate to the necessity, i.e., it must be reasonably warranted by the danger which it was intended to avert;

(iv)   it must be of a temporary character limited to the duration of the exceptional circumstances;

(v)   the temporary incapacitation of the authority (if any) which normally has the competence to act.

So much appears to be settled, but the difficulty is to determine what type of action can justifiably be done in pursuance of the doctrine. In English law, it has been stated, the executive, acting out of "an actual and immediate necessity arising in the face of the enemy and in circumstances where the rule *salus populi suprema* was clearly applicable," may take possession of a citizen's property for the defence of the realm without payment of compensation, unless by statute compensation is to be paid.[27] The doctrine operates therefore

---

27. *Att-Gen v. De Keyser's Royal Hotel* [1920] A.C. 508 — per Lord Moulton.

as an implied qualification upon individual human rights. Rights cannot be enjoyed absolutely, even where they are guaranteed in the constitution in absolute terms, since it is inconceivable that any court will enforce them at the expense of public safety. In an emergency, such as war, endangering the safety of the state and society, the necessity for safe-guarding the nation against destruction will justify actions which otherwise derogate from the guaranteed rights, and this must be so notwithstanding that the guarantee is not expressly made subject to such protective measures.

Is the doctrine, then, confined to cases of invasion of individual rights, or does it enable the executive to exercise legislative power during an emergency when the legislative authority is temporarily put out of action or a non-sovereign legislature to exceed the limits of its powers?

With regard to the English common law, the view has been expressed by Chitty that the King as head of state "is the first person in the nation... being superior to both Houses in dignity and the only branch of the Legislature that has a separate existence, and is capable of performing any act at a time when the parliament is not in being."[28] This view was expressed in 1820, but does it still represent the position today in English law? Glanville Williams thinks not. "The prerogative of necessity," he writes, "is now in disuse, because it is covered by and therefore superseded by statutes."[29] Elaborating on this he says:

> "The King cannot acquire new prerogatives by reference to state necessity ... However necessary the behaviour, the Government must today invoke the aid of Parliament if the behaviour involves breaking the letter of the law. It can act under the doctrine of necessity only to the same extent as a private person. Parliament's alleged failure to give adequate powers cannot be an excuse for conduct, because the necessity of powers claimed is for Parliament to decide, not for the judges over the head of Parliament. The question is not whether it is necessary to do the act but whether it is necessary to do it without the sanction of Parliament."[30]

On the other hand, in Greece, Italy, France and Germany, it

---

28. *Prerogatives of the Crown*, 1820 ed., p. 68.
29. ibid p. 231.
30. . p. 229.

seems to be generally accepted among writers on constitutional law that the doctrine may justify the exercise of legislative power by the executive. "Jurisprudence," declares a French authority, "was thus led to appreciate that there was a hierarchy in the juridical rules and that the executive authorities were behaving more in conformity with the spirit of constitutional institutions by a temporary encroachment on legislative prerogatives than by limiting themselves to a narrow conventionality or by remaining inactive when such inactivity imperils public order."[31] In Greece the courts have in many cases since 1945 upheld the exercise by the executive of legislative power in times of emergency by reference to the doctrine.

The danger is that the doctrine of civil or state necessity appears to be even more susceptible to abuse than emergency powers under the express provisions of the constitution. For it requires no formal declaration of an emergency,and,as will appear from the Pakistani and Cypriot cases discussed below, it may justify the assumption of powers going beyond those authorised by the constitution during an emergency. It has thus been described as the "plea for every infringement of human freedom. It is the argument of tyrants."[32]

As has been observed, the doctrine has had the most remarkable application recently in four of the emergent states, Pakistan, Cyprus, Nigeria and Rhodesia. The cases are extremely illuminating on the point and deserve therefore a somewhat detailed consideration. Only its application in Pakistan and Cyprus will however be here considered.

(i) Application of Doctrine in Pakistan, 1955

Before 1947 what is now Pakistan was part of India. It was separated from the latter and erected into a separate state under an arrangement which formed the basis for the grant of independence of the two countries. Shortly before independence

31. Quoted in *Att-Gen of the Republic v. Mustafa Ibrahim and Others* (1964), Cyprus Law Reports, 195 at p. 272 – per Josephides J.
32. Pitt, Speech in the House of Commons, Nov. 18, 1783, quoted in Glanvile Williams, op. cit. p. 223.

in 1947, the Viceroy of India,acting under directives from the·
British Government, issued an executive order setting up
separate constituent assemblies for India and Pakistan. By the
Indian Independence Act, which came into force on August 15,
1947, it was provided that the legislative powers of the two
countries shall in the first instance be exercised by their
respective constituent assemblies both generally and in
particular for the purpose of enacting a constitution. Until a
constitution was so enacted by the assembly the government of
each country was to be conducted under the existing
constitution contained in the Government of India Act, 1935, as
amended by the Independence Act; and the governor-general
for each country was to adapt the 1935 Act to bring it into
conformity with the new independent status of the country.
From the date of the Independence Act,the two constituent
assemblies immediately took in hand the task of providing a
constitution for their respective countries, but after seven long
years the Pakistani Assembly was nowhere near accomplishing
its task. Representations were made to the governor-general by
the various representative bodies in the country that the
assembly had turned itself into a permanent legislature and
had thereby become unrepresentative of the people. What was
more,conceiving itself as possessing the sovereign power of the
state on behalf of the people of Pakistan, the assembly in the
course of its seven years existence passed some forty-four
constitutional laws, which it put into force without submitting
them for the governor-general's assent as the Indian
Independence Act clearly required. (Ordinary enactments were
duly submitted for the governor-general's assent). These
purported enactments were thus clearly invalid and were
declared so by the Pakistani Federal Court.[33]

The governor-general then dissolved the assembly, basing his
action on the ground that it had proved itself incapable of
accomplishing the task set for it by the Independence Act; that
it had become unrepresentative and had lost the confidence of
the people, as the resolutions of the various representative

33. *Federation of Pakistan v. Khan* (1955), reported in Jennings, *Constitutional Problems in Pakistan,* 1957, p. 77.

bodies in the country made clear; and that it had become an illegal legislature by purporting to exclude the governor-general from the process of law-making. After dissolving the assembly, the governor-general issued an ordinance declaring a state of emergency and purporting, by virtue of his emergency powers under the Government of India Act, 1935, to validate with retrospective effect most of the void constitutional enactments of the dissolved assembly. The validation of these enactments so far as it purported to be based upon the governor-general's emergency powers under the 1935 Act was pronounced invalid by the court as going beyond the provisions of the Act.[34] "Under the Constitutional Acts," declared Chief Justice Muhammad Munir in the leading judgment, "the governor-general is possessed of no more powers than those that are given to him by those Acts. One of these powers is to promulgate Ordinances in cases of emergency, but the limits within which and the checks subject to which he can exercise that power are clearly laid down in section 42 itself... Any legislative provision that relates to a constitutional matter is solely within the powers of the Constituent Assembly and the governor-general is under the Constitution Acts precluded from exercising those powers."[35]

Thereafter the governor-general summoned a new Constituent Assembly for the purpose of making provision as to the constitution for Pakistan. He next proceeded by proclamation to re-validate the enactments which the court had earlier declared he had no power to validate. But whereas the earlier attempt at validation was based upon the governor-general's emergency powers under the 1935 Act, the basis of the new proclamation was the doctrine of state necessity. It was stated that the invalidation of the enactments having rendered unlawful all acts done thereunder, executive, administrative and judicial, the constitutional and administrative machinery had broken down, thereby threatening the state with imminent collapse; the validation of the enactments

---

34. *Usif Patel and Two Others v. The Crown* (1955), reported in Jennings, op. cit. p. 241.
35. ibid, pp. 249-50

was therefore necessary in order to preserve the state and society and maintain the *status quo* until the new constituent assembly had met and enacted the necessary validating laws. The proclamation was made subject to the opinion of the federal court. The governor-general now asked for the court's opinion whether, there being no legislature in existence competent to validate the void constitutional enactments of the dissolved assembly, "there is any provision in the constitution or *any rule of law* applicable to the situation by which the governor-general can by order or otherwise declare that all orders made, decisions taken, and other acts done under those laws shall be valid and enforceable, and those laws ... shall be treated as part of the law of the land until the question of their validation is determined by the new constituent convention."[36]

Among the questions referred for the court's opinion was whether the assembly had been validly dissolved. For if it had not, then the whole premise for the exercise of the power of validation claimed by the governor-general would not arise. It would suffice to say simply that the court unanimously accepted that under the circumstances the governor-general had power to dissolve the assembly and that the power had been validly exercised. Upon the crucial question concerning the governor-general's power to validate by proclamation the void constitutional enactments, the court was sharply divided, three for and two against. In the leading judgment delivered by Chief Justice Muhammad Munir, who went into a far-ranging examination of the doctrine of civil or state necessity, the majority affirmed the doctrine to be "implicit in the constitution of every civilised community."[37] On the premise stated in the Special Reference, namely that in consequence of the dissolution of the assembly and the invalidation of all the constitutional laws enacted by it during a period of seven years, the constitutional and administrative machinery of the state had broken down, so that the state itself stood in imminent

---

36. *The Special Reference by the Governor-General of Pakistan*, reported in Jennings op. cit. 259.
37. See *Federation of Pakistan v. Shah* (1955), reported in Jennings, op. cit. pp. 353, 357.

danger of collapse, and since the measures proposed by the governor-general for dealing with the situation were only temporary until the new constituent assembly had met to decide the matter finally, they (the majority) held that the retrospective validation of the laws by the governor-general was legally justified as a temporary measure by the exigency of the situation. In coming to this conclusion they relied upon the statement of the law by Chitty quoted above, but were nevertheless at pains to emphasise that the application of the doctrine in this case in no way implies that during an emergency the head of state steps into the position of the legislature as the sovereign legislative authority. On the contrary, legal sovereignty remains with whatever authority the constitution has invested it, and no transfer of it is or can be effected by the principle of imminent state necessity; all it does is to enable the executive to exercise legislative power temporarily on behalf of the incapacitated legislative authority, in order to save the state or society from ruination, but subject to the ultimate authority of the legislature, when it recovers from its incapacitation, to ratify or annul what the executive had done on its behalf. As Chief Justice Muhammad Munir said, the law of civil necessity "in no way interferes with, or affects, the sovereignty of the legislature."[38] The principle does not justify any claim of power to legislate independently and exclusively of the sovereign authority.

The minority maintained that the common law of civil necessity is confined to cases where in times of war or other national disaster the executive might interfere with private rights, but that it has never been extended to changes in constitutional law; and that so to extend it would be wholly repugnant to the Government of India Act which prescribed the circumstances and the limits within which the governor-general might exercise legislative power. Insofar as Chitty's statement of the law relied upon by the majority implied that the executive could exercise the legislative powers of parliament when that body is not in existence, that relates to "periods when, and to territories where, the power of the king was, in fact, supreme

---

38.   *Federation of Pakistan v. Shah*, Jennings op. cit, p. 357.

and undisputed. The records of these affairs are hardly the kind of scripture which one could reasonably expect to be quoted in a proceeding which is essentially one in the enforcement and maintenance of representative institutions."[39] One admits that the doctrine of necessity may justify executive encroachment upon the legislative field, and one may not quarrel with its application in the Pakistani situation,since what was done involved no separate legislative initiative on the part of the governor-general, but merely a confirmation of legislation already passed by the legislature.

Such, then, was the rather remarkable application which the doctrine has received in the extraordinary situation existing in Pakistan in 1955. With this may be compared the equally extraordinary experience of Cyprus in 1964.

(ii) Application of Doctrine in Cyprus, 1964

The application of the doctrine in Cyprus was a case of the legislature itself exceeding the limits of its powers under the Constitution, but the Cypriot precedent can only be understood against the background of the nature of the society and of the Constitution. The island state of Cyprus, comprising mainly two peoples of different race, nationality, religion and language — Greeks and Turks — is perhaps the most deeply riven of plural societies. So sharply divided and hostile are the two racial groups that relations between them have been marked by a state of extreme tension interspersed with periods of bloody civil conflict. The situation in the Island has been aggravated by the fact that the forces at work there are not confined within its boundaries,for the mother country of each of the two island communities, Greece and Turkey, have also been actively involved, and there has always been present a danger of war between the two countries on account of events in Cyprus. The other party in this tragic situation is Britain which had been administering the Island (from 1878) until its independence in1960. When independence began to be envisaged for the Island the hostility between the two island communities and

---

39. , *The Special Reference Case,* Jennings, op. cit. p. 342 — per Cornelius J.

the involvement of their respective mother countries assumed more menacing proportions, with the Greek majority, supported by the Greek Government, demanding union of the Island with Greece (Enosis) and the Turks pressing for partition. The fate of the Island in the event of the impending British withdrawal became thus an international issue engaging the vital interests of Greece and Turkey, with Britain more or less in the role of arbitrator. Meeting in Zurich and later in London in February 1959, the three countries undertook to guarantee the integrity of Cyprus as a sovereign state on the basis of certain heads of agreement, which were to be incorporated into its independence constitution as basic articles thereof. A joint commission consisting of members from Greece, Turkey and the two island communities was commissioned to draft the Constitution, which was completed in April and initialled in Ankara on July 29, 1960, by the parties' representatives. On August 16, 1960, the Island acceded to independence by virtue of an order-in-council (made under the Cyprus Act, 1960), which gave force of law to the draft constitution. The Constitution gave force of law to the treaty between Cyprus, Greece, Turkey and the United Kingdom whereby the independence, territorial integrity and constitution of the state of Cyprus were guaranteed by the parties, and its union with any other state or partition forbidden.[40] It reserved to each of the guarantor countries the right to intervene should there be an attempt to abrogate or subvert the "state of affairs established by the Basic Articles of the Constitution." The Constitution also gave force of law to the treaty of alliance between Cyprus, Greece and Turkey, providing for the stationing in Cyprus of Greek and Turkish military contingents for the defence of the island republic against any attack or aggression directed against its independence or territorial integrity.[41]

The conflicting interests represented in Cyprus have impressed upon the constitution a complexity and rigidity unparalleled anywhere else in the world. The feature that runs through it is the balancing of almost every conceivable power in

---

40.   Art. 181.
41.   Art 181. Both these treaties were scheduled to the Constitution.

the interest of the Turkish minority. All powers, executive, legislative and judicial are shared between the two communities in a manner that seems to caricature reason. In the same way, all public offices and amenities are to be apportioned on a pre-determined ratio of 7: 3. Commenting,in his usual telling language, upon this unique structure, Professor de Smith observed that "constitutionalism has run riot in harness with communalism."[42] "Two nations," he went on, "dwell together under its shadow in uneasy juxtaposition, unsure whether this precariously poised structure is about to fall crashing about their ears."[43] It did in fact crash between December 1963 and 1964, and it was the situation thus produced that gave rise to the application of the doctrine of civil necessity.

The specific issue concerned the impact of this crash upon the machinery for the administration of justice established by the constitution. The judicial system under the constitution consisted in its most important aspects of a supreme constitutional court composed of three judges, one Greek Cypriot, one Turkish Cypriot and a neutral president;[44] and a high court composed of four judges, two Greek Cypriot, one Turkish Cypriot and a neutral president armed with two votes as a counterpoise to the Greek majority.[45] Between them these two courts exercise the superior judicial authority of the country. There is also power given to establish inferior courts.[46] The high court is to determine the composition of such inferior courts in civil and criminal cases involving persons of different communities, but the court must in any case be of mixed composition with judges drawn from both the Greek and Turkish communities.[47] If only persons from the same community are involved in a case, the court must be composed solely of a judge or judges belonging to that community.[48] These provisions were incorporated into the constitution from

---

42. *The New Commonwealth and Its Constitution* (1964), p. 285.
43. *Ibid* p. 296.
44. Art 133, 1.
45. Art. 153, 1.
46. Art. 152.
47. Art. 153, 3.
48. Art. 159, 1 and 2.

the Zurich agreement, and became therefore in accordance with that agreement basic articles which "cannot, in any way, be amended, whether by way of variation, addition, or repeal."[49] The constitution itself is proclaimed the supreme law of the republic, and "no law or decision of the House of Representatives or any of the Communal Chambers and no act or decision of any organ, authority or person in the republic exercising executive power or any administrative function shall in any way be repugnant to, or inconsistent with, any of the provisions of this constitution."[50]

In July 1963 the neutral president of the Supreme Constitutional Court, a German, resigned; a successor, an Australian, appointed early in December was to assume duty in January 1964. Meanwhile on December 21 trouble flared up between the Greek and Turkish communities, thus making it impossible for the new president of the court to arrive in the country. And in May 1964 the neutral president of the high court, a Canadian, also resigned because of the political situation in the country. It should be mentioned here that the appointment of the president and other judges of the two superior courts is the joint responsibility of the president of the republic who must be a Greek and of the vice-president who must be a Turk. Neither can override the other in the appointment of the neutral presidents, but each has an overriding voice in the appointment of the judges assigned to his own community.[51]

From December 21, 1963, when the troubles started, the Turkish minority immediately organised themselves in armed revolt against the Greek-dominated government. The Turkish military contingent stationed in Cyprus under the provisions of the treaty of alliance moved out of their camp and took up positions outside Nicosia, the capital. The Turks established military control over their own quarter of Nicosia and over certain other parts of the country, to which access was barred to Greek Cypriots. Armed clashes occurred between groups

---

49. Art. 182, 1.
50. Art. 179, 1.
51. Arts 133, 2 and 153 1(2).

from the two communities, resulting in loss of life, damage to property, interruption of communications and a general breakdown of law and order in the areas affected by such clashes. To prevent further clashes while negotiations in international circles were going on to find a political settlement, a United Nations peace-keeping force was sent to the country with the consent of the government. Claiming that the Cyprus Government had lost its legality and had thereby forfeited any right to be recognised as the lawful government, the Turkish vice-president, ministers, members of the house of representatives and civil servants withdrew from participation in the government. Turkish judges of the district courts also refused to attend court except in one or two cases. The non-participation of the Turkish vice-president in the government made it impossible for the vacancy in the presidency of the high court to be filled or for a substitute to be found to the new Australian president of the Supreme Constitutional Court who had not turned up to take up his appointment because of the troubles. The result was that the two courts had been unable to function for some fourteen months, which meant that appeals in both civil and criminal matters could not be heard, and with the impossibility of forming mixed courts, the administration of justice and consequently the protection of the Rule of Law was all but paralysed.

The non-functioning of the Supreme Constitutional Court affected the governmental structure in other respects, since the court is the pivot of the constitutional system in the country. For in it is vested exclusive jurisdiction to interpret the constitution, to adjudicate upon the constitutionality of laws, upon any conflict of power between the organs and institutions of government,[52] and upon any question whether a law or decision of the house of representatives, including a budget, discriminates against either of the two communities.[53] In this latter case, the function of the court is more than that of a judicial tribunal, for it may either confirm or annul the alleged discriminatory law or decision, or return it to the House for

---

52. Arts 139-142, 144, 146, 147.
53. Arts 137 and 138.

reconsideration. Questions (not involving any issue of constitutionality) relating to abuse or excess of their powers by administrative authorities are also exclusively for the court to decide,[54] and it also decides whether a vacant post is to be filled by a Greek or Turk where the public service commission is unable to reach a decision upon the matter.[55]

It was in these circumstances that the house of representatives, sitting with only its Greek Cypriot members, on July 9, 1964, passed a law, the Administration of Justice (Miscellaneous Provisions) Law, to enable justice to continue to be administered pending a political settlement of the controversy. The law established a supreme court composed of the three Greek and the two Turkish judges of the Supreme Constitutional Court and the high court, and vested in it the jurisdiction and powers of those two courts. It also empowered the new court to determine the composition of subordinate courts without the requirement that in mixed cases such courts should contain a Greek and a Turkish judge. Its constitutionality was challenged on the ground that it contravened the basic articles of the constitution regulating the administration of justice and defining the jurisdiction and powers of the courts,which articles are made unalterable by the house of representatives or even at all.[56] A further ground of challenge was that the law had not been promulgated in accordance with the constitution, which required laws made by the house of representatives to be promulgated conjointly by the president and vice-president by publication in the official gazette in both the Greek and Turkish languages.[57] The law had been promulgated by the president alone and was published in the gazette only in Greek.

It was admitted that the law contravened the express provisions of the constitution in all the respects alleged, but it was nevertheless contended to have been validly enacted by virtue of the doctrine of civil necessity. In separate exhaustive

---

54. Art. 146.
55. Art. 25, 3.
56. *Att-Gen of the Republic v. Mustafa Ibrahim and Others* (1964), Cyprus Law Report, p. 195.
57. Arts 3, 1 and 2; 47(e), and 52.

judgments all three judges nominated by the full bench of the court to determine the case, examined the status and applicability of the doctrine in various jurisdictions, English, French, Italian and Greek, and came to the unanimous conclusion that, as in these other jurisdictions, the doctrine should be read into the written constitution of Cyprus as an inarticulate major premise thereof, and that so incorporated it operates to qualify, though not to abolish, the concept of the inviolability of the constitution's supremacy and consequently of the limitations which the constitution imposes upon governmental powers. Upon the question whether the situation existing in the country at the time the law was enacted justified the legislature in exceeding the limits of its power, the court held that the non- participation of the Turks in the government on account of the troubles which had developed between them and the Greek majority, had destroyed the premise upon which the constitutional structure was built, and had thereby created a situation which could not be met within the express provisions of the constitution, but which nevertheless called for action to ensure the continuance of a vital function of the state,namely the administration of justice, without which, law and order was bound sooner or later to break down. The maintenance of law and order at all times is an imperative necessity for the preservation of society and the state. As Justice Triantafyllides puts it:

> "Organs of government set up under a constitution are vested expressly with the competence granted to them by such a constitution, but they have always an implied duty to govern. It would be absurd to accept that if,for one reason or other, an emergency arises, which cannot be met within the express letter of the constitution, then such organs need not take necessary measures in the matter, and that they would be entitled to abdicate their responsibilities and watch helplessly the disintegration of the country or an essential function of the state, such as the administration of justice. Notwithstanding a constitutional deadlock, the State continues to exist and together with it continues to exist the need for proper government. The Government and the Legislature are empowered and bound to see that legislative measures are taken in ensuring proper administration where what has been provided for under the constitution, for the purpose, has ceased to function."[58]

---

58. ibid at p. 227.

To hold otherwise, he maintains,would amount to saying that "a state, and the people, should be allowed to perish for the sake of its constitution."[59]

It was argued that the doctrine was not applicable in the circumstances, since its application presupposes the existence of an emergency, and that since no emergency had been proclaimed in accordance with the provisions of the constitution,it must be assumed that no public danger threatening the life of the state existed such as would justify the legislature exceeding its constitutional powers. The constitution empowers the council of ministers, subject to a veto by the president or vice-president, to issue a proclamation of emergency, "in case of war or other public danger threatening the life of the republic or any part thereof."[60] In the opinion of the court,however, the exercise of power by an organ of government in excess of its ordinary constitutional competence, upon the ground of necessity to save the constitution and the state from destruction, does not depend upon whether a state of emergency has been formally proclaimed. "It would be an abdication of responsibility on the part of this court,"observed Justice Triantafyllides, "to close its eyes to the realities of the situation, because, for any reason,no Proclamation of Emergency has been made under Article 183, and to hold that everything is normal in Cyprus."[61] The court also held that,in any case, the provisions of Article 183 were altogether inadequate to meet the abnormal situation under consideration which had not been foreseen nor provided for by the framers of the constitution. The case therefore illustrates how much more sweeping are the powers that may be exercised by virtue of the doctrine of civil necessity than under the express emergency provisions of the constitution. For although the constitution empowers the council of ministers of legislate by ordinance on matters strictly connected with the state of emergency,[62] neither the proclamation of emergency nor any

---

59. At p. 237.
60. Art. 183, 1. The proclamation must be laid forthwith before the house of representatives which may confirm or reject it. Art. 183, 4 and 5.
61. Ibid, p. 226. See also Justice Josephides at p. 266 on this point.
62. Art. 183, 7(1).

such ordinance can suspend any provisions of the constitution except certain of the articles relating to fundamental rights and liberties.[63]

Granted that the situation created a necessity justifying the legislature in exceeding its powers, the crucial question still remains whether the provisions of the law were reasonably warranted by the necessity. This is an important condition for the application of the doctrine. Since what prevented the Supreme Constitutional Court and the high court from functioning was the vacancy in their presidentships and the impossibility of filling them, was the action called for not one that might enable those courts to function in some form or other, instead of their temporary replacement by a completely new court not contemplated by the constitution? The new Supreme Court, composed, as it was, of the three Greek and the two Turkish judges of the Supreme Constitutional Court and the high court, gave the Greeks a majority. If this was considered a satisfactory solution — and it must be noted again that the new court combined all the powers and jurisdiction of the two courts — then it would have been equally satisfactory to have provided for the appointment to the Supreme Constitutional Court of one additional Cypriot judge, preferably a Turk, since it is the Turks who stand in most need of the court's protection. The Law would then empower the president to make the appointment alone should the Turkish vice-president not be willing to countersign it. With regard to the high court, it would have been enough to empower it to function with its two Greek and one Turkish Judges. The Greek majority in the high court and the absence of the neutral president's neutralising extra vote would make it all the more desirable to appoint as the additional judge to the Supreme Constitutional Court a Turk. It is difficult to resist the inference that perhaps the main operative factor in merging the functions of the two courts in one supreme court was what Justice Vassiliades referred to as the "obstruction, delay and expense in ordinary litigation,"[64] caused by the dichotomy in

---

63. Art. 183, 2.
64. Ibid at p. 206.

the judicial system and the procedure requiring all constitutional questions arising in proceedings before the high court and the inferior courts to be referred to the Supreme Constitutional Court, and Justice Triantafyllides as "the need for maximum efficiency."[65]

Furthermore, the provision of the law empowering the new supreme court to assign a sole judge to try mixed cases was based upon the impossibility of forming mixed courts owing to the non-attendance of Turkish inferior judges. It was conceded, however, that the Turkish inferior judges resumed sitting again in June, so that on July 9 when the law was enacted this particular necessity had been removed. The argument that "it is likely that the same factor or factors which prevented them from attending in the past may at any moment prevent them again from carrying out their judicial duties,"[66] does not seem convincing,much less conclusive. Even if it were genuinely feared that they might absent themselves again in the future, the power of the court to dispense with mixed courts in mixed cases should have been made conditional upon that fear materialising.

In view of all this, one is inclined to question the correctness of the court's decision that the particular provisions of the law were legally justified by necessity. It is true that the law was a temporary measure, and in no way abolished the two superior courts established by the constitution, yet its provisions would appear somewhat disproportionate to the immediate necessity they were intended to meet. It may be conceded that the non-participation of the Turkish vice-president in the government justified promulgation of the law by the Greek president alone, but the justification for the non-publication of the law in the Turkish language is not so easy to accept, namely the absence from duty of Turkish officers in the printing department, who should have done the translation. One shares Justice Vassiliades" worry over this point. It was admitted that thousands of Turkish Cypriots were still to be found in areas controlled by the government, so that it would have been

---

65. At p. 236; also p. 239.
66. At p. 267 – per Justice Josephides.

possible to secure the services of one of them to do the translation. No effort in that direction was made. There was good reason for requiring laws to be published in both languages and stipulating that a law only comes into force on the day it was so published. Accordingly, even if we grant that the enactment of the law was justified by necessity, it should be deemed not to have come into force as far as the Turks were concerned. For (excepting for those of them who could read Greek) how otherwise could they inform themselves of its contents? The view of the court that, if the enactment of the law itself was justified by necessity, its non-publication in Turkish should not be allowed to defeat it seems to confuse validity with the coming into force of the law.

Chapter 12

A Society Infused with the Spirit of Liberty, Democracy, Justice, the Rule of Law and Order

Liberty lies in the hearts of men and women; when it dies there, no constitution, no law, no court can save it; no constitution, no law, no court can even do much to help it.

— Judge Learned Hand.

What the Spirit of Liberty, Democracy, Justice, the Rule of Law and Order Connotes and Requires

Liberty, democracy, justice, the Rule of Law and order are not just concepts or principles that may be secured by prescriptions in a constitution; they are more a matter of the spirit, of the heart, resting not only on the existence of a constitution that enshrines them, but more on attitude, temper, disposition or a moral sense inculcated by habit and by tradition. "What Habit as the basis of moral action is to an individual during the brief term of his existence here, Traditions are to a nation whose life extends over hundreds or thousands of years. In them dwells the moral continuity of its existence."[1]

The spirit of liberty, democracy, justice, the Rule of Law and order connotes and requires an attitude of obedience to and respect for the constitution, a democratic temper, a libertarian temper, an attitude of service and trusteeship and of commitment to the welfare of the people, a sense of civic

---

1. James Bryce, *Modern Democracies*, Vol. 1 (1920), p. 151.

responsibility, and an attitude against abuse of power. These attributes require amplification.

An Attitude of Obedience to and Respect for the Constitution

A constitution cannot be adequately sanctioned by organised force alone. More important is the sanction of a national attitude and tradition that regards the constitution as something inviolable, something so fundamental in the life of the nation that respect for it should be regarded as almost a kind of religion, and any violation of it as a sacrilege. In short, a constitution should enjoy sacrosanctity. It is no blasphemy to say this, since the Constitution of the United States does in fact enjoy something of this status. Among Americans it is worshipped and venerated almost as blindly as a religion. That is part of the explanation for its longevity. It has now endured for more than 200 years, and its endurance in perpetuity seems assured.

Respect for the constitution does mean that it should be treated as above the game of politics, not to be tampered with in order to buttress the political fortunes of the rulers. The use of the constitution as an instrument in the struggle for political power is perhaps one of the saddest reflections on African governments. Its effect has been to rob the constitution of any claim to respect and devotion. "In only three years and seven months of the new executive presidential system" writes a *New Nigerian* editorial, "the Legislative and executive arms have broken virtually every rule in the book."[2] It can indeed be said with truth that Nigeria's Second Republic (1979-83) was killed by the perversion of the relationships and procedures established by the Constitution[3] — by the transgression of constitutional limitations and restraints, and by abuse of power. The relationship between the federal and state governments, the legislature and the executive, the chief executive and his deputy, and between the state Governor and

---

2.   Thurs., 5 May, 1983.
3.   For a detailed account, see Nwabueze, *Nigeria's Second Experiment in Constitutional Democracy* (1985).

the state Police Commissioner was distorted and perverted either by a confrontational and arrogant attitude towards power,or by an inordinate ambition for it, by political indiscipline and intolerance. The arrogance of power on the part of its wielders was simply incredible. The unity of the executive, which is the organising principle of the presidential executive, was desecrated by rivalry between the state Governor and his deputy. The separation of power, on which stood the entire governmental framework, was assailed by mutual usurpations by the legislature and the executive of each other's functions, and by legislative and executive usurpations of, or interferences with, judicial power and the independence of the judiciary, that cornerstone of the rule of law. Other constitutional limitations and restraints upon power were similarly assaulted — the guarantee of fundamental rights, the guarantee of local government by democratically elected councils, the procedure for legislative and executive action, etc.

When the limits of power were not being transgressed, its exercise within those limits was abused for pervert or corrupt ends or for private or political advantage. The process of criminal prosecution, the prerogative of mercy, the procedure for the removal of judges,and the impeachment procedure were abused and perverted for political or personal reasons. The impeachment and removal of the Governor of Kaduna State, Alhaji Balarabe Musa in 1981 were blatant desecration of the Constitution. The entire administration of government,in particular the distribution of government patronages and amenities, was conducted so as to benefit members and supporters of the ruling party against others. The crowning height of all these irregularities, abuses and desecration of all standards of democratic behaviour was the massive and brazen rigging of the 1983 elections which involved the perversion of every aspect of the electoral process from the registration of voters to the collation and declaration of the election results.

2. A Democratic Temper

By a democratic temper is meant a spirit of fair play and of tolerance of other people's interests and opinions. It also demands of the rulers a willingness to accept that the power they exercise belongs to the people, that the people have a right to choose who should govern them and that their choice should be free and be respected. It is the absence of a democratic spirit that accounted for much of the perversion of the democratic processes of government in most developing countries of the world, as manifested in political coercion, electoral malpractices and the undermining of the freedom of the press and of assembly. Legal sanctions alone cannot guarantee observance of the rules of the political game.

3. A Libertarian Temper

A great American jurist, Judge Learned Hand, has said that civil liberties lie in "habits, customs — conventions if you will — that tolerate dissent... If such a habit and such a temper pervade a society, it will not need institutions to protect its civil liberties and human rights ; so far as they do not, I venture to doubt how far anything else can protect them: whether it be Bills of Rights or courts that must in the name of interpretation read their meaning into them."[4] The emphasis again is on *temper, habit and tradition.* Sir Ivor Jennings, the celebrated English constitutional lawyer, must also have had habits or conventions in mind as the only really effective guarantee of human rights and civil liberties when he said: "In Britain, we have no Bill of Rights, we merely have liberty according to law; and we think — truly, I believe — that we do the job better than any country which has a Bill of Rights or a Declaration of the Rights of Man."[5]

The truth of Judge Hand's statement is borne out by the incidence of frequent and widespread human rights violations in many countries with a constitutional guarantee of civil liberties. In Nigeria, for example, the *Shugaba Case* (1980) readily comes to mind.[6] While a Bill of Rights does serve as "the outer bulwarks of defence," making "the way of the

---

4. Learned Hand, An Address titled "A Fanfare for Prometheus" reproduced in *The Freedom Reader* ed. Edwin Newman (1963), p. 24; also reprinted in *The Spirit of Liberty: Papers and Addresses of Learned Hand,* ed. Irving Dilliard (1959), pp. 221-228.
5. Ivor Jennings, *The Approach to Self-Government,* (1958), p. 20.
6. *Fed. Minister of Internal Affairs & Others v. Shugaba Darman* (1982) 3 NCLR 915, 953; discussed in Nwabueze, op. cit. pp. 203-210.

transgressor, of the tyrant, more difficult,[7] it has not, generally speaking, prevented human rights violations. Such violations in the face of a constitutional guarantee of civil liberties can only be accounted for by the absence of a spirit or tradition of respect for human rights. They would have been unimaginable in Britain where respect for human rights and civil liberties is firmly rooted in British tradition and way of life.

As with a Bill of Rights, the establishment in the constitution of such other institutional safeguards like the *ombudsman* has in general not prevented governmental arbitrariness and interference with individual liberty. The institution of the *ombudsman* presupposes that the government of the day is desirous or at least willing to have complaints against its own administration, in other words, to have a watchdog over the way it administers the affairs of the nation, and that it is imbued with a spirit or temper for an open administration; without this, the *ombudsman* cannot be an effective watchdog of the citizen's rights against governmental arbitrariness.

From the standpoint particularly of democracy, a tradition or spirit of tolerance of dissent needs to be specially emphasised, since, like large-scale election rigging, intolerance of dissent has serious consequences for democracy. It usually, if not invariably, leads to the systematic victimisation and harassment by government of political opponents, repression of participation through the press and through the right to assemble peacefully to air or petition for grievances, the suppression of organised opposition, the emergence of a one-party state either *de facto* or *de jure* and (may be) the eventual intervention of the military, all of which pose for democracy the danger of its emasculation or demise.

4. A Spirit or Attitude of Service and Trusteeship and of Commitment to the Welfare of the People

The democratic principle of the ruler being a servant of the people and a trustee of their interest is more a matter of the

---

7.   Cowen, *The Foundation of Freedom*, (1960), p. 119.

spirit. It requires an attitude of honesty, fidelity, selflessness, disinterestedness, impartiality, objectivity, fairness, openness, devotion, courtesy, humility etc. These attributes need perhaps some elaboration. Arrogance and arbitrariness are a negation of the concept of service and the obligations of a servant.

The attributes of devotion, courtesy and humility speak for themselves. To be at a person's service is to be devoted to his welfare. The relationship of master and servant requires of the latter to be courteous, polite, respectful and humble towards the master as an acknowledgement of his authority. Discourtesy, disrespect or insubordination on the part of a servant imply a repudiation of the master's authority, and are therefore a proper ground for dismissal from service.

A self-serving servant is a contradiction in terms. It negates the very idea of service which implies, not service to oneself, but service to others. It is therefore of the essence of service that the servant must be selfless. The interest of the master or employer is the servant's only legitimate concern.

Related to the attribute of selflessness is that of disinterestedness. It is not enough that a decision or action by a public servant is not self-serving. He should have no personal interest in it at all even though the decision or action is not in fact influenced by self-interest. Disinterestedness is insisted on in order not to give any ground for suspicion as to the motivations for governmental decisions or actions. Governmental decisions and actions must not only be free of individual self-interest, they must manifestly be seen to be so.

The attributes of objectivity, fairness, openness and the absence of arbitrariness require that public servants are not to take decisions adversely affecting the legal rights of a member of the public without giving him an opportunity to be heard and without cogent reasons relevant to his case. For, what may have been thought a clear case may appear in a different light when the other side of it is put. The truth about any matter is seldom ever revealed by a one-sided view of it. There is always the danger that some relevant facts may have been overlooked or irrelevant ones admitted or that the facts may have been slanted or otherwise distorted by reason of bias on the part of an official, which may result not only from pecuniary or other personal interest but also from institutional interest or sheer over-zealousness.

Lastly, impartiality requires that a public servant should put his services at the disposal of the public without favouring any particular group, and that his decisions or actions should not discriminate between people on the basis of political opinion, ethnic origin, religion, etc.

Needless to say, a pervading attitude of fidelity, honesty and probity is required to eradicate corruption and the practice whereby the state is treated as an object of plunder to satisfy the interests of the rulers and their friends and relations, which is a negation of the democratic concept of government as a public trust. Corruption also suggests a lack of patriotic feeling, of a spirit to subordinate individual desire for wealth to the interest of the nation for development. Every abuse of public office, whether it be in the form of a kick-back, appointment or the siting of a development project based on selfish, sectional or political consideration, involves the sacrificing of the national interest, and manifests therefore a want of patriotic feeling. Nationalism is not enough if it is not infused by a patriotic feeling, strong enough to subordinate the selfish, sectional or political interest to that of the nation.

5. A Sense of Civic Responsibility

A sense of civic responsibility required for the success of democracy has both a positive and a negative aspect. On the positive side, it implies, for example, a spirit of co-operation in public affairs as well as a duty to vote at national, state or local government elections in order to ensure that only the right calibre of people get elected into government offices and assemblies; to pay taxes; to prevent the commission of an offence or to report it to the law enforcement agencies after it has been committed. The negative aspect enjoins the citizenry not to break or circumvent the law, or act outside and against it. A sense of civic responsibility calls for a pervading attitude on the part of all, rulers and the governed alike, to be governed by law and to conduct their affairs in accordance with it; it requires, in short, respect for the Rule of Law.

6. An Attitude or Habit against Abuse of Power

A democratic temper needs to be complemented by a disposition of self-restraint and moderation where an act, otherwise within power, would constitute an abuse of it, and by a statesman-like acceptance that the integrity of the whole governmental framework and the regularity of its procedures should transcend personal aggrandisement. It is of course important for such an ethic to get established and to be effective that the people themselves should be alive to cry out against any case of abuse. The force of public censure is perhaps the best guarantee against abuse of power. No matter what checks and restrictions are embodied in a constitution against tyranny and abuse of power, there can be no constitutional government unless the wielders of power as well as the governed are adequately imbued with such an ethic. In the words of Julius Nyerere, "when the nation does not have the ethic which will enable the government to say: 'We cannot do this, that is un-Tangannyikan' — or the people to say: 'That we cannot tolerate, that is un-Tanganyikan' — if the people do not have that kind of ethic, it does not matter what kind of constitution you frame. They can always be victims of tyranny."

The tradition should extend not only to public outcry or protest but also to a refusal to accept large-scale election rigging by a government or to submit to systematic oppression and tyranny. "If ever," wrote Senator Orrin Hatch, "more Americans... are content to surrender than are willing to defend freedom..., freedoms as we have enjoyed it will soon become as much a relic of history as the glory of Rome and Greece.."[8] Or, in the words of Sir Karl Popper, "the working of democracy rests largely upon the understanding that a government which attempts to misuse its powers and to establish itself as a tyranny (or which tolerates the establishment of tyranny by anybody else) outlaws itself, and that the citizens have not only the right but also a duty to consider the action of such a government as a crime,and its members as a dangerous gang of

---

8.   Orrin G. Hatch, "Civic Virtue: Wellspring of Liberty," in Toward The Bicentenial of the Constitution, published in *National Forum*, The Phi Kappa Phi Journal, Fall 1984, p. 38.

criminals."[9] John Stuart Mill is equally clear on this. "A people," he wrote,"may prefer a free government, but if, from indolence, or carelessness, or cowardice, or want of public spirit, they are unequal to the exertions necessary for preserving it; if they will not fight for it when it is directly attacked; if they can be deluded by the artifices used to cheat them out of it; if by momentary discouragement, or temporary panic, or a fit of enthusiasm for an individual, they can be induced to lay their liberties at the feet even of a great man, or trust him with powers which enable him to subvert their institutions; in all these cases they are more or less unfit for liberty: and though it may be for their good to have had it even for a short time, they are unlikely long to enjoy it."[10]

Abuse of office is one of the greatest dangers facing democracy in Africa, and this is accounted for largely by the absence of a tradition against it. To begin with, there is the relative impotence of extra-constitutional sanctions against the abuse of power. The social values of the advanced democracies enshrine a national ethic which defines the limits of permissible action by the wielders of power. This national ethic is sanctified in deeply entrenched conventions operating as part of the rules of the game of politics. Thus, although an action may well be within the powers of the President under the constitution, still he cannot do it if it violates the moral sense of the nation, for he would risk calling down upon himself the wrath of public censure. The force of public opinion is sufficiently developed to act as a watchdog of the nation's ethic,and no action that seriously violates this ethic can hope to escape public condemnation. More than any constitutional restraints, perhaps, it is the ethic of the nation, its sense of right and wrong, and the capacity of the people to defend it, which provides the ultimate bulwark against tyranny.

The traditional African attitude towards power is not of much assistance either. Tradition has inculcated in the people a certain amount of deference towards authority. The chief's

---

9.   Karl Popper, *The Open Society and Its Enemies* Vol. 2 (1966), p. 152.
10.   J. S. Mill, *Representative Government*: reprinted in *Unitarianism Liberty and Representative Government* (1910) Everyman's Library, p. 191.

authority is sanctioned in religion, and it is a sacrilege to flout it, except in cases of blatant and systematic oppression when the whole community might rise in revolt to destool, banish or even kill a tyrannical chief. Thus, while customary sanctions against extreme cases of abuse of power exist, there is also considerable toleration of arbitrariness by the chief. This attitude towards authority tends to be transferred to the modern political leader. The vast majority of the population, which of course is still illiterate and custom-bound, is not disposed to question the leader's authority, and indeed disapproves of those who are inclined to do so.

In a sense, therefore, the presidency in Africa is regarded by many in the light of the attitudes inculcated in them towards chiefly authority, and its power as the project of chiefly authority into the national sphere. The President, in effect, is the *chief* of the new nation, and as such entitled to the authority and respect due by tradition to a chief. This has not rested entirely on attitudes carried over from tradition. In places there has indeed been a conscious attempt to implant the attitude in the minds of the people, by, for example, publicly investing the President with the attributes of a chief. Thus, when he attended public rallies in Ghana, Nkrumah used to assume the style of a chief. He sat upon a "chiefly throne under a resplendent umbrella, symbol of traditional rule", and he took "chiefly titles meaningful to all major tribal units in Ghana: *Osagyefo, Katamanto, Kasapieko, Nufeno,* etc."[11] His opening of parliament was also done in chiefly style. His approach was "heralded by the beating of *fantomforom* (traditional drums). He was received by eight linguists representing the various Regions and each carrying a distinctive stick. A libation was poured and the president then entered the chamber to the sound of *mmenson* (the seven traditional horns).[12] Though this is explicable in part by Nkrumah's irredentist aspiration for the revival of the African cultural heritage, the political significance is obvious. It was intended to harness to the presidency the authority of tradition and the legitimacy which it confers. By

---

11.   H. L. Bretton, *The Rise and Fall of Kwame Nkrumah* (1966), p. 80.
12.   Bennion, *Constitutional Law of Ghana* (1962), p. 110.

aligning the presidency with the institution of chieftaincy in the public imagination, it is hoped to inspire public acceptance of the office and reverence for its authority.

Similarly relevant to the reality of presidential power in Africa is the African's conception of authority. Authority in African traditional society is conceived as being personal, permanent, mystical and pervasive.[13] The chief is a personal ruler, and his office is held for life, which pervades all the other relations in the community, for he is both legislator, executive, judge, priest, medium, father, etc. These characteristics are reflected in the   modern African presidency. The African President is both the executive and the chief legislator. His authority tends to be all-pervading. The mysticism of religion in which the authority of the chief is sanctified is also sought to be transferred to the presidency. Even the attribute of divinity, which also characterises certain of the traditional chieftaincies, had been claimed for Nkrumah, a claim in which he apparently acquiesced.

The office has tended to be an inheritance, which must be rendered secure by the liquidation of open and organised opposition. William Tubman of Liberia died in office after 28 years as President, Sekou Toure of Guinea after 26 years, Abdel Nasser of Egypt after 16, Jomo Kenyatta of Kenya and Sir Seretse Khama of Botswana after 15 years respectively. Lebua Jonathan of Lesotho, Hamani Diori of Niger and Kwame Nkrumah of Ghana were in office for 20, 14 and 10 years respectively before being overthrown in military coups, and Kenneth Kaunda of Zambia for 27 before he was voted out in a free multi-party democratic election. Habib Bourguiba of Tunisia, proclaimed life President in the Constitution, was dismissed after 32 years in office on ground of senility certified by a group of medical doctors. Julius Nyerere of Tanzania voluntarily retired after 27 years in office as did Leopold Senghor of Senegal after 21 years. Felix Houphouet Boigny of Cote D'ivoire, Sir Dauda Jawara of The Gambia, Mobutu Sese

13.   Alvin W. Wolfe, "African Conceptions of Authority," unpublished paper (1965); cited by K. W. Grundy and M. Weinstein, "The Political Uses of Imagination" (1961) *Transition* 31, p. 5.

Seko of Zaire, Gnassingbe Eyadema of Togo, Omar Bongo of Gabon and Muammar Gaddafi of Libya are still in office (June 1992) after 32, 27, 26, 25, 25 and 22 years respectively.

Like Habib Bourguiba of Tunisia, Kamuzu Banda of Malawi has had himself installed life President (he has been in office now for 28 years) as had Jean-Bedel Bokassa of the Central African Republic before his overthrow by the military in 1972. Other African Presidents, like Kwame Nkrumah and Kenneth Kaunda, rejected offers of a life presidency, just as Banda did for some time before finally succumbing to the pressure and the temptation. But all have said they would stay in office for as long as the people wanted them, which, given the indefinite eligibility for re-election, means in effect for life, the only difference being that every four or five years they will have to submit themselves to the ritual of an election. It was the ritualistic nature of the exercise perhaps that finally induced Banda, with his characteristic aversion to hypocrisy, to accept the life presidency.

Now, a life president, or one who has held office for 20 or 30 years, is a different kind of functionary from one who is limited to a maximum of two terms of four years each. His authority is bound to be greater, for after twenty or thirty years in office he is apt to become an institution himself, attracting loyalties of a personal nature.

This propensity to personalise rule and to perpetuate it indefinitely is perhaps the most outstanding contrast between the politics of the emergent states and those of the established democracies, especially Britain and America. In Britain politics has attained a happy equilibrium in which the alternation of government at not too distant intervals between two parties has become a political pattern. This owes to the good sense not only of the electorate but of the politicians themselves. It is unthinkable that a party in office should want to rig an election in order to stay in power. But what is equally, if not more, remarkable is the frequent change in the personnel of the rulers within the governing party. A British politician would not normally want to remain Prime Minister for as long as his party continues to win elections. No law forbids him to do so, but there is a general acceptance that the talent for leadership is not the exclusive property of any one individual. Many would be satisfied with two terms, some indeed would prefer to retire before the expiration of their second term, as did Harold Macmillan; this may be due partly to health and other personal reasons, but there is no doubt also a desire to give others within the party a chance to succeed to the leadership. (Margaret Thatcher breached this principle and had to be forced out.) And from the point of view of the nation, a change in leadership may guarantee against sterility, complacency and the danger of the cult of personality. Change may enable a fresh vitality and a fresh approach to be brought to bear upon the problems of government. "An untried president may be better than a tired one; a fresh approach better than a stale one."[14] There is yet another striking feature of the system of rulership in Britain. It is not considered "infra dig" for a person who has once been Prime Minister to serve as an ordinary minister under another leader. Each party has its own system of choosing its leader, and a previous appointment as Prime Minister carried with it no title to the continued leadership of the party in the future. A former Prime Minister who has lost in the contest for the party leadership will not necessarily feel embarrassment in serving as minister under a new party leader as Prime Minister, as happened in the case of Sir Alec Douglas-Home. The Prime Minister enjoys prestige and power no doubt, but he does not consider himself as uniquely set apart from the rest of the community.

In the United States the problem of succession to the rulership has received an equally happy solution, as a result again of the good sense of successive presidents from the first downwards. Until 1951 the American Constitution imposed no restrictions on the eligibility of a president to seek re-election indefinitely. At the time of the Constitution's adoption, most Americans wished indeed that George Washington, the first president, would retain his office indefinitely, so profound was the confidence and love they had for him. As a matter of general political principle, quite apart from the personality of Washington, the question of indefinite eligibility had provoked a disagreement of views. Washington himself and Alexander

---

14.   E. S. Corwin, *The President: Office and Powers*, 4th ed., p. 37.

Hamilton favoured it while Jefferson opposed it. Hamilton, in *The Federalist*, argued that a limitation on the number of terms permitted to a president would stifle zeal and make the president indifferent to his duty; that a president, knowing he would be barred from the office for ever after, might be tempted to exploit for personal advantage the opportunities of the office while they lasted; that an ambitious president might be tempted to try to prolong his term by pervert means; that it would deprive the community of the advantage of the president's previous experience in the office; and that it would lead to a lack of continuity in policy, and consequently to instability in administration.

Washington did, however, retire after two terms, much against the wishes and expectations of his countrymen. His example was followed by Jefferson, also against appeals from eight State Legislatures that he should continue in office. "If," he argued, "some termination to the services of the chief magistrate be not fixed by the Constitution, or supplied by practice, his office, normally four years, will in fact become for life, and history shows how easily that degenerates into an inheritance."[15] Since then the tradition has stuck that no person should be president for more than two terms. Until 1940, this tradition has been consistently observed except when, taking advantage of the uncertainty as to whether two terms meant two consecutive terms, Theodore Roosevelt sought (but failed) to be elected in 1912 for a third term some years after his first two consecutive terms. Tradition was finally breached when Franklin D. Roosevelt was re-elected for a third consecutive term in 1940 and for a fourth in 1944. But those were periods of grave emergency, the period of the Second World War. It is such emergency situations that present the strongest argument in favour of indefinite eligibility. In such a situation the prestige and authority of the president's personality might be invaluable in saving the life of the nation. This was the consideration underlying the break with tradition of Franklin Roosevelt's third and fourth consecutive re-elections. Roosevelt himself professed a desire to adhere to

---

15. Quoted in E. S. Corwin, op. cit., p. 332.

the tradition, and to relinquish office in 1941 to a successor if only he could do so with an assurance that "I am at the same time turning over to him as president a nation intact, a nation at peace, a nation prosperous, a nation clear in its knowledge of what powers it has to serve its own citizens, a nation that is in a position to use those powers to the full in order to move forward steadily to meet the modern needs of humanity, a nation which has thus proved that the democratic form and methods of national government can and will succeed."[16]

These are words which might be used by any African president to justify his rule in perpetuity, and it might even be more cogent and compelling in his case. As Corwin points out, this is just the "indispensable man" argument. To accept it, he says, "is next door to despairing of the country."[17] In a temporary emergency, like a war, it might perhaps be condoned, but in the context of the sort of emergency created by the development crisis in the emergent states it is a positive evil. For since the development crisis is a continuing "emergency," the argument tantamounts to making the presidency a life appointment. In any case, the Americans, after the Roosevelt experience, had to amend their Constitution in 1951 to give force of law to the tradition limiting the presidential office to two full elective terms or one full elective term plus more than half of another term inherited from a previous president.[18] African countries must do the same. After eight or ten years in office as president, no one should, in justice to the country and to other citizens, want to continue, and no nation, with the kind of ethic here suggested, should allow it.

Creating the Spirit of Liberty, Democracy, Justice, the Rule of Law and Order

Identifying what the spirit of liberty, democracy, justice, the Rule of Law and order requires poses perhaps less difficulty

---

16. Quoted in E. S. Corwin, op. cit., p. 336.
17. Ibid, p. 37.
18. XXII Amendment.

than suggesting how it may be created. A number of ways in which this may be done are here considered.

(a) A Selfless, Honest and Charismatic Leadership

Moulding or shaping societal behaviour — attitudes, dispositions and habits — in a desired direction is primarily a function of political leadership. It calls for a leadership that is at once dedicated, single-minded, selfless, disciplined, patriotic and highly motivated in the national interest. It must be a leadership whose sincerity of purpose is so transparent as to induce people to adopt the desired pattern of behaviour, and whose dedication to the cause is sufficiently total and selfless to inspire public confidence, a leadership that is seen to be practising what it preaches. People cannot be persuaded by the leadership to be tolerant, honest, etc. if the leaders do not themselves practise those virtues. Far from inspiring popular change in the desired direction, a leadership that is not seen to be practising what it preaches creates disillusion and disenchantment among the people.

This kind of leadership requires, in short, a national hero endowed with a mystique and charismatic appeal that can inspire personal loyalty and followership. Charisma and mystique in a leader are indispensable in shaping behavioural pattern in a society because they engender a belief and faith in him as a person whose precepts have to be obeyed. The prospect of such a leadership emerging may well be a tall order, a dream, in a country sunk deep in social indiscipline, corruption and abuse of office, and riven by ethnic or racial hatred and jealousy. Such a society may well need to be first cleansed by something like the French Revolution to pave the way for the emergence of the selfless, honest and charismatic leader of our conception. The absence of a leadership of this type is the primary problem of government in developing countries, particularly in Africa. As Africa embarks upon the transition from one-party or military rule to democracy, there is need for a complete change of guards, a complete change of leadership.

(b) Role of the Judiciary, the Mass Media and Education

The judiciary is in a unique position to create among the people an attitude of respect for the constitution and for human rights, a habit of order and regularity in the conduct of public affairs, and a commitment to legality and stability generally. The attitude of the people, both rulers and the ruled· alike, towards the constitution is conditioned to a large extent by the way in which it is interpreted and applied by the courts. Whether its prescriptions are to become active principles for restraining governmental actions depends to a great extent upon what the courts make of them. A liberal, purposive interpretation coupled with a courageous, dynamic application might be expected to impart vitality and reality to the provisions of the constitution, and to infuse in the rulers a consciousness of the peremptoriness of its commands, and the futility of disregarding them. A government, faced with such imminent risk of having its acts invalidated by an ever-watchful judiciary, might, it is to be hoped, make respect for the constitution a touchstone of all its actions. On the part of the governed, the effect would be to create a willingness, indeed eagerness, to seek the intervention of the court against any transgression of constitutional prescriptions by the government.

That has been the unique contribution of the judiciary in the United States in the development of a tradition of reverence for the Constitution which, as earlier stated, is one of the factors responsible for its sacrosanctity and longevity. From the early beginning of the Union, the Supreme Court, under the energetic leadership of its head, Chief Justice John Marshall, made the Constitution the controlling force in the government of the country, and so generated a feeling of reverence for its commands, which over the years have acquired the force of a tradition.

Writing about the role of the courts in the maintenance of democracy in America, Alexis de Tocqueville has said: "Scarcely any political question arises in the United States which is not resolved, sooner or later, into a judicial question. Hence all parties are obliged to borrow, in their daily controversies, the ideas, and even the language, peculiar to judicial proceedings; the spirit of the law, which is produced in the schools and courts of justice gradually penetrates beyond their walls into the bossom of society, where it descends to the lowest classes, so that at last the whole people contract the habits and the taste of the judicial magistrate."[19]

The active support of an enlightened, upright and independent press is also necessary for this purpose. Its instrumentality is indeed crucial in attuning people's minds and in rallying them in the desired direction. It is by means of newspapers that common sentiments, common principles and common attitudes and habits may be inculcated, fostered and disseminated among a large number of people.

Character training, discipline, the civic responsibilities of citizenship, moral values and the meaning and value of liberty and democracy must feature prominently in the content of education imparted in the schools, colleges and universities. It is from such early exposure that the youth can form the desired attitudes and habits. Education in human rights must be extended to the law enforcement agencies — the police, magistrates, judges and others including the personnel of the prison service and the military — with the object of inculcating in them the paramount importance of respect for human rights.

(c) Indoctrination

Indoctrination is a conspicuous technique employed by religion to inculcate and spread its beliefs and principles. Outside religion it can also be achieved through teaching in educational institutions and through the purposeful use of symbols and other ceremonial forms or observances. Among children in their formative years, a belief in the constitution, for example, can easily be inspired and nurtured by teaching. Hence the practice in some states in the United States of requiring by law instruction in the Constitution as part of the school curriculum. The aim, as declared in the relevant statutes, is to foster and perpetuate "the ideals, principles and spirit of Americanism."[20]

Symbols have great significance as an instrument of

---

19. op. cit., p. 126.
20. See, e.g. s. 1734 West Virginia Code, quoted in *West Virginia State Board of Education v. Barnette*, 319 US 624 (1943).

indoctrination. The flag in particular has been accorded the greatest symbolism in the United States in evoking among the people the spirit of Americanism. It is regarded as signifying "government resting on the consent of the governed; liberty regulated by law; the protection of the weak against the strong; security against the exercise of arbitrary power; and absolute safety for free institutions against foreign aggression.[21] Conscious of the value of symbols in fostering a national ethic, Congress has, by a joint resolution, required that a pledge of allegiance to the American flag should be rendered, on appropriate occasions,by standing with the right hand over the heart, and reciting: "I pledge allegiance to the flag of the United States of America and to the Republic for which it stands, one Nation indivisible, with liberty and justice for all". Compliance is optional, as no penalty is imposed for non-conformity.

Some states, however, have gone farther to make the flag salute a compulsory ceremony in their public schools, and to punish non-compliance by expulsion and by denial of re-admission until compliance, thus arousing conscientious objection by members of the Jehovah's Witness. Although they are prepared publicly to proclaim their respect for the nation's flag and to acknowledge it as a symbol of freedom and justice to all, they refused to salute it, on the ground that that would amount to worshipping an "image", contrary to the tenets of their religion. In an action challenging the constitutionality of flag salute as a compulsory, instead of a voluntary, ceremony in public schools, the Supreme Court at first sustained it.[22] It held that the flag being a symbol of national unity which in turn is the basis of national security, it should be within the power of the state to try to evoke in children through such a compulsory ceremony a love of nation and an appreciation of its hopes and ideals. In the words of the court:

> The ultimate foundation of a free society is the binding tie of cohesive sentiment. Such a sentiment is fostered by all those agencies of the mind and spirit which may serve to gather up the traditions of a people, transmit them from generation to generation,

21.   *Halter v. Nebraska*, 205 US 34; also *United States v. Gettysburg R. Co.*, 160 US 668 (1896).
22.   *Minersville School District v. Gobitts*, 310 US 586 (1940).

and thereby create that continuity of a treasured common life which constitutes a civilisation. We live by symbols'.[23]

That expresses eloquently the important role of symbols in the life of a people. Although the decision was overruled in a subsequent case three years later,[24] on the ground that "to believe that patriotism will not flourish if patriotic ceremonies are voluntary and spontaneous instead of a compulsory routine is to make an unflattering estimate of the appeal of our institutions to free mind",[25] the court still acknowledged symbols as an effective, if primitive, way of communicating ideals. It observed:

> The use of an emblem or flag to symbolise some system, idea, institution, or personality, is a short cut from mind to mind. Causes and nations, political parties, lodges and ecclesiastical groups seek to knit the loyalty of their followings to a flag or banner, a colour or design. The State announces rank, function, and authority through crowns and maces, uniforms and black robes; the Church speaks through the Cross, the Crucifix, the altar and shrine, and clerical raiment. Symbols of State often convey political ideas just as religious symbols come to convey theological ones. Associated with many of these symbols are appropriate gestures of acceptance or respect: a salute, a bowed or bared head, a bended knee.[26]

Apart from symbols and the gestures associated with them, other ceremonial forms or observances have also great value as a method of indoctrination. For like symbols, they serve to perpetuate ideals by fixing the mind in the contemplation of them, and by aiding it in embracing them warmly and holding them with firmness.

(d) The Role of Religion

Being a matter of the heart, of attitude and disposition, the spirit of liberty, democracy, justice, the Rule of Law and order rests upon morality. Liberty and justice are pre-eminently a moral value. Hence the age-old maxim that "only a virtuous people are capable of freedom," that liberty is meant only for a

---

23. Ibid. at p. 596 per Frankfurter J. delivering the judgment of the court.
24. *West Virginia State Board of Education v. Barnette*, 319 US 624 (1943).
25. Ibid at p. 641.
26. Ibid. p. 632.

moral people. Or, as Edmund Burke puts it: "men are qualified for civil liberties, in exact proportion to their disposition to put moral chains upon their appetites; in proportion as their love of justice is above their rapacity.[27] The creation and nurturing of the spirit of liberty, democracy, justice, the Rule of Law and order raises the question whether morality can be maintained without religion. And by religion is meant a system of belief in the existence of some supernatural being with power to change people's lives for the better or for worse, whether it be God, a god (or gods), the spirit of ancestors, etc. Like morality, religion is non-rational, resting entirely on faith. The existence of such a being, its power and how it works cannot be scientifically verified or tested; one simply believes or disbelieves it.

Religious beliefs have through the ages been the main anchor of morality, providing the necessary sanction and helping to transmit it from generation to generation. Such has been the linkage of the one with the other that it is said morality cannot exist without religion. Subscribing to this view, Will and Ariel Durant declare, after an 11-volume monumental survey of the history of the world from the earliest times,[28] that "there is no significant example in history, before our time, of a society successfully maintaining moral life without the aid of religion,"[29] maintaining that the provisional success of the experiment by the communist countries in dissociating themselves from religion "owes much to the temporary acceptance of Communism as the religion (or, as skeptics would say, the opium) of the people." They add in a pregnant comment that 'if the socialist regime should fail in its efforts to destroy relative poverty among the masses, the new religion may lose its fervour and efficacy, and the state may wink at the restoration of supernatural beliefs as an aid in quieting discontent."[30]

Alexis de Tocqueville has attributed the strength and resilience of liberty and democracy in the United States largely

---

27. Quoted in F. A. Hayek, *The Fatal Conceit* (1988) at p. 29.
28. Will and Ariel Durant, *The Story of Civilisation* in 11 volumes.
29. *The Lessons of History* (1968), p. 51.
30. loc. cit.

to the moral and religious character of her people. His oft-quoted words in this regard will bear repetition here. Said he:

> I sought for the greatness and genius of America in her commodious harbours and her ample rivers,and it was not there; in her fertile fields and boundless prairie, and it was not there; in her rich mines and vast commerce, and it was not there. Not until I went to the churches of America and heard her pulpits aflame with righteousness did I understand the secret of her genius and power.[31]

Liberty and democracy took root and flourished in the United States because, in the words of Senator Hatch, "the people were virtuous; they were virtuous because they were moral; and they were moral because they were religious."[32]

In an excellent summation of the role of religion in fostering happiness, discipline, harmony and stability in a democracy, Will and Ariel Durant have said:

> To the unhappy, the suffering, the bereaved, the old, it has brought supernatural comforts valued by millions of souls as more precious than any natural aid. It has helped parents and teachers to discipline the young. It has conferred meaning and dignity upon the lowliest existence, and through its sacraments has made for stability by transforming human covenants into solemn relationships with God. It has kept the poor (said Napoleon) from murdering the rich. For since the natural inequality of men dooms many of us to poverty or defeat, some supernatural hope may be the sole alternative to despair. Destroy that hope, and class war is intensified. Heaven and utopia are buckets in a well; when one goes down the other goes up; when religion declines Communism grows.[33]

They add in another poignant statement that "as long as there is poverty, there will be gods." We might perhaps modify this last dictum to read that as long as there are death, ill-health and poverty, there will be gods. It is the fear of death perhaps more than poverty that induces in men a belief in gods. Certainly, there would be less need for religion if death did not exist. With immortality, man would have been assimilated to a god.

It can thus be concluded that no society in which morality

31. *Democracy in America* ed. Richard Heffner (1956).
32. Senator Hatch, National Forum, The Phi Kappa Phi Journal, Fall 1984, p. 36.
33. *The Lessons of History* (1968) p. 43.

and religion are absent can ever attain and maintain liberty and democracy. This raises the question of the relation of the state to morality and religion. Two different issues are raised — the scope of freedom of conscience and religion, and the separation of the state and religion. I shall here concern myself only with one aspect of the question.

Given the indispensable role of religion in fostering happiness, discipline, harmony, stability, liberty and democracy, it is tempting to say that the state should positively support and promote religion, so long as it does so on the footing of the equality of all religions, and that it should not, by standing aloof completely in all matters of religion, lend encouragement to irreligion among its subjects. It should not, said Senator Orrin Hatch, adopt a position of "neutrality between religion and irreligion."[34] But such an approach ignores the interest of atheists and agnostics who, though a minority, have a right, in exercise of their conscience, not to believe or to disbelieve in any religion, and are entitled to demand that the state should not show favouritism towards religionists as against them. The notion that society has a duty to see that its members should be religious, said John Stuart Mill, "was the foundation of all religious persecution ever perpetrated." and it was so perpetrated in "the belief that God not only abominates the act of the misbeliever, but will not hold us guiltless if we leave him unmolested."[35] For this reason, state encouragement of religion, desirable as it might be, is inadmissible because it is incompatible with individual freedom of conscience, which includes freedom not to believe or to disbelieve without being subjected to discrimination or persecution on that account.

However, the state can lend its weight to religious beliefs, as by their enforcement by law, when they are the source of,or the sanction for, rules of morality accepted by the generality of members of the community who may include religionists as well as non-believers and dis-believers. It should not be blind to

---

34. op. cit. p. 37.
35. J. S. Mill, *On Liberty*, reprinted in *Utilitarianism, Liberty and Representative Government* (1910) Everyman's Library ed., p. 160.

religious convictions shared by the generality of the public,and which from part of the community's moral order. While it should not get involved in the promotion of religious teaching or dissemination of religious precepts, it can, without impropriety, throw its authority behind such of them as are accepted by the society as part of the moral principles governing its life.

So also the state *qua* state is not entitled to impose its own notions of morality upon the society. The view, adumbrated by Plato, that the state has the right and the duty to determine what standards of morality are to be observed in the community is not, as has been rightly said, acceptable to our modern thought. "It invests the State with power of determination between good and evil, destroys freedom of conscience and is the paved road to tyranny."[36]

The state is only entitled to enforce by law the morality that has passed the test of time and experience and been accepted as its common property by the generality of the society; it is not to make any judgment about the morality it is to enforce by law. "Naturally he (the law-maker) will assume that the morals of his society are good and true; if he does not, he should not be playing any active part in government. But he has not to vouch for their goodness and truth. His mandate is to preserve the essentials of his society, not to reconstruct them according to his own ideas."[37] But, short of a complete reconstruction, he can,within the limits acceptable to the prevailing public opinion in the society, reform the common morality to take account of changes in the moral attitudes and sentiments of the people.

---

36.   Devlin, *Enforcement of Morals* 1966), p. 89.
37.   Devlin, op. cit. p. 90.

Chapter 13

Balancing Liberty with Public Order/Security in a Democracy

> The challenge of democracy lies in combining the requisite stability and energy in government with the inviolable attention due to liberty.
>
> — James Madison

In a free society, as stated in chapter 7, it is reasonably justifiable for the state to have power to protect society against acts by individuals that might endanger public order or public security. In the constitutions of the developing countries in the Commonwealth, the necessary balance is expressed by the formula that the guarantee of liberty shall not "invalidate any law that is reasonably justifiable in a democratic society in the interest of defence, public safety, public order, public morality or public health." (The guarantee of the right to life and to personal liberty is not, however, affected by this qualification except during a period of declared emergency, nor is the prohibition of slavery, torture and inhuman treatment affected at all even during such an emergency).

But to say that in a free society liberty is qualified by the power of the state to protect society against acts by individuals that endanger public order/security provides but inadequate indication of the extent of limitation thereby imposed on government interference with liberty. What kinds of act by the individual would reasonably justify interference by the state in a democratic society in the interest of public order/security? What kind of relationship must exist between the act in question and public order/security to make interference reasonably justifiable in a democratic society? The formula in the Commonwealth Bills of Rights provides no answer to the question.

280

To answer the question, it seems necessary to draw a distinction between

(a) liberty as it pertains to the integrity and dignity of the human person, and

(b) liberty as it relates to human activities or conduct, including speech. Human activities or conduct need also to be differentiated into

(i) social, religious and economic activities, and

(ii) political activities.

(a) Integrity and Dignity of the Human Person

The human person has an inherent dignity, because it is made in the image of God, with a conscience or the faculty of judging right and wrong as well as a capacity for thought and for feelings and emotions, unlike other beings. The human soul, implanted in the human heart, belongs in the realm of the divine and the spiritual; it is the spiritual part of man, the divine nature of God manifested in man, and which, expressing itself in feelings, emotions and sensations, is supremely important to human happiness. Justice Louis Brandeis puts it eloquently thus:

> The makers of our Constitution undertook to secure conditions favourable to the pursuit of happiness. They recognised the significance of man's spiritual nature, of his feelings and of his intellect. They knew that only part of the pain, pleasure and satisfaction of life are to be found in material things. They sought to protect Americans in their beliefs, their thoughts, their emotions and their sensations."[1]

The divine and spiritual nature of man, the inherent dignity of the human being and the crucial importance of human thought, beliefs, emotions and sensations to human happiness entitle the human person to respect, and to protection against interference by the state as, for example, by holding him in slavery or servitude, compelling him by law or force to perform labour against his wish, subjecting him to torture, mutilation, acute mental or emotional suffering or other degrading treatment. Next to the taking of human life, perhaps the worst

---

1. *Olmstead v. United States*, 277 U.S. 438 (1928).

of all tyrannies is tyranny over men's mind, conscience, beliefs, feelings and emotions, which therefore makes constitutional protection an imperative necessity. What a person thinks in his mind or feels or believes in his heart, but does not manifest in speech or action or in any other overt way (e.g., refusal, on conscientious grounds, to do something required by law) can have no disturbing effect on public order, public security, public morality or public health as to justify the state to interfere with or control it for the purpose of maintaining those public interests. Human thought of course gives rise to action, for "it is what men think that determines how they act,"[2] yet human thought is not for that reason to be fettered until it is actually manifested in action. The exercise of thought, conscience, belief, feelings and emotions requires therefore to be put beyond the reach of governmental power; no room should be given for its control by the state. A man may be "punished for his acts (and utterances), never for his thoughts or beliefs or creed."[3] Only in an emergency endangering the life or well-being of the community may the exercise of these freedoms be controlled, and then only to an extent reasonably required for the purpose of dealing with the emergency situation.

In what circumstances the state may be justified in interfering with individual liberty of action by prohibiting or restricting it under pains of imprisonment (or other punishment) will be considered later. Here we are only concerned to consider when, an activity having been validly prohibited or restricted under pains of imprisonment, the actual incarceration of the human person by such imprisonment may justifiably be exacted by the state in a democracy. We begin by drawing a distinction between imprisonment for a criminal offence without trial and what is commonly known as preventive detention. It is generally recognised that the detention of a person without trial, when

2. J. S. Mill, *Representative Government*; reprinted in *Unitarianism, Liberty and Representative Government* (1910) p. 198.
3. Justice Williams O. Douglas, "The Manifest Destiny of America," article reproduced in *The Freedom Reader* by Edwin S. Newman, 2nd ed. (1963), p. 26.

duly authorised by law, is justifiable to an extent, say, two or three months, "reasonably necessary to prevent him from committing a criminal offence."[4] This is not to say that preventive detention without trial is good or desirable. For, while it may be justifiable to detain a person in order to prevent him from committing a criminal offence, the power lends itself very much to abuse. This is because the grounds on which it is suspected that a person may, if left at large, commit a criminal offence may be flimsy and tenuous. The suspicion may be based on activities which have no criminal tendencies or intention at all but are simply offensive to the government or inimical to its political interests. This is the cardinal danger of any system of preventive detention. It is fraught with the tendency on the part of government to equate activities that threaten its personal political fortunes with a criminal threat to the security of the state. Political opponents of government thus face the risk of being clamped into detention, ostensibly to prevent them from committing subversion or other criminal offences against the state, although no shred of evidence exists of any preparations for it or of anyone having contemplated it at all. "It is," said John Stuart Mill, "one of the undisputed functions of government to take precautions against crime before it has been committed, as well as to detect and punish it afterwards. The preventive function of government, however, is far more liable to be abused, to the prejudice of liberty, than the punitory function; for there is hardly any part of the legitimate freedom of action of a human being which would not admit of being represented, and fairly too, as increasing the facilities for some form or other of delinquency."[5]

Imprisonment without trial, not for the purpose of preventing a person from committing a criminal offence, but for a criminal offence allegedly committed already, is justifiable only if the person detained is in fact guilty of the offence in question. In other words, guilt is the sole justification for imprisonment for a criminal offence. It is oppressive and unjust to imprison a

---

4.   See the Bills of Rights in the Constitutions of Commonwealth countries.
5.   J. S. Mill, *On Liberty*; reprinted in *Unitarianism, Liberty and Representative Government* (1910) Everyman's Library, No. 482, pp. 164-165.

person or to punish him in any other way for an offence of which he is innocent. Nothing outrages human feelings and depresses the spirit more than the false accusation of a criminal offence and the infliction of punishment on an innocent person for it.

The only justification for incarcerating the human person by imprisonment for a criminal offence allegedly committed is through an impartial trial and conviction by an independent tribunal. This is the view underlying the requirement in the Bills of Rights in Commonwealth countries that a person detained for a criminal offence must be brought before a court within one day, or two days if there is no court within a radius of 40 kilometers from the place of detention. Only a court can authorise his detention beyond a period of one or two days. If trial is not to take place within two months, then the court is obliged to order his release either conditionally or upon conditions necessary to secure his appearance at the trial, unless the offence is a capital one in which case no right to bail is given. Without conviction and sentence after trial by a court, it is unjustified and oppressive to imprison a person for a criminal offence merely because the authorities are satisfied that he has committed the offence in question. Imprisonment in those circumstances violates the dignity of the human person because it outrages human feelings and depresses the spirit.

Nor should trial and conviction for a criminal offence be conducted otherwise than by the regular courts of law which are characterised, as a court of law is, by independence in terms of their powers and the appointment and tenure of their members and by a trial procedure that guarantees their impartiality and the absence of bias. Special tribunals not forming part of the judicature as constitutionally established should not try, convict and punish people for criminal offences. There are compelling reasons why only courts of law strictly so-called, and not special tribunals, should be invested with jurisdiction in criminal cases. First, conviction of a person for a criminal offence carries a distinct "moral obliquy and social stigma." It is an expression of society's disavowal of his conduct as a deliberate flouting of its values, a condemnation of him as unworthy of its membership. "To be branded an anti-social is half-way to being deemed an outlaw."[6] It is intolerably unjust to be so treated if the conviction is false. "A false conviction is a lie; it proclaims that the person convicted has done something he has not done. It is, moreover, a particularly damaging lie, in that in making imputations against a man's character, it impugns him as the individual he is, and assails his status as a responsible member of society... To impute misdeeds, is, therefore, to deny one's identity by making out that one is not the person one is."[7] This element of public disgrace, it has been said, is the worst part of criminal conviction.[8]

The moral obliquy and social stigma of criminal conviction have practical legal consequences. Criminal conviction brands a person with an indelible stamp of someone unfit to be employed, to be admitted into decent institutions or societies or to be trusted. The disability arising from a conviction is prescribed by the law itself in cases where the offences involve dishonesty. Thus, a person convicted of such an offence is disqualified by law from holding certain public offices or from functioning in certain capacities.

The imposition of punishment following upon a conviction carries the matter further, by giving society's disesteem a *tangible* form in the way of some unwelcome incarceration, like imprisonment. It thus gives weight to society's verbal condemnation and disesteem of a person flouting its values.

To condemn and disgrace a person as a flouter of society's values, and to punish him accordingly, imperatively requires that the process used must be such as guarantees the independence and impartiality of the tribunal and the other safeguards of a fair trial, such as the presumption of innocence, the requirement of proof beyond reasonable doubt, the rules of admissibility or inadmissibility of evidence, etc. This is necessary to guard against as much as possible the possibility of an innocent person being convicted. The injustice of a false conviction and punishment is the worst injustice imaginable. Nothing outrages human feelings and depresses the spirit more

6.   J. R. Lucas, *On Justice* (1980), p. 138.
7.   J. R. Lucas, op. cit. pp. 137-138.
8.   J. R. Lucas, op. cit. p. 133.

than a false conviction for a criminal offence and the infliction of punishment on an innocent person for it.

Evidently, the kind of processes best calculated to reduce to the barest minimum the chances of a false conviction and punishment is that in which the trial is conducted by independent, trained and experienced judges who are learned in the law and versed in the difficult art of sifting evidence and judging the demeanour of witnesses, and who have been reared in the legal tradition of individual liberty, which insists, rightly, that it is better for nine guilty persons to go free than for one innocent man to be incarcerated. Clearly therefore, conviction for a criminal offence and the infliction of punishment therefor, with their attendant moral obliquy, public disgrace, disabilities and unwelcome incarceration, does imperatively require the processes of the ordinary courts of law.

It is for these reasons that criminal conviction and punishment has been held to pertain *exclusively* to judicial power.[9] Judicial power is not necessarily involved because a dispute involves two opposing parties, or because the issue to be determined affect their legal rights or other questions of law, or because a determination of the dispute is made binding on them.[10] While these are necessary attributes of judicial power, they are not exclusive to it, but can also and often do form part of administrative power. But conviction and punishment for a criminal offence goes much beyond that. It determines authoritatively and conclusively the legal standing of a person as a member of society, and incarcerates him by infliction of physical pain, the deprivation of personal liberty or property.

There is another reason why a tribunal composed, in whole or in part, of persons who are not independent of the Executive should not convict and sentence for a criminal offence. The Executive is the accuser in a criminal trial, and it simply affronts justice that it should also, through its functionaries or

---

9.   *Waterside Workers' Fedn. of Australia v. J.W. Alexander Ltd.,* (1918) 25 C.L.R. 434, 444.
10. *Shell Co. of Australia Ltd. v. Fed. Com. of Taxation,* [1931] A.C. 275 (P.C.).

other person appointed by it, be the judge of the guilt or otherwise of an accused person. Justice can only be seen to be done if the trial is conducted by persons who are in no way connected with the Executive, either as its appointee to the membership of the tribunal or as its paid functionary.

The affront to justice and liberty is greater where the trial is by a military tribunal. As the U.S. Supreme Court has observed, civil liberty and the trial of civilians by a military tribunal "cannot endure together; the antagonism is irreconcilable; and, in the conflict, one or the other must perish."[11]

Intolerable as it is that special tribunals should be authorised to convict and punish for criminal offences, it is outrageous that their decision, especially a sentence of death, should be unappealable to the ordinary courts of law. That a tribunal, even an ordinary court, should be authorised to impose the death penalty without an appeal to a higher court is, to say the least, careless of human life. It makes light of what is really a most sacred thing.

The objective of expedition and the avoidance of undue technicality in the trial of economic or anti-social crimes, which is no doubt the reason for the use of special tribunal in such cases, can be achieved within the framework of the ordinary court system. The Chief Justice can be empowered to constitute a separate division of the court, manned by such number of judges as he may deem necessary, to be engaged solely in the trial of such cases, with a specific direction to try them by a summary method and to dispose of each case within a specified time limit without prejudice of course to the validity of the proceedings where, for any reason, they cannot be concluded within the specified time limit.

The division of the court charged with the trial of such cases can also be specifically directed by statute to decide according to the substantial merits of each case, unfettered by strict legal forms, but with due observance of the rules of evidence and other safeguards of a fair trial in criminal cases. Such direction is not without precedent, and has been held not to deprive a

---

11. *Duncan v. Kahanamoku*, 327 U.S. 304, at p. 324.

tribunal of the character of a court or its decisions the character of judicial decisions.[12]

(b) Rights Pertaining to Human Activities

Human conduct or action is the external manifestation of human desires, human will and intellect. The imposition of legal restrictions on human conduct or action may involve either the incarceration of the human person (as by imprisonment) or the deprivation of property (as by fine or forfeiture) as a punishment for those who violate the restrictions or, more commonly, the frustration of their desires and will for those coerced by the threat of legal punishment to abstain from the prohibited conduct or action in question. Apart from the fact that the unimpeded exercise of individual freedom of choice is itself a value of great importance to human life, the frustration of human desires and will may involve the infliction of a special form of suffering. This, as Professor Hart has pointed out, is particularly so in the case of laws enforcing a sexual morality, which "may create misery of a quite special degree" arising from the individual being compelled to repress his sexual impulses in obedience to such laws.[13]

Yet the repression of the desire to engage in an activity prohibited by law is not, except in the case of a small minority of people, "a recurrent and insistent part of daily life," such as to affect "the development or balance of the individual's emotional life, happiness and personality,"[14] as in the case of imprisonment or torture or other inhuman treatment or of each.

However that may be, the real issue with which we are concerned is to determine when the state may be justified in interfering with individual liberty of action by prohibition or other restriction under pains of legal punishment such as

12. *Peacock v. Newton Merrickville and General Co-operative Building Society (No. 4) Ltd.*, (1943) C.L.R. 25; *R.V. The Commonwealth Court of Conciliation and Arbitration (The Tramways Case)* (1914) 18 C.L.R. 54; *British Imperial Oil Co. Ltd. v. Fed. Com. of Taxation* (1925) 35 C.L.R. 422, 438 - 50.
13. H. L. A. Hart, *Law, Liberty and Morality* (1963) p. 22.
14. Hart, loc. cit.

imprisonment, fine or forfeiture of property. (The conditions under which actual incarceration of the human person by imprisonment may justifiably be effected have already been considered). It is not enough, as earlier pointed out, to say that, in a democracy, individual liberty to engage in activities — social, political, economic and religious — may be justifiably restricted by law in the interest of public order, safety, public security, public health, public morality, economic well-being and general well-being. We need to know when or in what circumstances control or restriction in these public interests is justified.

(i) Freedom of Social, Religious and Economic Activities

The first principle here, as established by a long line of decisions of the U.S. Supreme Court, is that a law which "makes the peaceful enjoyment of freedom which the Constitution guarantees contingent upon the uncontrolled will of an official — as by requiring a permit or licence which may be granted or withheld in the discretion of such official — is an unconstitutional censorship or prior restraint upon the enjoyment of those freedoms."[15] It follows that where freedom of action (which includes private enterprise) is guaranteed in the constitution — it is not guaranteed in the Commonwealth Bills of Rights except to a limited extent — then, the requirement of a licence from the state for carrying on any activity is, in general, a denial of the right and unconstitutional.

Apart from a licence requirement, a law restricting freedom of social, religious and economic activities (where such is guaranteed in the constitution) is warranted only if it has a substantial, rational and proximate relation to the appropriate public interests and is not otherwise unreasonable or discriminatory.[16] In a case before the High Court of Zambia, the issue was whether the power given by the Exchange Control Regulations of Zambia to customs officers to open and search without warrant postal packets reasonably suspected of

---

15. *Staub v. Baxley*, 355 U.S. 313 (1956).
16. See, e.g., *Lockner v. New York*, ibid; *C.B. & R.R. Co. V. McGuire*, 219 U.S. 549 (1911).

containing articles or currency notes being imported into or exported out of the country in contravention of the Regulations was unconstitutional interference with the freedom of correspondence and expression guaranteed by the Constitution.[17] The court held that, to be reasonably required, the connection between a regulatory legislation and public order, public safety, etc., must be a proximate one; that is to say, its bearing on public order, public safety, etc., must be reasonably close and not too remote or far-fetched. It must also be rational, in the sense that it must suggest itself to a reasonably intelligent mind.

Now, exchange control, being a very vital aspect of a country's development, has certainly some bearing on public order and safety. The question however is whether this bearing is sufficiently proximate and rational to make exchange control reasonably required in the interests of public order and safety and thereby to justify interference with the individual's freedom of expression. The court held, rightly, that it was not. In the words of the learned judge:

> It could conceivably happen that complete financial anarchy might so weaken the economy that internal disaffection might be caused, leading to rioting and civil disturbance. So might widespread unemployment caused, say, by overpopulation. So might prolonged drought which disrupted agricultural production. One might think of many things which could, ultimately, affect the public safety. None of them would however, have the quality of proximateness which would justify involving this exception. Nor do I think that exchange control is sufficiently proximate to public safety to warrant the present legislation being adopted in the interest of public safety.

The reasoning in this case is a gratifying repudiation of an earlier decision by another judge of the same court. A regulation made by the Government under the Education Act required children in government or government-aided schools to sing the national anthem and to salute the national flag on certain occasions.[18] The requirement was challenged on the ground that it was an unconstitutional interference with the freedom of conscience guaranteed by the Constitution. This depended on whether the regulation was reasonably required in

17. *Patel v. Att-Gen of Zambia*, 1968 S.J. Z 1.
18. *Kachasu v. Att. Gen for Zambia*, 1967/HP/273.

the interests of public safety and public order. Chief Justice Blagden held that it was. His reasoning was that the singing of the national anthem and the saluting of the national flag were necessary to inculcate among the people, especially among children in their formative age, a love of nation, and a consciousness of common belonging. And the need for national unity, he further reasoned, was much greater in an emergent state like Zambia with its seventy-three distinct tribal groupings, divided not only by language and culture but also by economic and other interests.

All this must be admitted. Yet the question is whether the compulsion of children to sing the national anthem and salute the flag was reasonably required in the interests, not of national unity, which was not one of the specified public interests, but of national security. The Chief Justice had reasoned that since "national unity is the basis of national security", then, whatever was reasonably required in the interests of national unity must also be reasonably required in the interests of national security. But surely the connection between the singing of the national anthem or the saluting of the flag and national security is an ultimate, not a proximate, one. The danger to national security in school children not being made to sing the national anthem or salute the flag is rather remote. Indeed, the U.S. Supreme Court has held that it was not permissible under the U.S. Constitution to use compulsion to try to achieve national unity. "To believe that patriotism will not flourish if patriotic ceremonies are voluntary and spontaneous instead of a compulsory routine is to make an unflattering estimate of the appeal of our institutions to free minds."[19] Accordingly, it held, reversing its earlier decision,[20] that the compulsory flag salute and singing of the national anthem were unconstitutional.

The limitation thus imposed on governmental control of freedom is all the more remarkable because the "reasonableness of each regulation depends on the relevant facts", with the result that "a regulation valid for one sort of

19. *West Virginia State Board of Education v. Barnette*, 319 U.S. 624 (1943).
20. *Minersville School District v. Gobitis*, 310 U.S. 586 (1940).

business, or in given circumstances, may be invalid for another sort, or for the same business under other circumstances."[21] In upholding a building zone law which excluded from residential districts apartment houses, business houses, retail stores and shops, and other like establishments, the U.S. Supreme Court observed that "regulations, the wisdom, necessity and validity of which, as applied in existing conditions, are so apparent that they are uniformly sustained, a century ago or even half a century ago, probably would have been rejected as arbitrary and oppressive. Such regulations are sustained, under the complex conditions of our day, for reasons analogous to those which justify traffic regulations, which, before the advent of automobiles and rapid transit street railways, would have been condemned as fatally arbitrary and unreasonable... A regulatory zoning ordinance, which would be clearly valid as applied to the great cities, might be clearly invalid as applied to rural communities."[22] This approach to the matter has enabled the court to overrule the line of decisions which invalidated laws fixing minimum wages and maximum working hours or prices, as well as certain laws regulating business activities.[23]

(ii) Freedom of Political Activities

The U.S. Supreme Court has laid it down that the test of substantial and rational connection applied in ordinary cases is not enough when freedom of political discussion, press and assembly is concerned. A restriction on these rights, the political freedoms, is valid only if "the words used are in such circumstances and are of such a nature as to create a clear and present danger that they will bring about the substantive evils that Congress has a right to prevent."[24] This has become known as the 'clear and present danger' test. Expatiating on this test in 1927, Justice Brandeis said:

---

21. *Nebbia v. New York,* 291 U.S. 502 at p. 524 (1934) – per Justice Roberts.
22. *Village of Euclid v. Ambler Realty Co,* 272 U.S. 365.
23. *Lincoln Federal Labour Union v. North Western Iron and Metal Co.,* 335 U.S. 525 (1949).
24. *Schenek v. United States,* 249 U.S. 47 (1919), per Justice Holmes delivering the unanimous opinion of the court.

Those who won our independence by revolution ... did not exalt order at the cost of liberty. To courageous, self-reliant men, with confidence in the power of free and fearless reasoning applied through the processes of popular government, no danger flowing from speech can be deemed clear and present, unless the incidence of evil apprehended is so imminent that it may befall before there is opportunity for full discussion. If there be time to expose through discussion the falsehood and fallacies, to avert the evil by the processes of education, the remedy to be applied is more speech, not enforced silence. Only an emergency can justify repression. Such, in my opinion, is the command of the Constitution.[25]

The test was again in 1945 affirmed by Justice Stone for the court:

Any attempt, he said, "to restrict these liberties must be justified by clear public interest, threatened not doubtfully or remotely, but by clear and present danger. The rational connection between the remedy provided and the evil to be curbed, which in other contexts might support legislation against attack on due process grounds, will not suffice. These rights rest on firmer foundation. Accordingly, whatever occasion would restrain orderly discussion and persuasion, at appropriate time and place, must have clear support in public danger, actual or impending. Only the gravest abuses, endangering paramount interests, give occasion for permissible limitation."[26]

The justification that has been proffered for the "preferred position" of the freedoms of speech, press, assembly and processions is not that they are more natural than freedom of social, religious and economic activities; both are a manifestation of the human will and intellect, the ability to act, and are therefore equally natural to man. It is simply the indispensability of speech, assembly and procession in maintaining the openness of the political process and in ensuring that "government may be responsive to the will of the people and that changes may be obtained by lawful means."[27] Speech concerning public affairs is said to be "more than self-expression; it is the essence of self-government."[28] Archibald Cox has put the point somewhat more appealingly.

Where the channels of debate and representative self-government are open it is fair to say to one claiming under the due process

---

25. *Whitney v. California*, 274 U.S. 357 (1927).
26. *Thomas v. Collins* 323 U.S. 516, 530 (1945).
27. *Stromberg v. California* 283 U.S. 359 quoted with approval in *New York Times Co. v. Sullivan* 376 U.S. 254 at p. 269 (1964).
28. *Garrison v. Louisiana* 379 U.S. 64, 74-5 (1964).

clause that a law is so unjust as to be unconstitutional, 'You must seek correction through the political process, for the judiciary to intervene would be a denial of self-government.' This is no answer, however, when the statute under attack closes the political process to particular ideas or particular groups, or otherwise distorts its operation. Then the correction must come from outside and no violence is done to the principles of representative government if the Court supplies the remedy.[29]

It is right to point out that the "clear and present danger" test has not had an unbroken or unchallenged application. In two cases in 1919 and 1925,[30] it was abandoned in favour of the "dangerous tendency" test, which resulted in certain convictions for sedition being sustained. But these were majority judgments maintained against the vigorous dissents of Justices Holmes and Brandeis. Re-stated and refined in the Holmes and Brandeis dissents in these two cases, the "clear and present danger" test was soon re-established as the law in cases involving freedom of speech. In 1951, however, the meaning and application of the test again came under consideration in an appeal by eleven leaders of the Communist party against their conviction for advocating the overthrow of the Government.[31] The Court, by a 6-2 majority, upheld the convictions. Although the majority judgment professes to have applied the "clear and present danger" test, in fact the test, as applied, seems to have been modified to one of "clear and probable danger," the modification being predicated upon the distinction between advocacy and discussion. Justice Frankfurter, in a separate concurring judgment, even attacked the test, saying that it was never meant to be a "technical legal doctrine" or "to convey a formula for adjudicating cases." And Justice Jackson, also concurring, thought the test inappropriate to "modernised revolutionary techniques used by totalitarian parties;" he would confine it to the issue of criminality of "a hot-headed speech on a street corner, or circularisation of a few incendiary pamphlets..." The two dissenting judges, Justices Douglas and Black, maintained that, on a strict application of the "clear and present danger"

---

29. Archibald Cox, *The Warren Court* (1968) pp. 9-10, 94-5.
30. *Adams v. United States*, 250 U.S. 616 (1919); *Gitlow v. New York*, 268 U.S. 652 (1925).
31. *Dennis v. United States*, 341 U.S. 494 (1951).

test, the appellants were entitled to be discharged; "free speech," said Justice Douglas"... should not be sacrificed on anything less than plain and objective proof of danger that the evil advocated is imminent." In spite of attacks on it, the "clear and present danger" test remains the law in the U.S., at least in sedition cases.[32]

These great liberal pronouncements of the U.S. Supreme Court, which ring like a freedom charter, are in refreshing contrast to the unprogressive stand against liberty taken by the Nigerian Supreme Court in two decisions in 1961 handed down in judgments that are completely barren of any insight into the problem of balancing posed. The leader of the minority Dynamic party, Dr Chike Obi, was charged with sedition for a publication entitled *The People; Facts that you must know*, in which appeared the words: "Down with the enemies of the people, the exploiters of the weak and the oppressors of the poor ... the days of those who have enriched themselves at the expense of the poor are numbered." The Nigerian Criminal Code makes it an offence of sedition intentionally to publish words calculated to excite hatred, contempt and disaffection against the Government. Dr Obi's defence was that, having regard to the guarantee of freedom of speech in the Constitution, it was not reasonably justifiable in a democratic society to punish a man for making a statement which merely exposed the government to hatred, contempt or disaffection, without any repercussion for public order or security. Dr Obi was convicted.

In upholding the conviction Chief Justice Ademola on behalf of the Supreme Court, ruled, without going into discussion of the problem posed, that "it must be justifiable in a democratic society to take reasonable precautions to preserve public order, and this may involve the prohibition of acts which, if unchecked and unrestrained, might lead to disorder, even though those acts would not themselves do so directly."[33]

The conviction of Dr Obi clearly does not satisfy any of the three tests applied in the U.S. Supreme Court in sedition cases.

---

32. For a more resent discussion of the test, see *New York Times Co v. Sullivan*, ibid; *Garrison v. Louisiana*, ibid.

33. *D.P.P. v. Obi* (1961) 1 All N.L.R. 186, 196.

The publication in question posed no clear and present or clear and probable danger to public order or security nor did it have any dangerous tendency towards violence. It is doubtful even whether it had a substantial and rational connection to public disorder; the connection was pretty remote, if not altogether non-existent. It appears clearly to have been intended simply to induce the people not to vote for the government at the next election; it was certainly not an advocacy for the overthrow of the government by unconstitutional means.

The Nigerian Criminal Code also makes it an offence to publish false news likely to cause fear and alarm. In supporting the conviction of a newspaper for violating this prohibition, Chief Justice Ademola, for the Supreme Court, merely said:

> I do not think it necessary to enter into any lengthy consideration of the question presumably posed. Suffice it to say that section 24 of the Constitution of the Federation relating to Fundamental Human Rights guaranteed nothing but ordered freedom and that the section of the Constitution cannot be used as a licence to spread false news likely to cause fear and alarm to the public."[34]

That is all there was in the judgment on the problem posed. No one disputes that what the Bill of Rights guaranteed is ordered freedom, that is to say that it presupposes an ordered political society. But the problem is where the line should be drawn. Is the mere *likelihood* of causing fear and alarm to the public enough? And how likely was that danger in the circumstances of the particular publication? How much fear and alarm would create sufficiently substantial danger to public order or safety to justify criminal punishment?

Happily, the Court of Appeal, in a recent appeal from Anambra State in 1983, had held it to be inconsistent with the guarantee of freedom of speech in the Constitution to punish as sedition, utterances or publications which expose the government to contempt or hatred but which fall short of an incitement to violence or other unlawful action.[35]

---

34.   *The Queen v. The Amalgamated press (of Nigeria) Ltd* (1961) 1 All N.L.R. 199, 201-2.
35.   *Nwankwo v. State*, FCA/E/111/83 delivered on 27/7/83.

Chapter 14

Democratising the Economy

> The road to freedom is not a road from one system to another
> (communism and capitalism), ... The battle of systems is an illiberal
> aberration.
>
> — Sir Ralf Dahrendorf.

Transition from a Communist Economic Order to the Open Society

The transition from a communist economic order to a market economy and private enterprise would involve the dismantling of the whole communist structure of the society and economy by means of denationalisation and privatisation and by the repeal and replacement of numerous other socialist laws and institutions. The process is now in progress in all the countries of Eastern Europe as existing laws and institutions are being reviewed with a view to their modification to ensure their conformity with democratic standards. Yet, considering that in most of these countries some 90 per cent of industrial enterprises and 90 per cent of employment were owned or provided by the state, the process is bound to be long and tortuous. The progress may be slow, but some caution is also needed, for as Misha Glenny has warned, "subjecting these economies to the ruthless logic of a completely free market would result in social upheaval and a second more threatening phase of revolution."[1]

Sir Ralf Dahrendorf has also rightly cautioned that the collapse of socialism/communism in Eastern Europe and the former Soviet Union should not be seen as the triumph of

---

1. Misha Glenny, *The Rebirth of History* (1990), p. 18.

capitalism as such, but rather as the triumph of f~~ dom over system. "The countries of East Central Europe," ys, "have not shed their communist system in order race the capitalist system... the road to freedom ' from one system to another, but one that leads into the open spaces of infinite futures, some of which compete with each other."[2] For him, "the battle of systems is an illiberal aberration. To drive the point home with the utmost force: if capitalism is a system, then, it needs to be fought as hard as communism had to be fought. All systems mean serfdom, including the 'natural' system of a total 'market order' in which no one tries to do anything other than guard certain rules of the game discovered by a mysterious sect of economic advisers."[3] What is needed, he maintains, is a "combination of democracy and planning, of economic freedom and demand management, of individual choice and redistribution, of liberty and justice."[4]

Democratising the African Economies

Liberalising Economic Activities

The statute book of most African countries abounds with laws regulating various aspects of the economic life of the country in a manner which no American government would dare do — laws fixing minimum wages; prohibiting general wage increases; pegging income from dividends; fixing prices for various commodities; controlling fees and fares chargeable respectively by certain professionals and operators; controlling rent and the use and disposition of land; requiring a licence for or otherwise restricting the carrying on of certain professions, trades or industrial activities; controlling the import and export trade, interest rates, credit, banks and banking, the corporate form of business organisation and dealings in stock and shares including their prices, trade union activities, etc.

The state in Africa also engages in a vast amount of direct economic activities, ranging from manufacturing and other

---

2.   Ralf Dahrendorf, *Reflections on the Revolution in Europe* (1990), pp. 36-37.
3.   Ibid p. 37
4.   Ibid p. 50.

industrial enterprises, commerce to agriculture and agro-allied enterprises. In terms of value, government direct economic enterprises account for about 70% of the total value of investment in both the public and private sectors of the economy. Government direct involvement in economic activities results in the restriction of private enterprise because such activities are often operated as monopolies with the consequent exclusion of competition and other market forces or are otherwise granted a favoured status, in the form of exemptions and immunities, *vis-a-vis* private enterprises operating in the same field of activity.

No doubt, many of the state regulations and controls of private enterprise are necessary and desirable in the interest of social justice and the protection of the general public. In the circumstances of Africa, a certain amount of government involvement in economic enterprise is also dictated by the inadequate capital, skilled manpower, managerial skill and other resources available to the indigenous private sector, by the reluctant response of its expatriate counterpart to the demands of industrialisation, by the need for government to control, through direct ownership of industries of basic and strategic importance to the economy, such as exploration and mining of mineral, iron and steel, fertiliser production, and by the long period of gestation entailed in some of these enterprises, which might make them unattractive to private investors desirous of immediate returns on their investment.

Notwithstanding this, however, democratisation requires that the economy of these African countries should be considerably de-regulated, and that government enterprises should be privatised to a large extent. Happily, this is already happening in many of the countries as part of the structural adjustment programme.

Freeing the African Economies from Subservience to Foreign Economic Interests

Just as democracy in a national community implies that there should be no subservience or servility in the relations of the classes *inter se,* so also does it require that the nation itself, as an independent political entity, should not be subservient to foreign economic interests in the direction and management of the economy. The dominance of foreigners, a small minority, in the "commanding heights" of the African economies as regards both jobs and ownership of business enterprises is an affront not only to democracy but also to social justice. It has meant that many vital economic decisions and their implementation are dictated by interests other than those of the African nations concerned. It has enabled the foreign economic interests to continue to exploit the African countries economically more or less as before independence. Political independence needs to be matched by economic independence to bring about meaningful national independence and social justice.

Whilst many African countries have since taken steps to rectify the situation by indigenising most of the foreign business enterprises, a new form of economic dependence has arisen as a result of the debt burden and the foreign-imposed structural adjustment programme, which has put the countries adopting the programme under the tutelage of foreigners, the World Bank and the IMF, enabling the latter to dictate the economic policies of the countries concerned. "How is it then possible to speak of democracy," asks Niandou Souley, where the "crisis of African economies is taken care of by non-African actors?... The tutelage of the international financial institutions restricts the African States' liberty of choice. It thus takes the form of a denial of democracy since this very liberty of choice is an essential implication of democracy. If Africa wants to give itself the chances of a real and lasting democracy, it will have to take up the economic challenges implied by democracy.[5]

Eradicating (or at least reducing) Poverty and Illiteracy

Poverty-stricken people are too engrossed in the struggle for subsistence and survival to care much for political rights. The maintenance and defence of liberty and democracy demand therefore a heightened effort to improve the standard of living of the people through the provision of employment, social welfare

---

5.   Niandou Souley, "Economic Crisis and Democratisation in Africa," in B. Caron *et al. Democratic Transition in Africa* (1992), p. 382.

services, assistance and incentives. Democracy or popular participation must be seen, not as an end in itself, but only as a means to an end, a means for trying to uplift the conditions of life of the people. And to ensure the attainment of the desired end, it should not be left to the elected governors and legislators to pursue it or not as they deem fit. We need an ethic that would make them to accept it as their moral duty. A moral obligation to pursue the welfare of the people should of course be reinforced by also making it a legal duty imposed through the Constitution. That is what social democracy is about. But full development cannot even be attained through the processes of popular government, by the state providing employment and social welfare services and assistance; to attain full development, social democracy must be combined with liberal democracy, with the liberty of the individual to employ his initiative, resourcefulness and enterpreneurship.

Poverty can hardly be eradicated in a predominantly illiterate society; the one is inseparable from the other. To eradicate or reduce poverty, illiteracy must also be eradicated.

An illiterate people is greatly handicapped in exercising political freedom/democracy. A people's native wit and intelligence, as sharpened by political discourse and by practice and experience in matters of politics, certainly stands to be enhanced by education. In its original meaning, democracy was indeed meant for small, simple face-to-face communities where it was possible for the population to gather together in one place to conduct their affairs, which were necessarily simple and limited in scope. Except in some of the Greek city states and in Rome, the necessity did not often arise for the complex process of elections with its sophisticated trappings of secret ballot, ballot papers, ballot boxes, etc. The process and its trappings could be operated successfully only among an educated people while an informed and intelligent choice between candidates, judged by the quality of their election campaign speeches, or between the programmes of competing political parties for handling the affairs of a modern state, with their vastly expanded scope and complexity, also requires a certain level of education. Even the modern state itself, in the complexity of its structures and relations and the issues confronting it, is beyond the understanding of an illiterate people.

The same goes, to the same or lesser extent, for the other political rights. Freedom of the press has no meaning for a person who can neither read nor write. Criticism by speech or by peaceful assembly or procession and even the freedom to organise in opposition to the government require ability to understand the issues at stake and the shortcomings of the government's approach to them. An illiterate people can understand and act only as concerns actions or inactions that affect them directly, and then mostly as directed by the educated elite. The choice of a political party to join is also decided for them by the educated elite, which exposes them to manipulation and exploitation by the latter; the initiative to form a political party is clearly beyond them. Nor can the right to participate in the executive and legislature as elected members thereof be enjoyed by an illiterate person, the possession of a certain level of education, often specifically prescribed in the constitution itself, being a condition for election to those bodies.

It is true, as Lord Bryce said, that "a democracy that has been taught only to read, and not also to reflect and judge, will not be the better for the ability to read." Political education therefore consists in the ability not only to read, but to think critically, and not to take a stand without considering the two sides to any matter in issue. Above all, education must go hand in hand with the involvement of the people in self-government in order that practice may vivify knowledge.

The eradication of illiteracy must therefore be vigorously and relentlessly pursued through a programme of a compulsory, universal and, if possible, free education at the primary level, supported with adequate educational facilities at all levels, as well as a programme of, and vigorous campaign for, adult literacy.

Index